RELIGION AND IDENTITY IN MODERN FRANCE

*The Modernization of the Protestant
Community in Languedoc
1815-1848*

James C. Deming

University Press of America,® Inc.
Lanham • New York • Oxford

Copyright © 1999 by
University Press of America,® Inc.
4720 Boston Way
Lanham, Maryland 20706

12 Hid's Copse Rd.
Cumnor Hill, Oxford OX2 9JJ

Library of Congress Cataloging-in-Publication Data

Deming, James C.
Religion and identity in modern France : the modernization of the
Protestant community in Languedoc, 1815-1848 / James C. Deming.
p.   cm.
Includes bibliographical references and index.
1. Huguenots—France—Languedoc—History—19th century. 2.
Languedoc (France)—Church history—19th century.   I. Title.
BX9456.L36D45 1999 284'.5'0944809034—dc21 99—20611 CIP

ISBN 0-7618-1382-9 (cloth: alk. ppr.)

♾™ The paper used in this publication meets the minimum
requirements of American National Standard for Information
Sciences—Permanence of Paper for Printed Library Materials,
ANSI Z39.48—1984

For Christy

CONTENTS

TABLES AND FIGURES

PREFACE

This book began as a doctoral dissertation that set out to explore the political attitudes of French Protestants between the empires of Napoleon Bonaparte and his nephew Napoleon III. Southern France was chosen because it was here that the Huguenots' descendants lived in sufficient density to be a political force and that a specifically Protestant identity was discernable. As thus envisioned the study would be a Huguenot parallel to Brian Fitzpatrick's book on Catholic royalism, filling the gap between James N. Hood's work on Protestant-Catholic relations during the French Revolution and that of Stuart Schram and André Siegfried on French Protestantism's identification with leftist politics in the Third Republic and after.

In researching the question, however, it became evident that a simple equation of Protestant with the French Left, though true in general, needed some nuance. At the same time a deeper question began to emerge from the documentation; that of the role of the Reformed religion in forming the Protestant identity from which its political expressions arose. Specifically, I became interested in the how changes in religious attitudes and expression effected Protestant corporate identity. These changes of course did effect Protestant political expression. While the nature of this impact was the explicit topic of earlier articles, the present study is more concerned with how religious change, and in particular the religious awakening in French Protestantism known as the *Réveil*, altered the nature of Huguenot identity and effected Protestantism's relation to the emerging society of modern France. In other words, this book is interested in how religious change helped set ajar the doors that had enclosed French Protestants in the south of France within a closed confessional identity set apart from broader society, and eased its insertion into modern France.

In conducting a study of this extent and duration, I have benefitted greatly from the assistance of many. Thanking them here is weak recompense for their generous efforts. I can only wish it were in my power to acknowledge them in a manner that more nearly equated to what is their due. Research was assisted by a Faculty Research Grant from Princeton Theological Seminary, a Research Development Grant from Penn State University, and a Zahm Travel Grant and Dissertation-Year Fellowship from the University of Notre Dame. The research itself was conducted in the Archives du départment du Gard in Nîmes, the Archives nationales, the Bibliothèque nationale and the Bibliothèque de la Société d'histoire du protestantisme français in Paris, and the Manuscript Library of the School of Oriental and African Studies in London. Their staffs showed every courtesy and their knowledge, efficiency and gracious assistance made the long hours of research pass as enjoyably and profitably as possible. A delightful afternoon was spent with Pastor Michel Jas of the Reformed Church of Nîmes, discussing Cathar and Protestant history. Raymond Huard offered much helpful guidance on the research and direction for this study, as did Brian Fitzpatrick of the University of Ulster, who was also generous enough to take an interest in a somewhat bewildered American graduate student and introduce him to the curiosities and mysteries of the Gard.

I have profited from the readings of an earlier version of this study by Marvin R. O'Connell, Mark Meyerson, and Nathan Hatch. Thomas Kselman has been involved in this study from the very beginning. Its successful completion is in no small part due to his insight, suggestions and encouragement. Roberta and Tom Spencer graciously opened their home during a crucial stage of writing. Preparation and proofreading of the manuscript was assisted by Haruko Nawata Ward and Marianne Delaporte. Lynn O'Grady graciously and patiently assisted with the index. A special thank you to Hannah and Jacob who, though not understanding why it was taking me so long to write one book when by the end of the first grade they had published several, patiently endured their father's divided attention. The greatest debt, however, is owed to Christy. Her assistance has come in every form and at every stage. Without her confidence and support, both gentle and aggressive, this project would not have been possible.

INTRODUCTION

Much has changed in France since the nineteenth century, not the least being the place of religious minorities in French society. This book is a case study of one such minority community during the turbulent decades when the foundations of modern French society were laid between the collapse of the Napoleonic Empire in 1815, and the establishment of the Second Republic in 1848. Its subject is the Reformed Protestants living in Languedoc in the region centering on the department of the Gard. The focus is on how these descendants of the Huguenots adjusted to increasing religious toleration and their inclusion into national society after more than a century of persecution. As this was a community in which religion was an integral part of its identity the study is necessarily concerned with the place of religion and religious change in this process.

Protestantism in France has received surprisingly little attention from contemporary historians. Its importance is recognized for the Reformation and Wars of Religion, but based on most history texts the Protestant faith seems to have disappeared from France after the Revocation of the Edict of Nantes.[1] The deprivations of 1685-1787 were severe, forcing hundreds of thousands of Huguenots to flee their homeland, but French Protestantism survived. In fact the historian of Protestant memory, Philippe Joutard, has argued that the Revocation became "the founding event of French Protestantism as a whole." Thus, Protestant invisibility in histories of modern France may be more a reflection of their nearly complete assimilation into contemporary French society than of historical reality.[2]

Undoubtedly they were a small minority, less than three percent of the population in 1851, but their economic and political influence far exceeded their numbers, and as the anti-Protestant polemic of the nineteenth century indicates this did not go unnoticed. Some, such as Jules Michelet, Lucien Prévost-Paradol, and Marc Sangnier, respected Protestantism for its resistance to tyranny and as a model for a religion in modern society. More often Protestants were linked with Jews and Free Masons as subversives undermining the integrity of France and conspiring to impose upon the nation a godless republican society. Thus Felicité de Lamennais, in his *Essay on Indifference*, blamed the Protestant Reformation as a foundation for modern religious indifference. Louis Veuillot, editor of the Catholic newspaper *L'Univers*, declared "Protestantism has destroyed human society," and expressed his regret that Luther was not burned and Jan Hus wasn't burned sooner. In the charged atmosphere of the Dreyfus affair and the separation of church and state, Edouard Tavanier identified a *parti protestant* "organized for treason and plunder." Charles Maurras combined race with religion, stating that Protestants "in politics, in philosophy, in the arts and letters, are first of all anti-Latins." And Georges Thiébaud claimed Protestants were the most influential, the most dangerous and the most guilty of the "suspect minorities" and therefore were the first to be battled.[3]

Surprisingly, considering the precariousness of their place in French society and the rhetorical power of the charges leveled against them, French Protestants did not entirely contest the critique to which they were subjected, but instead embraced it. Much of the controversy that surrounded Protestants reflected their general identification with the Left in French society. In part, their support of leftist causes was a function of the attempt during the Ancien Regime to eradicate Protestantism and the emancipation of Protestants under the Revolution. The fact that Roman Catholicism and Protestantism's critics largely aligned with the Right only reinforced this tendency by Protestants to champion modern society. Thus, not long after the White Terror in southern France ravaged the Protestant community at the close of the First Empire, Samuel Vincent, pastor for the Reformed Church of Nîmes, proudly declared Protestantism was "the base of the vast system of individualism that constitutes modern civilization."[4] Even socially and politically conservative Protestants accepted the virtues of constitutional and representative government, the rights of the individual, and the benefits of a religiously neutral if not anti-clerical state. They only tended to separate from their coreligionists in their abhorrence of the type of political and social radicalism they associated with the Jacobin Terror and the dechristianization campaign of 1793-1795.[5]

French Calvinists also believed, however, that there was a basic affinity between Protestant theology and the ideals of a modern liberal society.[6] They identified as the *principe Protestant* the right of free inquiry which was rooted in the doctrine of the priesthood of all believers. Protestantism, it was argued, made individuals equal before God and personally accountable for their faith. This meant one must be able (some would say demanded) to read and interpret the Bible for oneself, and be free to arrive at his or her own understanding of their relationship with the divine. This right to spiritual free inquiry was the religious corollary to the equality of citizens and the freedom of thought and expression championed by the French Revolution. Consequently, as France moved towards a liberal society French Reformed Protestants were inclined to interpret their own broadening social access not as their absorption into the national culture, but as an indication of the Protestantization of France.[7]

This affinity for modernization could not obscure the impact the process was having on their own community. While Protestants may have been tempted to herald the final victory of the Reformation in France they were also aware that their community was not only changing, but in fact feared it was disintegrating. This was particularly evident in Bas-Languedoc where the Reformed population had a powerful self-identity as a distinct community rooted in religious dissent from the Roman Catholic majority. This identity was forged in the experience of violence and repression, the memory of which was kept alive by the tie of these events to specific locations and the passing of their meaning down from generation to generation. To this day the region holds nearly a mystical place in the consciousness of French Protestants. It had the largest concentration of Calvinists in France, with nearly 40 percent of the Reformed population in 1851 living in departments of the Ardèche, Gard, Hérault and Lozère. It was the land of the Protestant Camisard rebels and the heartland of the *Eglise du désert*. It is the setting for much Protestant literature and is the site of the contemporary Musée du Désert commemorating French Protestantism's *time on the cross*.[8] Protestants were also a significant proportion of the local population. In the department of the Gard, in which they were most concentrated, Reformed Protestants accounted for a third of the population, and in several cantons of the Cévennes Mountains were an overwhelming majority.

This numerical strength merged with Protestant economic power, based upon their dominance of the silk industry and local finance, and the history of confessional violence to accentuate religious differences to create a society severely polarized between Catholics and Protestants.

Louis XVI's Edict of Toleration of 1787 gave Protestants legal status, but local confessional relations were further stressed and politicized by the differing fortunes of the two communities during the French Revolution and Empire. The period under study opens with the restoration of the Bourbon Monarchy, which was occasion in the south for the White Terror in which Catholic vigilantes wrecked vengeance on the Reformed community for indignities suffered under the Revolution and Empire. The level of violence and lack of government intervention that made this episode possible was not matched again, but confessional tensions remained a continuing feature of local society that could erupt into violence at the slightest provocation.[9]

Consequently, the Reformed community of southern France entered the nineteenth century an integrated confessional community well aware of its vulnerability in the midst of an often hostile Catholic majority. As such it favored a tolerant society both in principle and for the sake of its own security. But while religious toleration offered Protestants many advantages it also raised new challenges. First, for a sub-culture that was to a large degree defined by its distinctiveness and even resistance to the majority, inclusion in the larger society could in itself be disorienting. The fact that under the Organic Articles of 1802 the French Reformed Church was not only tolerated but received government funding only added to the problem, particularly since that support came at the cost of alterations in ecclesiastical structure and the loss of some the Church's freedom of action. Second, the removal of civil disabilities exposed the community fully to the economic and social forces altering the shape of French society, but from which repression had at least partially sheltered it. As elsewhere the spread of a commercial economy, the introduction of industrial forms of production, and the quickening pace of urbanization raised economic tensions and political and social rivalries that sorely stressed communal bonds. This internal fragmentation was all the more threatening for southern Protestants who were well aware of their vulnerability in the midst of a hostile majority.

It is not surprising, given the centrality of the Reformed faith and the structures of its Reformed Church to the identity and organization of the Protestant community, that this climate of crisis and change would be reflected in the religious life of the community. Central in this regard was the *Réveil*, or awakening, of French Protestantism in the first-half of the nineteenth century. This renewal had two distinct but related aspects. One was the energy and resources that went into rebuilding and extending the institutions of the Reformed Church. As internal tensions increased

Reformed elites looked to the Church's educational, charitable and spiritual resources to reinforce the bonds of community.

Related to this institutional renewal, but more independent of ecclesiastical control, was the spiritual renewal that occurred in the Reformed population. This second aspect of the Réveil was part of the broader evangelical awakening that swept through European and American Protestantism in the eighteenth and early nineteenth centuries.[10] At one level it looked to the past for inspiration in its stress on the *essential* Christian doctrines of the Protestant Reformation, but it also introduced an emphasis on personal conversion and a reliance on the affections as much or more than the intellect for verification of one's faith. This movement helped revivify spiritual life from the malaise in which Enlightenment theology and the Revolution's attempt at dechristianization had left it. In this regard and in combination with the institutional recovery that was taking place, the Réveil could be seen to reinforce the religious foundations of a community decaying under the pressure of economic and social divisions. But in its heightened spirituality, insistence on doctrinal conformity, and emphasis on the individual and voluntary action, the Réveil also further eroded the integrity of the community by providing a vehicle for independent action that challenged the legitimacy of traditional communal authorities, and by shattering the religious solidarity by creating a distinction between those who were awakened and those still spiritually asleep. As the movement progressed the religious complexity grew considerably beyond this basic division. Within the established church bitter disputes developed between the doctrinaire orthodox faction, or evangelicals, who championed the Réveil, and their more theologically liberal opponents. Far less numerous, but symbolically more disruptive of communal life were those who abandoned the Reformed Church entirely to join autonomous churches established by English Methodists, missionaries from Switzerland or a variety of independent evangelists.

At the same time, however, the emphasis the awakening placed upon individual responsibility and action, its reliance on persuasion and voluntary associations, and its tendency to recast authority on a consensual basis, forced the Reformed Church and other communal institutions to adjust their structures, and the Reformed community to alter its self-perception, in ways that were more amenable to new patterns of social and political organization. These structural and conceptual adjustments facilitated the integration of this once isolated minority into French national culture. Protestantism as a common cultural heritage remained, but as a system of faith it became more a matter of private belief than of communal practice. This secularization of Protestant identity allowed a diversity of political, social and religious expression that facilitated interaction and forms of identification between Protestant groups and individuals, and the larger French society.

This study examines a localized community as it integrated into the larger society. Given that confessional identity was a central aspect of this community's self-understanding, the part religious experience played in the process is necessarily essential. To ignore it would be to miss one of the primary ways by which Protestants thought of themselves and interpreted the world in which they lived. Using a mixture of regional, civil, and ecclesiastical sources it is possible to follow the internal dynamics of the community as it struggled to adapt to the challenges of a changing social and political order yet maintain its own integrity and identity. Records of the consistories of the Reformed Churches and pastoral conferences provide a valuable window into the ordinary institutional and religious life of the church, the relations between the church and the community, and the issues and controversies with which they were concerned. Particularly important to this study were the archives of the Consistory of the Reformed Church of Nîmes. Unlike many rural consistories which only met a few times a year, that of Nîmes convened every two weeks and maintained unusually complete records of its sessions and correspondence. This preponderance of evidence skews the perspective towards that of the Nîmois, but it is also a reflection of the importance of Nîmes for the Protestant community of southern France. Though in the course of the nineteenth century Nîmes lost to the Consistory of Paris its unofficial status as the capital of French Protestantism this did not mean it answered to the new center. The Reformed Church lacked a centralized structure and all influence was strictly informal and depended on factors such as demographics, geography and wealth. In this regard Nîmes was an important counter-weight to the consistory at the nation's capital, particularly for the jealously independent Reformed Churches of the Bas-Languedoc.

Beyond its contribution to the history of French Protestantism, as a case study this book has much to offer for understanding the nationalization of French society. More than two decades ago Eugen Weber's groundbreaking study, *Peasants into Frenchmen,* presented an influential argument for the historical process by which provincial France was assimilated into national culture. France in the nineteenth century was a hodgepodge of disparate regions sharing little more than a common government. In terms of language, culture and religious traditions it was otherwise quite diverse. But the government working out of Paris reached into the farthest recesses of the country through an expanding network of roads, railroads, schools, elections and military service to pull the provinces out of their backwardness and isolation to create the national culture. Weber was not alone in making this argument. Earlier André Siegfried described politics in the west of France as "traditionally distinct from that of modern France, and neither questions of religion, economics or politics are approached, perceived or resolved in the same manner as elsewhere." In addition, much of what Weber argues seems to echo the perceptions of republicans as they struggled against their Royalist and clerical opponents in the 1880s and 1890s. But in its simple elegance and narrative power Weber's argument is persuasive.[11]

This book joins with the work of several other historians who have begun to modify this model of modernization as a missionary effort by Paris to the nation. Beginning with Maurice Agulhon's study of the department of the Var and Edward Berenson's book on the connections between popular religion and the dissemination of democ-soc ideals during the Second Republic, it was noted that regional culture played more of a role in the spread of such supposed movements of the center as republicanism. More recently other historians have used local studies to show that nationalization was more of a dialogue between Paris and the provinces than effective colonization. By shifting the focus away from the capital to the internal character and dynamics of local communities they have drawn attention to the way regional cultures could mediate between center and periphery.[12]

Strong religious affinities were one of the aspects of local society that, according to the imperialist model of nationalization, would fade away with integration into the national culture. Reflecting a version of positivism by which secularization was an inevitable corollary to modernization, religion was often regarded as atavistic behavior obstructing integration and progress. Thus, the famous Geneva-St. Mâlo line was seen to divide the religiously skeptical, republican north from the practicing, royalist, and agrarian south. Testimony of anticlericals foretelling the demise of religion and the hand wringing of church officials over the irreligion of the age combined with evidence of declining rates of religious practice seemed to confirm the thesis. But again a closer look reveals a more complex situation. Popular religion may not have been so much in decline as changing in form in ways traditional expectations and measures would miss. Despite the advance of modernity, there was still much in life that technology, politics and social theories could not explain or whose explanations provided little comfort to those suffering through the death of a loved one or trying to cope with economic hardship. At the same time religion was assumed to be dying out, pilgrimages increased, spiritism was wide-spread, and prophets and their messages were followed closely in the media.[13]

Neither did popular religiosity necessarily work against the formation of a national culture. With the advent of railroads and national media, religious sites like Marpingen, Lourdes and Fatima drew pilgrims from across the nation and Europe, and religious figures such as Thérèse de Lisieux become national and international icons. At a more localized level, Suzanne Desan uses a case study of the Yonne to document the remarkable resiliency and power of adaptation of lay Catholicism in the French Revolution. Catholic lay women and men found ways to reconcile their religiosity with goals of the Revolution despite the efforts of revolutionary cadres in Paris to dechristianize the country. At the other end of the nineteenth century, Caroline Ford has shown that Catholicism was an important vehicle for the politicization of the Breton population.[14]

Protestantism showed a similar capacity to revitalize and mediate. Here pressure to embrace nationalization was enhanced by the fact Protestants felt their security and prospects for the future depended on the successful imposition of liberal society from outside the region since there seemed little likelihood the local Catholic majority would voluntarily accept a religiously neutral society. On the other hand, there was much liberalism carried with it they felt was destructive. With some success they resisted or were able to mitigate the consequences. Key to the ability of Protestants to make these adjustments were changes in the religious life of the community. The Reformed faith lay at the heart of the identity of southern Protestants and the Reformed Church was the community's central organizing institution. The challenges and controversies confronting the Church often reflected the divergent concerns and desires of various groups within the Protestant population. At the same time that religious change was an expression of social forces, spiritual beliefs shaped the nature of that society, and the solutions to religious questions settled upon by individuals inside and outside the Church influenced personal and social behavior and attitudes.

This concern with the relation of religion and society takes the implications of this study from the fields of Church history and the history of modern France to that of the sociology of religion. Peter Berger and Robert Luckmann have argued that part of the secularization of modern culture is the development of a separation between public and private. The public sphere contains those aspects of society that have been the most fully rationalized, such as the economy and politics. The private sphere is characterized by areas in which rationalization has been less thorough.   Therefore, as modern society develops, religion in its resistance to rationalization increasingly became confined to the private sphere.[15]

There is little question that belief in the French Protestant community was became a more personal matter.   Karel Dobbelaere is correct, however, in pointing out that the categories *public* and *private* are not objective constituents of society. "They are *social* definitions used by participants, and just what they constitute varies according to the social agents involved."[16] [emphasis in text]   That is, public and private are concepts that are defined in social discourse by the actors themselves (and, I would add, by historians as well).   When Protestants attacked Methodist evangelists as agents of discord and dragged their wives and daughters out of prayer meetings, or when evangelicals protested consistorial opposition to their charitable projects, they were in essence disputing the boundary between public and private.   Thus, one of the sub-texts to debates within the French Reformed community was exactly where or if the line between private religious belief and the realm of public life should be drawn.   But as Brian Wilson has argued, even if the line was established the spheres still impacted each other.   Religious belief may have become an increasingly private matter, but the decisions individuals made in this regard had implications for the availability and nature of social assistance, the distribution of power and influence in the community, and the contours of communal identity.[17]

In pursuing this investigation the first two chapters of this book establish the setting and historical background for the Reformed community in Bas-Languedoc.   Chapter 1 describes the demographics of Protestant settlement in Bas-Languedoc, and its economic and social character. It draws attention to the ways in which patterns were changing and the pressures these alterations were placing on the fabric of the community. Chapter 2 follows the history of Protestantism in the region from the Reformation to the White Terror in 1815. It focuses on the impact repression and the polarized Protestant-Catholic relations had in forging Reformed identity.   The exigencies and experiences of persecution not only had a direct impact on identity, they also had a determining effect on the organization of the community and the place of the Reformed faith, and the Reformed Church in communal life.

The next three chapters describe the Réveil in the Reformed community of southern France. Chapter 3 looks at the condition and structure of the Reformed Church, and follows its institutional recovery of French Protantism, both from within the established church and the network of voluntary agencies that surrounded it. Chapter 4 focuses on the spiritual awakening that paralleled, but operated independently of the institutional renewal. Chapter 5 examines the tensions and debates that surrounded this spiritual Réveil. It is particularly concerned with how religious controversies reflected underlying tensions, but also on how the Réveil opened up new avenues of expression in the community that broke with customs and social norms of the past and threatened to overturn the traditional order.

This is followed in Chapter 6 with a look at responses by the established church to the challenges presented by the Réveil. This section focuses on charitable assistance and religious rituals to show how competition between evangelicals and liberals for influence in the community led to an expansion and differentiation in social assistance, and introduced new forms of worship and standards of religious devotion that generalized the impact of the Réveil throughout the religious life of the Reformed community. The chapter ends with a look at the national conference in Reformed Protestantism held in Paris soon after the February Revolution of 1848. Though this meeting had no official standing it was the first nation-wide meeting of the Reformed Churches of France since the mid-eighteenth century. At the conference a clear majority of the delegates showed themselves determined to maintain the integrity of Reformed Protestantism despite the many differences dividing them.

By way of conclusion the book looks at the celebration in 1859, of the three hundredth anniversary of the founding of the French Reformed Church. The event was marred in southern France, however, by the Bishop of Nîmes' use of the occasion to publish a pamphlet that challenged the Protestant community's right to celebrate the anniversary since they no longer followed the religion established by Calvin and enshrined in the Reformed Confession of La Rochelle of 1559. His assault struck a sensitive nerve and provoked several immediate and passionate responses from Protestant ministers. In them can be seen in some detail the effort the Reformed community made to come to grips with what it meant to be a Protestant in nineteenth-century France. The specifics of this case are particular to the Reformed Protestants of Languedoc, but to the degree that religion formed the identity of communities of other faiths and in other places it is informative of how they too balanced and maintained local and national affiliations in the midst of the formation of modern France.

CHAPTER 1

CONTEXT

In the nineteenth century the most distinct feature of the region of Languedoc centering on the department of the Gard was the religious diversity of its population. As with other parts of France it was mostly Roman Catholic with a fair-sized Jewish community in the cities of Nîmes and Montpellier and a compliment of skeptics and Free Thinkers as well. More unique was that nearly a third of the region's population was Protestant. The presence of this large minority transformed the area's religious variety into a confessional division that was reflected in its demographic, social and economic features.

The region was diverse in other ways as well. It had three distinct geographic regions, the costal plain, the Garrigues which was an arid plateau, and the Cévennes Mountains. It had an active urban life, dominated by the cities of Nîmes and Montpellier, but was also profoundly rural with numerous isolated hamlets. In the mountains and during periods of bad weather travel was even more difficult.[1] Economic activity too, was varied. There was a large and active artisanat, much of which was involved in the production of textiles with the beginnings of industrialization visible in textile manufacturing and in the expansion of coal mining and railroads. In agriculture, some regions still followed the traditional practices of polyculture, while others produced for the marketplace, specializing in crops such as wine or mulberry leaves.

The region spanned the line between the heights of Haut-Languedoc and the plains of Bas-Languedoc. It was bounded geographically by the Massif Central to the north, the Rhône River to the east and the Mediterranean Sea on the south. The coastal regions were mostly marshy flats from the Camargue in the Gard to the Etang de Thau south of Sète.

This rose into the coastal plain, a twenty to thirty mile wide band of fertile land arching from Béziers to Roquemaure on the east bank of the Rhone. North of this were the barren Garrigues, which one writer likened to a Middle Eastern landscape.[2] This stony, barren terrain stretched north into the Vivarais and northwest to the foothills of the Cévennes. Protestants were largely concentrated within a rough triangle stretching from Sète and Montpellier to the southeast, Nîmes to the east, and Mende in the north. Above the towns of Alès and Anduze were the Cévennes Mountains themselves, which were the spiritual and demographic heartland of Occitan Protestantism.

Administratively the jurisdictions were carved out of the old province of Languedoc by the Constituent Assembly in 1790, and included much of the department of the Gard, the western Hérault and southern Lozère, as well as parts of the Ardèche and Aveyron. It is arguable that Montpellier, with its ancient university and law courts, was more important intellectually and culturally, but the geographic, demographic and cultural center of Protestantism in southern France lay in the department of the Gard and its capital, Nîmes.

Though the number of Protestants in the region (about 30 percent of the population in the Gard) was in itself unusual, their geographic concentration increased their importance in local affairs. For the most part the Protestant community was concentrated in the Garrigues and the hills of the Cévennes. The only area of fertile soil in which Protestants were numerically dominant was the region of the Vaunage in the valley of the Vidoure River that formed the boundary between the departments of the Hérault and the Gard. In the Gard, more than 40 percent of the population, but only 18 percent of the Protestants, lived in Nîmes or on the fertile soil of the eleven cantons lying east of the city. To the west and north, Protestants made up a significantly larger proportion of the population. In twelve of these cantons they were a majority. In three others they made up more than 40 percent of the inhabitants. And in four cévenol cantons at least eight of every ten residents were of the Reformed faith. This pattern held in the neighboring departments of the Hérault and Lozère as well. The six thousand Protestants of Montpellier were notable in terms of wealth and education, but were only a small percentage of the city's inhabitants. More important were the Calvinist concentrations around Marsillargues in the Vaunage, and Ganges in the foothills of the Cévennes. Similarly there was a small Protestant community in Mendes, but they were far more numerous in the rural cantons bordering the Gard, especially in the Valle de France and Florac which were nearly entirely populated by Protestants.[3]

This geographic confessional division continued within cantons, towns and cities. It was not uncommon for one commune to be completely Catholic and the next nearly entirely Protestant. The town of Aiguesmortes, for example, was less than 2 percent Protestant, but a few kilometers away the commune of St-Laurent-d'Aigouze was nearly two-thirds Protestant. In the Cévennes, three-fourths of the residents of Valleraugue were Reformed, while just down the road they were fewer then one hundred of the two thousand inhabitants of St-André-de Majaneoule. It was the same situation in the city of Nîmes. In 1852, this city had more than 50,000 residents, 14,000 of whom were Protestant. This Reformed population was strongly concentrated in the northern and western neighborhoods. Sections 1 and 2 of the city were more than half Protestant, but Sections 3 through 9 were 90 percent Catholic.[4]

Despite this concentration in Nîmes the vast majority of Protestants lived in the countryside and earned their livelihood directly from the land. Over 60 percent of the department's adult population was occupied in agricultural production. A rather large proportion of this population were property owners (See Table 1.1). Nearly 70 percent of those deriving their living from the land owned property. More than 80 percent of these lived entirely from this land, 72 percent by working the soil themselves, and 12 percent by renting their holdings to others. Only 9 percent of the agricultural population farmed as sharecroppers or rented the land they worked, and more than a third of these also owned some land. However, many did not own land or did not own enough to feed themselves and their families. Thus, nearly a third of the total rural population worked at least part of the year as agricultural day-laborers, but ownership of some land remained common as more than a fifth of the 47,804 journaliers were also propriétaires. These earned or supplemented their income by alternating work in the grain, wine and silk harvest with the gathering of salt from the salt marshes along the coast. Understandably then, the proportion of day laborers was substantially higher south of a line running from Nîmes to Roquemaure, where this labor was most needed. Here in the coastal plain, half of the agricultural work force was identified as journaliers, compared to less than a third in the rest of the department. This same region held slightly more than 14,000 (11 percent) of the Gard's 126,000 Protestants, of which 11,000 lived in the canton of Vauvert. In contrast close to 90 percent of the Reformed community and 75 percent of the department's agricultural population lived in the Cévennes and Garrigues. In these regions nearly three-fourths of those

Table 1.1
Agricultural Population of the Gard, 1851

Canton	Agricultural Population	% Protestant	% Propriétaires/ Cultivateurs	% Day laborers
Arrondissement of Alès				
Alès	7,176	30	37	39
St-Ambroix	7,707	16	69	22
Anduze	3,733	84	54	22
Barjac	2,448	13	79	16
Génolhac	5,500	10	62	29
St-Jean-du-Gard	1,878	89	43	23
Lédignan	2,047	77	51	31
St-Martin-de-Valgalgues	4,822	33	72	11
Vézénobres	3,604	72	67	23
Arrond. Total	38,915	38	59	25
Arrondissement of Nîmes				
Aiguesmortes	720	19	25	71
Aramon	5,234	0	39	35
Beaucaire	4,556	0	40	51
St-Gilles	2,561	18	7	78
St-Mamert	4,293	61	51	35
Marguerittes	3,850	1	43	49
Nîmes	7,022	26	13	39
Sommières	6,588	61	45	28
Vauvert	6,589	69	25	58
Arrond. Total	41,413	29	33	45
Arrondissement of Uzès				
Bagnols	7,811	0	57	27
St-Chaptes	4,572	50	68	24
Lussan	2,657	24	100	24
Pont-St-Esprit	6,656	0	69	24
Rémoulins	3,115	0	49	41
Roquemaure	5,881	0	39	48
Uzès	5,557	28	50	35
Villeneuve	3,628	0	42	41
Arrond. Total	39,877	12	58	33
Arrondissement of Le Vigan				
Alzon	1,498	19	55	33
St-André-de-Valbrgn	2,345	93	67	16
St-Hippolyte-du-Fort	1,832	58	41	30
Lasalle	2,881	86	42	33

Continued on next page.

Table 1.1 - Continued

Canton	Agricultural Population	% Protestant	% Propriétaires/ Cultivateurs	% Day laborers
Quissac	2,021	54	52	32
Sauve	1,588	66	41	44
Sumène	3,220	28	53	19
Trèves	1,714	1	73	5
Valleraugue	2,879	45	67	27
Le Vigan	3,873	41	37	34
Arrond. Total	23,851	49	52	27
Department Total	144,056	30	50	33

Source: Census of 1851. ADG 6M 111.

involved in farming made their living entirely from their own land. This high percentage of landowning meant that individual holdings were quite small, but as Emilien Frossard observed of the region around Alès, "today there is not a crevice in the rock which is not filled by a mulberry or chestnut tree. . . . Here the land is extremely divided. Each family possesses a fraction of soil on which it labors to render productive the smallest parcel."[5] Through hard work and efficient use of every piece of soil, peasants earned a degree of economic independence which could translate into a social and psychological independence not always present to the same degree in other populations.

Although predominantly rural, Bas-Languedoc was not able to feed itself. Since much of the food supply had to be imported, the additional cost of transportation meant residents paid significantly higher prices for their bread than elsewhere in France. Thus, in 1817 the Prefect of the Gard worried about the late arrival of grain from Toulouse, and in 1834, low water on the Saône created a grain shortage that raised the price of bread in Nîmes to nearly twice that in Lorraine. Part of the shortfall in foodstuffs was due to the lack of good land. It was only on the fertile coastal plain that cereals could be grown with success. Consequently, inhabitants in many areas, and particularly those of the Cévennes, relied on alternative crops such as chestnuts for their dietary staple and feed for their animals. In addition, while traditional forms of polyculture were still prominent, farmers in some regions were starting to specialize in specific crops.[6] Even landowners in the fertile coastal plain were shifting from wheat to other crops that seemed more profitable.

One such crop was wine. Viticulture had been expanding slowly in the region for several centuries. In part this was a consequence of the demise of communal grazing lands, forcing villagers to give up their stock animals and plant a cash crop. Some of these vineyards, especially those along the Rhône, had a fair reputation outside the immediate region, but most wine was destined for the local market or converted into eau-de-vie.[7] With the expansion of the railroads in the 1840s, and a shift towards monoculture in other regions of France, demand grew for cheap *vin ordinaire*. It was met by increased planting of vignoble. In the first-half of the century growth in viticulture was not too dramatic, but in later years it picked up pace. In 1844, 71,306 hectares in the Gard were planted in vineyards. Prior to the devastation wrought by the phylloxera epidemic in the late 1860s the total stood at more than 104,000 hectares, with much of the growth taking place in the Vaunage, while the Hérault produced only a quarter of its needs in wheat due to the amount of land given-over to growing grapes.[8]

The other crop to rise in importance was the cultivation of mulberry trees (See Table 1.2). These trees were valued for their leaves which formed the sole ingredient in the diet of the silk worm. They had been introduced in the regions of Uzès, Alès and Anduze several centuries earlier with its fortunes rising and falling according to conditions of economy and fashion. After the uncertainty of the Revolutionary period and the English blockade during the Empire, the silk market grew in the first-half of the nineteenth century, and with it the planting of mulberry trees expanded. From 1839 to 1852, the amount of land given over to mulberries increased by 22 percent. These trees provided a convenient means for subsistence farmers to supplement their income, particularly in those regions where poor soil prevented the cultivation of cereals and grapevines.[9]

The increased commitment to mulberries was a function of the importance of the silk worm for the Gardois economy. As Frossard observed, "the handsome and abundant production of silk occupies the inhabitant of the Cévennes during a large part of the year, puts all arms to work during the good season and feeds our mills in Bas-Languedoc." From the time they hatched in late spring, until they built their cocoons for winter hibernation, silk worms fed continuously on the mulberry leaves fed to them by their breeders. In late summer the cocoons were harvested, boiled in water to be loosened and drawn into thread. In mulberry leaves and cocoons alone, silk worms added more than 25 million francs to the economy of the department of the Gard in 1841.[10] These were only two parts in the multi-stepped process required for the production of silk cloth. The thread was then woven and dyed, or blended with other fibers, depending on the finished product. The spinning of silk thread and its

Table 1.2
Plantings in Mulberry Trees

	Mulberries (hectares)	Percent of Land	Value of Mulberries	Value of Cocoons
Arrondissement of Alès				
Alès	1352	17.5	--	--
St-Ambroix	2150	14.5	–	--
St-Jean-du-Gard	490	8.2	--	--
St-Martin-de-Valgalgues	621	10.7	--	--
Vézénobres	781	5.0	--	--
Arrond. total	6260	7.9	5,310,159f	8,372,000f
Arrondissement of Nîmes				
Aramon	211	1.5	--	--
St-Gilles	316	1.7	--	--
St-Mamert	371	2.2	--	--
Marguerittes	268	1.7	--	--
Arrond. total	1510	0.9	30,881f	40,823f
Arrondissement of Uzès				
Bagnols	500	2.0	--	--
St-Chaptes	728	4.2	--	--
Lussan	1458	5.8	--	--
Pont-St-Esprit	1700	5.8	--	--
Uzès	589	2.0	--	--
Arrond. total	5403	3.1	3,241,012f	4,651,556f
Arrondissement of Le Vigan				
St-André-de-Valborgne	605	5.1	--	--
Lasalle	588	4.6	--	--
Sumène	645	5.6	--	--
Valleraugue	406	3.5	--	--
Le Vigan	449	2.7	--	--
Arrond. total	3281	2.6	2,781,465f	4,269,276f
Department Total	16,454	3.0	17,333,655f	11,363,518f

Source: Hector Rivoire, *Statistiques du Gard* (Nîmes, 1842), 67, 796-797.

creation into a finished product could be performed year-round, but the early stages of silk production were seasonal. Often they were carried out during a farmer's spare hours, and particularly by their wives and children. In a good year a family could add the equivalent of a hundred-days' wages for a month and-a-half of work.[11]

While production of silk cloth rose steadily after 1817, its profitability was subject to severe fluctuations. To respond to increasing competition from cheap cotton goods flowing out of the English midlands and the continuing shift in economic strength from the Mediterranean to the

Atlantic, silk producers in Nîmes and the rest of the Gard concentrated on the lower-end of the market. Accordingly, their manufactures shifted from taffeta to cheap silk and cotton blend stockings, known as *bonneterie*, handkerchiefs and shawls (Table 1.3).

Table 1.3
Textile Production in Nîmes, 1825-1840

Year	Workers Employed	Taffeta Pieces	Shawls and Handkerchiefs	Total Pieces	Value (x 1,000F)
1825	4,180	3,750	83,000	161,900	13,947
1826	19,790	3,300	45,000	96,200	18,000
1827	15,580	1,930	28,800	73,190	12,602
1828	15,200	1,600	27,200	68,100	11,750
1829	14,300	900	162,000	201,900	9,000
1830	15,300	300	350,000	490,000	9,000
1831	13,100	600	360,000	505,000	8,700
1832	14,950	800	550,000	768,000	15,600
1833	16,080	850	725,000	1,030,250	19,600
1834	15,960	840	605,000	884,340	17,700
1835	15,400	690	760,000	955,290	12,000
1836	14,800	650	690,000	874,050	12,000
1837	9,600	250	1,510,000	1,511,250	6,000
1838	11,250	200	1,685,000	1,686,000	8,000
1839	11,750	200	1,405,000	1,405,900	9,500
1840	10,350	150	1,190,000	1,190,650	8,500

Source: Rivoire, *Statistiques du Gard* (Nîmes, 1842),. 68-69.

Though these articles were more affordable for the general public, they were quite susceptible to economic fluctuations. In Nîmes, the center of the region's silk industry, employment in textile manufactures reached a peak in 1826, of more than 19,000. Five years later, it dropped by a third. A few years after that it was back up to 16,000, but then began a gradual decline to little more than 9,000 in the mid-1840s. In 1851, more than 10,500 were still engaged in the manufacture of cloth, yet the city as a whole had grown by a third during the previous decade. The value of the textiles fluctuated even more. Between 1826 and 1831, the value of cloth manufactures in Nîmes declined by half. Two years later they more than doubled. After that, reflecting the shift to shawls and handkerchiefs, value again declined until in 1840, it fell below the 1831 level. Thus, while employment in the Nîmois textile industry dropped by 35 percent from 1833 to 1840, receipts shrank 56 percent. The decline of the textile industry in Nîmes did not necessarily indicate a similar decline in the region as a whole. Though Nîmes dominated the industry, cloth was manufactured in the other towns and communes as well. In part this was due to the lack of an adequate water supply in Nîmes which hindered expansion of production. But entrepreneurs also encouraged production in the countryside to escape the higher costs and restrictions of the urban labor force. Thus, part of the decline in textile manufacture in Nîmes was due to the dispersal of production into the countryside where it was a cottage industry. The statistician Hector Rivoire in 1842, cited more than a dozen towns that were important centers for the manufacture of *bonneterie*, where the weavers worked "for the fabricants in the region or for the fabricants of Nîmes." This rural competition prompted some Nîmois workers, inspired by the Lyon silk workers' rebellion of 1834, to go into the countryside and smash their rivals' looms.[12]

Despite this hostility weaving continued as a rural occupation. The census of 1851, showed twenty cantons outside of Nîmes with more than 300 individuals involved in textile production. For the Gard as a whole, more than 30,000 men and women, or approximately 15 percent of the adult population, were involved in the manufacturing of cloth. Twenty-one thousand of these were engaged in small artisanal or domestic production, with more than a quarter listed as masters.[13]

Whether located in Nîmes or in the towns and communes of the Garrigues and Cévennes the manufacture of textiles in Bas-Languedoc underwent significant structural changes during the Restoration and July Monarchy. It began with the introduction of the Jacquard loom in 1819, which made it easier to weave designs directly into the fabric. By 1825, more than half the looms in Nîmes were of this type.[14] At the same time small mechanized mills were introduced alongside artisanal and cottage based forms of production. The shift to large-scale production progressed rather slowly as the relative costs of machinery and power were high for a region with a large inexpensive labor-pool. Eventually this worked against the industry because when it became necessary to mechanize further to remain competitive the textile industry could not compete with the wine industry for scarce capital. Yet during the Restoration and Orléans Monarchies, there existed a sometimes uneasy blend of rural and artisanal production with machine production.[15]

In the countryside the spinning of silk thread was increasingly concentrated in small mills or *filatures*. In the early 1840s, Rivoire listed seventy-four mills of more than twenty employees, with a combined work force of 3,718, including 3,049 women and 339 children. Most of these small factories were located in the northern towns of the department, such as Anduze, St-Jean-du-Gard, Uzès and Bagnols. As local production of finished silk products declined, the producers of raw and spun silk were able to survive by supplying producers outside the region.[16] Nîmes had only six filatures, employing 223 people, but held nearly all of the small cloth producing mills or *fabriques*. There were forty-five fabriques of shawls in Nîmes, with a work force of 5,406; forty-one factories made silk blend stockings, gloves and cloth, employing 1,530 workers; four mills employed 325 people in the manufacture of rugs; and three fabriques, with a total of 480 employees specialized in dying and printing the manufactured cloth. For the department as a whole, Rivoire provides a figure of 16,957 people working in 249 establishments having more than twenty employees each and engaged in some aspect of the manufacture of textiles.[17]

More modern types of heavy industry were also beginning to appear. Two smelters were operating in the arrondissement of Alès in the early 1840s, taking advantage of the coal and iron deposits located north of Alès in La Grand' Combe and Portes. Together these two enterprises, one at Robiac and the other in Alès, employed more than 800 workers and had an annual production of nearly 20,000 metric tons. An additional foundry had just begun producing in Alès. In Nîmes there were two smaller foundries employing more than one hundred men, producing a little less than two thousand metric tons of milled iron and machinery. Nîmes also was the site for a fledgling gas company producing 250,000 cubic meters of gas and more than a thousand metric tons of coke.[18]

The expansion in metallurgy was founded upon growth in mining. In 1835, the basin north of Alès produced 45,000 tons of coal. Ten years later this had grown to 415,000 tons. The fortunes of both mining and smelting in the Gard were enhanced by the opening of a rail link between La Grand' Combe, Alès and Beaucaire in 1838, and the extension of the Paris-Lyon-Mediterranean Railroad in 1844, through Nîmes to Montpellier. As a result, the mines and smelters of Alès were able to compete successfully with those of the Loire in a regional market stretching from the Basses-Alpes to the Haute-Garonne. By 1851, there were eleven blast furnaces and three metal foundries processing the mineral resources of the Gard.[19]

These enterprises attracted an increasingly large and varied labor force. Approximately one thousand workers were employed in the casting mills and smelters and nearly three thousand were miners according to the census of 1851. Some of these workers were from Belgium, Piedmont and England. Others were French, but from outside the region. In

Table 1.4
Population of the Gard, 1831-1851

Canton	% Protestant (1851)	Popultion (1831)	Popultion (1851)	Population Change	% Change
Arrondissement of Alès					
Alès	29.47	16,647	24,328	7,681	46.1
St-Ambroix	15.83	13,973	18,251	4,278	30.6
Anduze	83.99	9,215	9,905	690	7.5
Barjac	12.82	5,250	6,316	1,066	20.3
Génolhac	10.18	10,979	11,680	701	6.4
St-Jean-du-Gard	88.89	5,650	6,032	382	6.8
Lédignan	76.45	4,591	4,769	178	3.9
St-Martin-de-Valgal.	32.51	7,611	13,982	6,371	83.7
Vézénobres	71.88	6,372	6,909	537	8.4
Arrond. Total	38.07	80,288	102,172	21,884	27.3
Arrondissement of Nîmes					
Aiguesmortes	19.00	4,372	5,632	1,260	28.8
Aramon	0.01	11,483	12,366	883	7.7
Beaucaire	0.24	13,867	16,015	2,148	15.5
St-Gilles	18.16	7,444	7,925	481	6.5
St-Mamert	61.19	7,001	7,186	185	2.6
Marguerittes	0.67	7,197	7,614	417	5.8
Nîmes	27.33	45,574	58,921	13,347	29.3
Sommières	61.40	15,813	16,024	211	1.3
Vauvert	69.30	15,710	16,898	1,188	7.6
Arrond. total	29.41	128,461	148,581	20,120	15.6
Arrondissement of Uzès					
Bagnols	0.32	16,027	16,493	466	2.9
St-Chaptes	49.91	8,334	8,973	639	7.7
Lussan	23.70	6,121	6,595	474	7.7
Pont-St-Esprit	0.20	14,647	16,510	1,863	12.7
Rémoulins	0.15	6,194	6,621	427	6.9
Roquemaure	0.09	11,093	12,062	969	8.7
Uzès	28.09	14,489	15,559	1,070	7.4
Villeneuve	0.11	6,847	7,112	265	3.9
Arrond. total	11.71	83,752	89,925	6,173	7.4
Arrondissement of Le Vigan					
Alzon	19.13	4,377	4,542	165	3.8
St-André-de-Valbgn.	93.06	4,407	4,411	4	0.1
St-Hippolyte	57.81	7,922	8,502	580	7.3
Lasalle	86.18	6,416	6,446	30	0.5
Quissac	53.88	4,499	4,870	371	8.3
Sauve	66.14	5,327	5,263	(64)	(1.2)

Continued on next page.

Table 1.4 - Continued.

Canton	% Protestant (1851)	Population (1831)	Population (1851)	Population Change	% Change
Sumène	27.71	7,176	7,359	183	2.6
Trèves	0.53	3,604	3,401	(203)	(5.6)
Valleraugue	45.24	6,521	7,423	902	13.8
Le Vigan	40.97	14,639	15,002	363	2.5
Arrond Total	49.26	64,888	67,219	2,331	3.6
Department Total	30.95	357,389	407,897	50,508	14.1

Sources: Derived from Census of 1831,ADG 6M 105; Census of 1851, ADG 6M 111.

addition to these, the area of Alès and La Grand' Combe was attracting a large number of individuals from the surrounding countryside.[20] As a result the area around the mines and foundries grew markedly. Alès grew from 12,077 in 1831, to 18,871 in 1851. Robiac doubled in size, from 1,209 to 2,463 during the same period, and La Grand' Combe, which was not listed in the 1831 census, had a population of 4,730 in 1851. Over all, the cantons of Alès, St-Ambroix and St-Martin-de-Valgalgues grew 68 percent in the twenty years between 1831 and 1851. No other part of the region had as dramatic a population increase. Nîmes itself had a raw population gain only two-thirds that of the cantons of the Alès basin.[21]

While the demographic changes in the arrondissement of Alès dwarfed those elsewhere, during the July Monarchy the region was beginning to experience the massive population shifts that would eventually leave the countryside relatively depopulated. The people of Bas-Languedoc were traditionally quite mobile. Men and women would descend from the slopes of the Cévennes to work the harvests, collect salt, or seek temporary employment in the towns and cities of the plains, while shepherds took their flocks and herds into the mountains for the summer's grazing. By the middle of the 1840s, however, these seasonal migrants were not always returning home.[22] Between 1836 and 1851, the departments of Lozère and Ardèche had a net migration loss of more than 20,000. During the same period, the Gard gained 12,700 residents as a result of immigration from other departments. The department of l'Hérault grew by 14,200, the department of the Vaucluse, across the Rhône, by 1,900, and the Bouches-du-Rhône had an in-migration of 54,700 reflecting the growth of the ports of Marseille and Toulon.[23] Population changes between departments can mask equally important changes in demographic patterns within the departments. Leslie Page Moch has shown the importance of Nîmes as a destination for migrants from the towns of Villefort and Langogne in the Lozère, as well as Le

Vigan within the Gard. To this terminus could be added Montpellier, the port of Aiguesmortes and the mines and foundries of the region of Alès.[24] By the middle of the nineteenth century the towns of Villefort, Langogne and most other cevenol communes suffered from a loss of local industry as poor lines of communication and cheap outside products displaced local artisans and merchants. As a result, many inhabitants of these remote areas traveled south in search of better opportunities.

The plight of Le Vigan was somewhat better than many areas due to its position as a regional administrative, commercial and industrial center. Despite this, however, the canton of Le Vigan showed a gross population increase of only 2.5 percent during the July Monarchy and Second Republic, and the town itself grew even less.[25] As a whole the Gard grew by fifty thousand people, of which Jean Pitié estimates 12,700 migrated into the department. This would mean a natural increase of 10.6 percent between 1831 and 1851, or an annual rate of .53 percent. This is deceptive. Only nine cantons achieved this rate of growth, and even then growth varied considerably from one commune to the next (Table 1.4). Thus, while the canton of St-Martin-de-Valgalgues grew by 83.7 percent, five communes had less than 10 percent growth, and two of these actually declined in size. In fact, the cities of Alès and Nîmes and the mining centers of Robiac and La Grand' Combe, together accounted for more than half of the total increase. Excluding these four centers population growth for the rest of the department was less than 7 percent. Several places did not achieve even this level of growth. Demographic expansion was particularly weak in the Cévennes, where the cantons of Génolhac, St-Jean-du-Gard, St-André-de-Valborgne, Lasalle, Valleraugue, Trèves, Le Vigan, and Sumène grew less than 4 percent in twenty years.[26]

These comparisons are crude and do not take into account birth and death rates, yet it seems clear that by the late 1840s the region of the Cévennes was experiencing a mild demographic crisis. Population in the area was not yet in decline, but it was nearly static and considerably less than what would be expected from natural increase. The fact that demographic trends varied markedly from one commune to the next would seem to indicate that the flat rate of demographic growth was due less to fertility and mortality rates than to mobility. People were abandoning the remote regions of the department for more urban settings.[27] These figures indicate the population shifts taking place within the department itself, and particularly in the Cévennes, in addition to immigration from the departments of the Massif Central. This was not yet l'exode rurale, but it was a foretaste of what was to become a major demographic transformation.

These population movements were a visible indication of the tightening economic and social situation in Bas-Languedoc. It has already been seen that in cevenol and sub-cevenol regions levels of land ownership were quite high and the average size of holdings was quite small. Much of this land was also of poor quality, and not suitable for growing cereals. In order to maintain themselves the peasants of the region shifted to cash crops like mulberries and, in the lower regions, the vignoble, and supplemented their income by raising silkworms and participating in the silk and grape harvests.

Closely related to these agricultural circumstances was the presence of a large artisanat, particularly in textiles, which turned the raw cocoons into hose, gloves, shawls and rugs sold on the national and, through the fair at Beaucaire, the world market. Originally, production of these goods had been almost entirely performed in Nîmes, but as demand declined and competition increased, textile manufactures moved increasingly into the countryside. Thus, the region's population, and particularly those areas in which Protestants were concentrated, was highly commercialized and susceptible to the fluctuations of the market.

During much of the July Monarchy the market for silk was good, but the competitive pressures which prompted entrepreneurs to move production into rural areas continued to build. Lowering costs by further dispersion of the steps of production was no longer a practical solution. Rural manufacturing had nearly reached the saturation point, and the rural population had become quite dependant upon the silk industry for its existence, and accordingly less able to absorb reductions in income. Therefore, when an economic crisis developed its impact was more generalized and severe. One such decline followed the July Revolution of 1830. Another occurred in 1834, and continued on into 1838. In October 1834, the Municipal Council of Nîmes allocated 57,500 francs for public works projects and poor relief. In 1835 and 1836, the national government committed 15,000 francs for relief in the same city, and in 1837, raised the sum to 20,000 francs. It was also in this period that cholera swept through the region, striking the lower classes particularly hard.[28] The economy recovered slowly from these shocks, but in 1847, a new crisis took hold and fed the events and passions raised by the Second Republic.[29]

In this climate of economic uncertainty it would be natural to assume that social tensions would increase. They did, but not to the degree that might be expected. For most of the first-half of the nineteenth century the major source of civil strife was not social class but confessional differences between Protestants and Catholics. Frequently this could have a social aspect, particularly since the Protestants dominated the bourgeoisie, but under the limited franchise of the July Monarchy this hostility was political rather than social.[30] Economically the two confessions were essentially segregated. Merchants and artisans of both confessions tended to have employees and clients drawn mostly from their own religion. As Brian Fitzpatrick concluded in his study of Catholic royalism during the July Monarchy:

> The remarkable tranquility of the working populations of the Gard in contrast to those of other industrial regions, including the nearby Lyonnais, is a reflection both of the extent to which social elites, particularly the Catholic elite, continued to influence their co-religionists well into the nineteenth century, and of the extent to which the popular classes continued to identify conflict in terms of sectarian antagonism.[31]

As a result of confessional patronage, class tensions remained largely submerged beneath those arising from religious differences.

This did not mean such tensions were not present. The best evidence comes from the Second Republic and early years of the Second Empire when the Reformed community visibly divided between Orléanists, Bonapartists and Republicans.[32] Indications of social tension are also found in records from the previous period. In the region of Le Vigan one's class could be distinguished by dress, language, food and even when one ate.[33] The social question was pertinent enough in the late 1830s to prompt Félix de Lafarelle, a Legitimist elected to the Chamber of Peers in 1842, and to the Consistory of Nîmes in 1845, to write and publish a detailed study of the issue.[34]

The elites of society and the higher authorities were suspicious of the common people to the point that having popular support in a dispute could immediately raise suspicions of anarchism or socialism. Thus, Jean-Paul Hugues, serving as the assistant to the Protestant pastor in the town of Gallargues, had to defend himself against charges of anarchism because he had the backing of the common people in a dispute with the regular pastor. Similarly, another assistant pastor, François Reboul, had a complaint filed against him by the commissar of police in Sommières for campaigning among the Protestants in the surrounding towns and countryside and among the poor in his bid to secure a vacant pastorate.[35]

The clearest example, however, of social tensions within the Reformed community of the Gard, comes from the cevenol town of Valleraugue, more than three-quarters Protestant. In 1844, a popular disturbance necessitated the occupation of the town by a company of soldiers. It resulted from charges of moral impropriety leveled against a local pastor by several of the town's notables. His forced resignation became intertwined in a pre-existing dispute between urban elites and the rural population over a recent change in local taxes. The residents of the countryside rallied around the embattled pastor, boycotted the official church, set up religious services of their own, and built a structure in which to hold these services. Ultimately this venture into religious separatism lost energy and failed, but it revealed the tensions lying below the surface of Protestant solidarity, and the ability for these pressures, once emerged, to assume a religious guise.[36]

Such social tensions were not confined to the region of Valleraugue. In this respect Bas-Languedoc was similar to the Var, the Lyonnais, and the alpine regions.[37] The transition from old regime to new was still underway. Agriculture was shifting from polyculture and subsistence farming to monocultural production of cash crops. In many regions holdings were small and a peasants' livelihood depended upon the market for finished silk. In this way the fate of the peasant was tied with that of the small artisan in textiles, and the two worlds frequently over-lapped. The silk worker turned the product of the farmers labor into a finished product which was sold on a world market. In the course of the nineteenth century this market was increasingly vulnerable to competition from mechanized producers in France, England, and elsewhere, changes in fashion, the onset of disease, and the vagaries of a commercial economy. In economic crises small landholders and artisans suffered alike. Their vulnerability was visible in the need for government relief in the cities and the first signs of permanent migration from the more isolated and least productive areas. Larger landowners, producers and merchants, however, could afford to wait out a crisis and perhaps even increase their holdings at the expense of the less fortunate.

In these circumstances class conflict was a natural result, and this became particularly evident during the Second Republic, as well as a few incidents in earlier years. Yet on the whole, the region appeared unusually calm when it came to the *social question* in comparison to its neighbors. There were no major strikes or other large public demonstrations of economic concerns between the Restoration and the Second Republic.[38] This may have been a product of the overriding concern with confessionalism. Society was divided less according to issues of class and economics than that of religion. There existed a hostility between Catholic and Protestant populations rooted in centuries of conflict and violence, and which often superseded all other questions. Thus, while the Reformed community of southern France experienced many of the same social and economic stresses that placed the *question sociale* at the forefront of public debate, religious identity supported a thin plaster that united merchant and artisan, peasant and landlord against the menace of the Catholic majority.

CHAPTER 2

ORIGINS OF A CONFESSIONAL COMMUNITY

In 1875, the Prefect for the department of Lozère wrote his superiors in Paris about a large gathering of Protestants in his region to worship at the site of earlier gatherings of the Huguenot Church of the Desert. To illustrate his unease over this assembly he told of a conversation he had with a "highly honorable" noble about why political troubles always seemed to be used by Protestants and Catholics as a reason to shoot each other. The noble explained that in the preceding century the forebears of these Protestants had nailed his great grandfather alive to a barn door near his chateau. Given the opportunity, the aristocrat concluded, "I would shoot them like they were rabbits." This story, coming from the last quarter of the nineteenth century exemplifies the conditions that set Bas-Languedoc apart from the rest of France. This particularity was frequently cited by those charged with governing the region, who complained about the special challenges they confronted on a nearly daily basis. As the Prosecuting Attorney for the region argued in 1849, in urging the that a court of appeals be maintained at Nîmes, the city sat "between the Protestant populations of the Cévennes and the Catholic populations of the plain, and, holding 60,000 inhabitants from the two confessions, the least political commotion throws these two long hostile populations into direct confrontation."[1]

The confessional enmity testified to in these and similar examples characterized the religious complexity of Bas-Languedoc and was central to the perception among the Protestants of southern France that they formed a distinct community from the Catholic majority. While economic and political factors, especially the union of throne and altar in French absolutism, were also involved in creating this Protestant identity, "an unique tradition of hostility between organized groups, growing out of centuries of religious intolerance, was the most clearly distinctive aspect of [the] society."[2]

The "tradition of hostility" began in the Wars of Religion and in time hardened confessional differences into a cultural distinction. As Janine Garrison has argued, the Huguenots in particular came to define themselves in opposition to their Roman Catholic neighbors.

> One discerns among the Protestants, first by culture then by nature, the exaltation of those values which signified their difference [from French society]. Changed by its history, this religious society cemented itself together, and that which initially was the affirmation of its difference (even claiming it as a right), progressively transformed itself into permanence in difference.[3]

In the nineteenth century French Protestants continued to take pride in their distinctiveness from the Catholic majority. They saw their minority status and history of suffering as verification that they were a chosen people in whom lay the true hope of the nation. In this manner the crusading and evangelical spirit of primitive Calvinism remained fresh into the modern era.

This sense of a special calling was encouraged by Reformed theology. The Calvinist doctrine of predestination held that God's grace was limited to a select few, and that God in divine omnipotence had chosen those who were destined for Hell as well as for Heaven. Thus the world was divided between the saved and the damned, with neither peace nor compromise possible between the two. In the climate of Reformation polemics and the violence of the Wars of Religion, the differences between Protestants and Catholics could be interpreted apocalyptically as a battle between God's elect and the forces of evil. The atrocities committed by both sides turned this dualism into a self-perpetuating reality. Each round of violence spawned resentments and confirmed prejudices that were baptized theologically and fed into new confrontations, reconfirming and strengthening the divisions between the two populations.

While confession-based hostility and oppression encouraged the transformation of French Protestantism into a distinct community, it did not mean the Huguenots were unanimous in spirit and purpose. Neither were they exempted from the economic and social changes that were altering the structures of French society. External threats to their security, however, encouraged Protestants to display outward solidarity, while internal tensions tended to be papered over rather than risking the debates and dissension that could lead to their resolution. In addition, the revocation of the Edict of Nantes ended formal contacts between French Protestants and the rest of Protestant Europe, isolating them from theological and ecclesiastical developments that might have aided their adjustment to changing social and intellectual conditions. Consequently, though Protestants were united in their common consciousness as a distinct religious community, in the early nineteenth century it was a community marked by lines of fracture from unresolved strains and differences.

Viewed historically southern France seems to have been fertile ground for religious dissidence. In the fifth century the indigenous population held stubbornly to the Nicean creed despite the Arianism of their Visigothic conquerors. In the twelfth and thirteenth centuries, the region was nearly lost by the Roman Church to the Cathar and Waldensian heresies.[4] Some historians have argued these heresies prepared the ground in which Lutheran, and later Calvinist teachings would sprout and flourish among the women and men of Languedoc. In Nîmes and the surrounding towns and cities of the region Lutheran teachings and reforms began to appear in the early 1530s. The first executions for heresy took place in Nîmes in 1537, and were followed by similar burnings for false doctrine in Beaucaire and other towns of Languedoc.[5]

Persecution encouraged the replacement of this early Lutheranism with the organizational and doctrinal program of Calvinism that was more decentralized and less dependent on civil authority for its survival. In Nîmes in early 1560, the first celebration of communion according to the Reformed rite took place. Within a few years Reformed congregations directed by consistories of pastors and lay elders, and meeting regularly in regional synods, existed in nearly every city and town of Bas-Languedoc, a process greatly aided by the passage through the region of Pierre Viret, Calvin's colleague from Geneva. The region was also one of the few in which the Reformed faith moved outside of an urban environment and gained a strong peasant following. As Théodore Bèze noted with some surprise:

> It was during this time [the reign of Henri II] that the natives of the mountains of the Cévennes (a harsh, inhospitable country if ever there was one in France, and that would seem the least capable of receiving the Gospel on account of the rudeness of the spirit of the inhabitants), nevertheless received the Truth with marvelous ardor.[6]

In fact they may have been too ardent. It was here that the first Calvinist rebellions occurred in 1560, and a year later Calvin himself reprimanded the faithful of the Cévennes for their excessive enthusiasm for destroying crosses and statues.[7]

Throughout the Wars of Religion, Languedoc was dominated by the Huguenots, and the Catholic population suffered accordingly. One of the most remembered examples was the Michelade of September 29, 1567, that took place after municipal elections removed Huguenots from the city's administration. On the feast of St. Michael the Calvinists seized control of the city, slaughtering eighty priests and laymen in the process, many of whom were buried alive in a well.[8] Two years later the Catholic population struck back and sacked the Protestant temple at Nîmes. In February 1575, Protestants and "peaceful" Catholics signed a treaty of union. Catholic worship was only restored the following year, and incidents between the two communities continued into the reign of Henri IV.

Henri IV's promulgation of the Edict of Nantes formally concluded the Wars of Religion. It also granted various legal and religious privileges to Protestants which served to institutionalize their domination of Bas-Languedoc by giving them control of the urban centers of Montpellier, Nîmes, Alès, and Anduze as a guarantee of the terms of the edict. The Edict of Nantes, combined with the conversion of Henry IV from Calvinism to Roman Catholicism, was perhaps more restrictive for French Protestantism than it was liberating. The King's conversion assured the Catholicity of the state. At the same time, the Edict of Nantes assured the presence of the Reformed Church, but limited public Protestant worship to the lands of Protestant nobles and the two hundred fortified towns and villages granted to the Huguenots as security. Reformed worship was banned from all Catholic episcopal sees, and new congregations could not legally form after 1598. Thus, the peace and liberty of the Edict of Nantes essentially ended further Protestant expansion, sealing their minority status in a Catholic state.

Exhausted by thirty years of civil war and generally content with the compromises that brought them to an end, relations between Protestants and Catholics remained relatively calm for the rest of the reign of Henry IV. This detente ended in the 1620s as the Calvinist duc de Rohan led the south and west into revolt against the monarchy. The Huguenots, however, were far less effective in this uprising than they had been under Henry of Navarre. Still, from 1622 to 1629 the region was in a nearly constant state of unrest, suffering the ravages of royal and rebel armies alike. Finally, at the close of the decade Cardinal Richelieu orchestrated a campaign that crushed the rebellion. After the successful siege of La Rochelle in 1628, the King's army entered Languedoc to reduce the last Huguenot strongholds. Alès surrendered without resistance and Nîmes decided to negotiate. Louis XIII then issued the Edict of Alès of 1629, which stripped the Huguenots of their political and judicial privileges, but left their religious freedoms intact. This was the last revolt attempted by southern Calvinists until the revocation of the Edict of Nantes.[9]

Passivity, however, did not improve Huguenot fortunes. The monarchy openly discriminated against Protestants in the granting of offices and favors. Calvinists no longer dominated the government of the region, and as time passed their religious liberties were eroded. Protestants were gradually forced out of the faculty of the College of Nîmes until in 1644, the Jesuits assumed control. In 1639, the Bishop of Nîmes seized a Protestant leprosarium and gave it to the Ursulines. The buying of conversions also began in the years following the Edict of Alès. During his tenure as Garde des Sceaux, Michel de Marillac used cash subsidies to secure the conversion of eighty Reformed pastors, thirty-one of whom were in Languedoc.[10]

This combination of persuasion and suppression to win converts gained momentum under the reign of Louis XIV who, in his commitment to the principles of royal absolutism, entered into a Huguenot policy that culminated in 1685, with the revocation of the Edict of Nantes. In a society in which the Church registered births, marriages and deaths, and was the chief means of informing the public of state affairs, religious pluralism was an implicit denial of the equation of the state with the person of the king. It was therefore at least a latent threat to royal power. In the case of the Huguenots, Reformed theological emphasis on the priesthood of all believers and its representational form of church government, ran counter to the principles of authority and hierarchy characteristic of an absolutist state. In addition, their presence was a destabilizing factor in local affairs, and they had demonstrated on several occasions a willingness to engage in armed challenges to monarchical will. With Louis XIV's entry into an aggressive foreign policy against which the most stalwart opponent was the Calvinist William III, King of the Netherlands and later of England and Scotland, the presence in France of a large Reformed population could assume a sinister aspect.

For its part, Protestantism in France was losing momentum, and Protestants themselves continued to affirm their loyalty and obedience to the king. Despite their earlier rebellions, Protestant leaders now frequently argued in favor of the divine right of kings. As one pastor declared in a sermon:

> We believe that our kings recognize nothing above them in the world than God; that they hold their crown only from the first and eternal King of kings; that it cannot be separated from them except by Him alone; that they are not responsible for their actions to anyone on earth; that their subjects cannot be released by anyone, no matter whom this might be, from the fidelity they have sworn.[11]

The logic of *une foi, une loi, un roi*, however, worked against them. Louis XIV was content for a time to continue offering privileges and monetary compensation to encourage conversions, but this proved expensive and the results were not altogether satisfying. Instead, the government shifted strategies and began applying the terms of the Edict of Nantes with rigor, enforcing to the letter laws that had assured the presence of the Reformed faith in France and turning the Edict into an instrument for Protestantism's suppression. The National Synod of the French Reformed Church in 1660, was the last allowed by the King. In 1664, the government began disbanding congregations that had formed after 1598. Seats on municipal councils and university degrees were reserved to Catholics. Protestant schools were limited to a single teacher whose instruction could not have any religious content. Reformed pastors were similarly restricted in the performance of their duties. Conversions to the Reformed religion were forbidden. Catholics were not allowed to even enter a Protestant place of worship, infractions being punished by the suspension of worship in that place. Consequently, there were several cases of zealous Catholics walking into Protestant temples in order to provoke their closure. Similarly, Huguenot children could be taken away from their parents if they expressed a desire to convert to Catholicism, leading to numerous coerced conversions. Finally, in 1681, the practice of billeting royal troops in Huguenot homes began. These *dragonnades* were marked by beatings, imprisonment, torture, theft, rape and murder of Protestants at the hands of the soldiers. As one bishop stated, "the dragoons here have been good missionaries."[12]

One Huguenot response to these trials was to view them as a manifestation of God's punishment. Holding to their responsibility for loyalty and obedience towards the king as ordained of God, French Calvinists interpreted their sufferings as another indication of their special calling. God was punishing them for their disobedience in order to further purify them to fulfill their purpose. Thus a cevenol prayer composed soon after the Revocation confessed:

> Often you admonished us. Often you warned us by the mouth of your servants, but we closed our ears and hearts to your remonstrances and your warnings. Often you made us feel your rod, but we did not profit from it. We have seen the desolation of many churches, but the examples of your anger little subdued our hardness. You destroyed our temple because we profaned it by our impiety. There one read your word, and we filled this holy place with murmurs and profane conversations. There one preached your gospel, and we entertained our spirits with thoughts of the world. We departed from it as corrupt as when we entered.[13]

This heightened call of obedience to God led some to the conclusion they could not do so and also always obey the King. On May 3, 1683, several of this mind met in the home of the Nîmois lawyer Claude Brousson. Pledging "to live constantly in purity, sobriety, modesty, humility, good faith, equity, charity, piety and zeal for the glory of God," they approved Brousson's plan to resume worship services in private homes. In practice the Reformed bourgeoisie and a large part of the pastoral corps refused to participate in the project. Only in St-Hippolyte, and in the Vivarais were services actually held on a regular basis. According to Pastor Jean Claude, the "malcontents" attending these services amounted to only "a handful of persons, [and] only further enhanced the resignation and the obedience of our body."[14]

In the absence of mass resistance the government persisted towards its goal of reestablishing religious uniformity in France. In doing so there were those Calvinist ministers who actually sympathized with the project. They saw reunion with the Catholic Church as a real and desired possibility if certain concessions were secured, such as communion in both species, the singing of Psalms in French, modifications in the cults of the Virgin and of the Saints, and a declaration of the inviolability of the Four Gallican Articles. Pope Innocent XI, however, refused to make any concessions. In the face of his opposition, supported by the Jesuits, the Assembly of the Clergy in June of 1685, rejected a compromise. Instead, it pushed for new measures against the Protestants.

Louis XIV complied. Over the next few months most of the remaining temples were destroyed and Protestants were forbidden to travel to attend services in those temples that still existed. In the second half of 1685, with a new intendant in place, dragonnades were applied to Languedoc. In September, thirty-three temples were destroyed in the diocese of Nîmes. On October 4, the pastors of Nîmes, Saint-Cosme, Cheiron and

Paulhan led thousands of their parishioners to the cathedral of Nîmes where they abjured Calvinism. Three days later the town of Anduze surrendered, thereby extending the suppression of the Reformed religion into the Cévennes. At the same time thousands of others made their way into exile or prepared to do so.[15]

In the wake of mass conversions such as these, Louis XIV promulgated the Edict of Fontainebleau of October 15, 1685, which declared that since the "greatest part of the Reformed Protestant Religion" had embraced the Catholic faith it was "useless" to maintain the Edict of Nantes. Therefore he formally revoked the terms of the earlier edict. By this act of administrative efficiency the exercise of the Reformed religion in any public or private place was prohibited. Reformed pastors were ordered to convert or leave the realm within fifteen days. All children had to be baptized and raised in the Roman Catholic Church. Further, "anything in general, which could appear as a concession, whatever it might be, in favor of the said religion" was forbidden. Finally, Protestants were not allowed to leave the realm under threat of incarceration in the galleys and the confiscation of their property.

The Reformed pastorate was the first to suffer and experienced the most severe losses. It is estimated that of the six to seven hundred pastors then active in France, more than a third entered the Catholic Church. Most of the rest went into exile. Very few stayed to minister to their congregations. Most who did were in the Vivarais and the Cévennes. As for the Protestant laity, tens of thousands had already, or were about to emigrate. Samuel Mours has estimated that 200,000 French Calvinists sought refuge in a foreign state. Of these only about 14,500 were from Bas-Languedoc, the Vivarais and the Cévennes. All told, Mours figured that 40 percent of Protestants in the north fled the country, but only 8 percent of those in Bas-Languedoc and the Vivarais, and a mere 5 percent of cevenol Calvinists sought foreign refuge.[16] In part this is because the simple Huguenot artisans and peasants of this region were unable to flee because of geographic distance and poverty. But even among the bourgeoisie and nobility many Calvinists seemed to hope they could continue to live peacefully under the conditions of the final article of the edict of revocation. This article stated that those who had not converted:

> waiting for the time when it pleases God to enlighten them, . . . will remain in the towns and places of our realm . . . and there continue in their commerce and to enjoy their goods, without being either troubled or hindered under pretext of the said so-called Reformed Religion, under the condition that they make no exercise or assembly under pretext of prayer

or of worship in the said religion.[17]

In practice, this declaration was ignored or interpreted *à la rigueur*. Instead of seeking accommodation the government instituted a final dragonnade. Deprived of their leaders, most of the Reformed populace gave in quickly. The maréchal de Noailles, charged with the project in Languedoc, wrote "I no longer know what to do with the troops because the places where I send them convert so quickly and generally that all one is able to do is bed them for a night."[18] Thus, the first four days of the dragonnade in the cevenol town of Lasalle produced 425 conversions. By the end of the year eight hundred of the 1,375 Calvinists in Lasalle had been received into the Catholic Church.[19]

Under pressure the vast majority of the Reformed population did like their brothers and sisters at Lasalle and became Catholic. Many, however, did so in form, but not in conviction. They received the mass and had their children baptized to escape the dragoons, and to retain their positions and rights of inheritance, but did little else. In the countryside they sometimes waited only until the pressure eased somewhat before returning to the practices of their old faith. Thus, the curate of Gallargues came back to his church after being ill for several months to find it virtually empty and had to appeal to the civil authorities to force the residents back into the pews. At the same time many Huguenots began to gather secretly in caves, basements and fields for Reformed worship. In the Cévennes, enough were attending these services at the end of 1686, for the government to consider relocating the population en masse to other parts of the nation.[20]

Such behavior deepened suspicions about the sincerity of the conversions of all former Calvinists. This scepticism fed into the emergence of a new social classification, the *nouveaux convertis*, who were treated by the Catholic clergy, the civil authorities and the larger population with much the same suspicion and disdain with which the Spanish had viewed converted Jews and Moors. While such feelings naturally followed the suppression of the French Reformed Church wherever it had been established, in the region of Nîmes and the Cévennes, where the Huguenots had lived in significant concentration and their exodus into exile was relatively light, these feelings were even stronger. In addition, the rebelliousness of some of recent converts did little to assuage the distrust of all. Clandestine *assemblées du désert* continued, and in the near total absence of trained pastors and notables these meetings took on a character disturbing even too many Protestants.

In the Cévennes several laymen, usually artisans and a few peasants with one or two from the professions, like the lawyer Brousson began to call themselves preachers and took on the pastoral duties of the absent ministers.   Despite lacking any theological training they delivered sermons, distributed the Eucharist and baptized in their own right. Frequently they were chosen by those they served, and it was on this foundation of popular approval that they exercised the right to a act as ministers.[21]

The illegality of these meetings, the absence of ordained pastors, and their replacement by non-ordained men of the popular classes discouraged most Huguenot notables from participating. Some, particularly those who found refuge outside of France, continued to claim that those Protestants still in France were obligated either to obey the king or seek exile. Participants in the clandestine services, on the other hand, began arming themselves for protection in case of discovery. In addition, several preachers formed ties with foreign governments during the War of the League of Augsburg. Encouraged by states allied against Louis XIV, they attempted uprisings in September 1689, and March 1690. For the most part these rebellions only succeeded in confirming French suspicions of Calvinist loyalty and the rightness of Louis XIV's decision to revoke the Edict of Nantes.[22]

Calvinist *prédicants*, meanwhile, continued to stress the need for their listeners to repent their conversions to Roman Catholicism and return to their former calling. The combination of this prophetic spirit, inherent in Calvinism's use of the Old Testament, and the deprivations and insecurities Protestants suffered gave rise to what Philippe Joutard has termed an "epidemic of prophetism."[23]   The first of these prophets, or *inspirés*, was Isabeau Vincent, a fifteen-year-old Dauphinaise. Beginning in early 1689, according to an eyewitness, she would, while apparently asleep, "expound upon some passage of the Holy Scripture after which she [explains] its application to the present goods and evils of the Church and the repentance of the sinner, who is always the principal target of all her exhortations."[24] Others began to have similar experiences and people gathered to hear their message. Though this first wave of prophetism was soon suppressed by the authorities, in the fall of 1700 it reemerged. By this time Claude Brousson had been captured and executed at Montpellier, and the rest of the *prédicants* had either followed him into death or fled into exile. Deprived of even these untrained ministers, the Calvinists of the Cévennes welcomed the inspirés as their new spiritual leaders. Over time, however, the messages of the inspirés became increasingly militant, as they exhorted their listeners to take direct action against the Catholic Church. Inspired by such exhortations a group of men in July 1702, murdered the abbé du Chaila. The assassination of this zealous hunter of heretics was the opening act of the War of the Camisards.[25]

The Camisard rebellion was of major importance for shaping the identity of Protestant and Catholic populations alike in the eighteenth and early nineteenth centuries. Unlike the Wars of Religion and the rebellions of the seventeenth century, the War of the Camisards was both popular and religious. Neither the Protestant nobility nor the bourgeoisie played a significant part in it. The most successful Camisard chieftain, Jean Cavalier, was a baker's son. The rebels were closely tied to the people of the locales in which they operated, upon whom they depended for men and supplies. They used guerilla tactics, and their targets were principally religious: Catholic priests, shrines, and churches. When they attacked a chateau it was to gain arms or free prisoners, not to protest noble privilege or royal taxation.

In the conduct and suppression of this rebellion both sides met atrocity with atrocity. For example the Camisards slaughtered the people of Fraissinet-des-Fourques who were known for their cruelty towards the Protestants of the area. The Catholic village of Saturargues met a similar fate. The royal forces, for their part, surprised a group of three hundred Protestants worshiping in a mill near Nîmes. Montrevel, the maréchal de France, ordered that the doors be locked and the mill set on fire. All within died except a young girl who escaped only to be hung the following day.[26] Unable to suppress the rebels in a conventional manner the government deported entire cevenol towns while the army carried out a scorched-earth strategy to deprive the Camisards of their basis of support. Meanwhile, the Catholic population, frustrated by the failure of the royal troops to guarantee their security, formed their own bands of counter-Camisards, called the Cadets of the Cross or the White Camisards, and carried out attacks on Protestants.

Most of the violence was confined to the period of 1702-1704, at which time Cavalier negotiated an amnesty for the rebels and the freedom to emigrate for those who desired it. Yet sporadic attacks continued through 1710.

While the percentage of Protestants who participated in the rebellion was quite small, many more were sympathetic to the cause, and supported the rebels with food and secrecy. The same was true for the Cadets of the Cross, a fact which helps to explain the way these events became ingrained in the collective memory of the people of Bas-Languedoc. The

War of the Camisards became so embedded in the popular mythology of the region that Joutard has found several cases in which events occurring as late as the separation of Church and State in 1905, were assimilated in popular memory as another episode of the War of the Camisards.[27]

Not all Protestants viewed the Camisards favorably. Many, particularly among the bourgeoisie, were appalled by the rebels' violence. Their opinion of the inspirés, whose fanaticism they felt was responsible for Camisard violence, was perhaps even lower. One such critic was Antoine Court, the son of a family of *nouveaux convertis* that continued to practice the Reformed faith in secret. Born in 1695, Court grew up in a time and place well aware of the rebellion. In fact, he may have begun his ministerial career as one of the prophets. He later abandoned prophetism, and by 1714, committed himself to a policy of non-violent resistance to the government's injunctions against Protestant worship.

In August of 1715, a month before the death of Louis XIV, Court met in a secluded place in the Cévennes with eight other Protestant preachers, none of whom were seminary trained or even ordained in an official manner. At this meeting, the first synod of the French Reformed Church of the Desert, they set out to rebuild the institutional structure of the French Reformed Church, and to put it on a more moderate foundation than that of the inspirés and the Camisards.[28] Like the inspirés, they urged Protestants to "leave the Babylon" of Catholicism, but stressed submission to the civil authorities in all things except religion. Under their ministrations consistories reformed, church discipline was restored, synods met regularly, and a seminary was founded in Lausanne to train French youths to pastor the reconstituted congregations. With the reestablishment and spread of Reformed institutions the Protestant population's attachment to the inspirés and Huguenot militancy lessened. This regularized and more pacifistic form of worship in turn attracted more of the *nouveaux convertis* back into the Reformed faith.

Persecution, however, did not end with a more peaceful orientation by Protestants. Instead the *Eglise du désert*, in this regard, was a victim of its own success. It set out to combat militancy through the extension of organized worship services led by trained pastors, and governed by duly appointed lay leaders. The establishment of a regularized church, however, increased Protestant visibility and attracted the government's attention. Continued repression, in turn, limited the size and effectiveness of the pastoral corps, and discouraged many lay people, particularly the upper bourgeoisie and nobility, from returning to the church. Facing adversity and lacking sufficient clergy and a significant educated laity, doctrine and theology assumed a diminished role in Calvinist life. Consequently, as James Hood has argued, the Reformed community tended to distinguish itself from the Catholic majority according to fraternal loyalties rather than doctrinal distinctions. French Reformed Protestantism became a "religion of social cohesion" more than one of spiritual theology.[29] In addition, the absence following the revocation of the Edict of Nantes of the more cultivated classes left Protestants largely without civil and social leaders. At first this void was filled by the prophets and Camisard chieftains, but as their influence waned they were replaced in this role by the few itinerant preachers and particularly the boards of lay elders that governed local congregations. Consequently, French Protestants tended to look to the Church for temporal as well as spiritual leadership, and the consistories of pastors and laymen that administered local congregations were seen as the guardians of Protestant interests. The French Reformed Church thereby provided organization and direction to the Calvinist population while also serving as a symbol for communal identity.[30]

The last wave of government sponsored repression occurred between 1743 and 1763, at the end of Louis XV's reign. Several Calvinists were executed. Many more were imprisoned or sent to the galleys, and their goods confiscated. Though during the Seven-Years War rumors circulated of a plot linking the Prince of Conti, the Protestants of the south and west, and the British, the scheme never materialized. Huguenot leaders disclaimed any involvement in the plot and fervently protested their continued loyalty, despite their sufferings. The fact the government believed that such a scheme was possible or even probable enough to institute precautionary measures, indicated the level of suspicion and marginalization in which Protestants continued to exist in France. For Calvinists, their sufferings illustrated in vivid detail the civil and social differences between Catholics and Protestants, and further reinforced their tendency to consider conflict and violence, regardless of its origins, from a confessional point of view.[31]

After 1763, however, civil administrators, sensitive to philosophe criticism and determining that persecution was only encouraging radical responses, followed a policy of de facto toleration. Though still standing outside the law, the end of aggressive measures against Protestants allowed the Reformed Church to consolidate and further regularize its institutions. An increasing number of the bourgeoisie and some of the nobility began to return to the church of their ancestors. Declining repression also increased the stability and status of the Reformed pastorate. Ministers who had kept on the move due to their few numbers and the threat of arrest, now took-up residence among their congregations, and overall were better paid and educated.

This increased security, however, was now marred by squabbles within the Protestant community. The stability of the pastorate could create tensions within congregations between pastors and independent-minded lay leaders accustomed to running the church without ministerial interference. Disputes also developed between churches. Church leaders had tried to maintain associational ties through colloquies and synods, but prolonged persecution limited their effectiveness, and a considerable amount of congregational particularism developed.[32] As stability led to improved contact between churches these differences became more troublesome.

Particularly disruptive were disagreements between urban and rural churches that lay behind debates over national ecclesial governance. Several pastors, mostly of urban churches, felt the existing system of periodic colloquies and synods was inadequate for contemporary circumstances. Paul Rabaut, pastor at Nîmes, presented a plan for the creation of a central committee to administer the Church between synods. Rural congregations opposed this plan, fearing a central committee would give urban churches too much influence.[33] The initiative was defeated at the National Synod of 1763, but Rabaut and his allies did not let the matter die. For their part, rural churches rejected efforts to reconvene the National Synod fearing they would be forced to accept a central committee. As a result the National Synod did not meet again in the eighteenth century, greatly hindering efforts to resolve problems of doctrine and governance that emerged.[34]

One such issue flowed from differences in piety and theology that followed the *embourgoisement* of the church. Under persecution themes from the *inspirés* persisted in Reformed popular piety. It was characterized by a strong biblicism and Old Testament prophetic quality that elevated heroic stands for the faith while beseeching the divine for deliverance. One was either a Protestant and sympathetic to the cause or one was an enemy. From this sort of viewpoint Pastor Rabaut could claim,"reasonable Catholics without doubt [are] actually Protestants."[35] Conversely, as the bourgeoisie returned to the Reformed Church, they brought with them Enlightenment forms of thought. For French Protestants, the attraction of these new ideals was enhanced by the philosophes' championing of the Huguenots as victims of religious fanaticism. Younger and wealthier members of the Reformed community readily adopted philosophe rationalism. An entire generation of pastors was steeped in natural theology at the seminary at Lausanne directed by the encyclopedist Polier de Bottens. Thus, while most Huguenots regarded the Bible as the foundation of knowledge, were inclined to cheer defiant stands for the faith and saw the world through a Protestant/Catholic dualism, those touched by the Enlightenment viewed such tendencies as deplorable displays of superstition and fanaticism.[36]

The impact of the Enlightenment was further enhanced by Louis XVI's promulgation of the Edict of Toleration in 1787. This legislation, which owed much to the philosophes' campaign against religious bigotry, allowed Protestants to legalize births, marriages and deaths that had taken place under the auspices of the Eglise du désert. Though Protestants acted quickly to take advantage of the measure, in general they were far from satisfied with the law as it did not grant either freedom of worship or the right for Protestants to hold public office. The monarchy was ready to acknowledge the unreasonableness of persecuting people on the basis of religion, but was still unwilling to regard French Calvinists as full members of the nation. In southern France, where concentrations of Protestants were such that regular worship was the norm and several Calvinists held local government positions, if strictly applied the Edict of Toleration could actually be a step backwards.

Almost as soon as the Edict of Toleration became law, however, French society was caught into the whirlwind of the Revolution. The Estates-General were convened by the King to propose reforms to help bring the state out of its fiscal crisis, but it quickly became the platform by which the old political and social structure, based on corporate privileges and hierarchy, was dismantled. In its place a new civil society was proposed founded upon individual rights and equality before the law and state. French Protestants were early and enthusiastic supporters of this program seeing in it the fulfillment of their hopes for toleration and equality in a France founded upon principles with which they were already familiar in the spiritual realm.

In the Sénéchausée of Nîmes, Protestant wealth, education and eagerness to participate again in public life enabled them to secure six of eight places in the region's delegation from the Third Estate to the Estates-General. They took with them to Versailles a cahier de doléances calling on the King to complete the work he began with the Edict of Toleration.[37] Protestant hopes were realized not by the King, but in the National Assembly which stated in the Declaration of the Rights of Man and Citizen that "no man shall be disturbed in his opinions, even religious." In December 1789, this principle was regularized by the Constituent Assembly's granting to Protestants all rights of French citizens.

Though there was opposition to incorporating heretics into the nation, Catholic opposition to the Revolution crystallized more fully around the Civil Constitution of the Clergy. In the department of the Gard this hostility focused on the Reformed community which, because of the Revolution had been able to gain considerable political and social influence. They clearly dominated the National Guard in many towns, including that of Uzès and Nîmes where they were less than a third of the population. As the fortunes of the Catholic Church declined, the clergy joined with some of the former oligarches in opposition to the Revolution, and began to recruit support among Catholic workers, many of whom were employed by Protestant manufacturers.

Tensions coalesced around departmental elections in June 1790, which gave Protestants control of the departmental council. On June 13, the National Guard of Nîmes clashed with Catholic militants. That night word of the dispute spread into the countryside, and in the morning thousands of guardsmen, "poorly armed, without munitions, and without order," converged on the city from the Protestant regions to the west and north. For two days they terrorized and plundered the city in what was called the *bagarre*, or "sacking," of Nîmes. In its wake were three hundred dead, only twenty-one of whom were Protestant, and more than 120 houses destroyed, most belonging to Catholics. More than 1,200 Catholic families fled the city fearing for their safety.[38]

Civil authorities and the leaders of the Reformed community cast the *bagarre de Nîmes* as a battle against a counterrevolutionary rebellion, but it also revealed the continuing hostility between Catholics and Protestants. This enmity possessed political and economic dimensions in the changes effected by the Revolution and in tensions between the Protestant dominated bourgeoisie and their Catholic workers. But a strict socio-economic reading does not explain why Protestant workers did not join with their Catholic counterparts, nor does it explain the confessional focus of the violence. Political and social factors may have provided the occasion, but it is impossible to separate these from religious identification.

The riot in Nîmes was only the most violent of several similar episodes replicated on a lesser scale in other towns and villages. In Sommières, Catholic and Protestant National Guard companies faced off in 1791, while the exclusively Catholic royalist camps of Jalès, meeting three times on the borders of the Gard between 1790 and 1793, were suppressed by National Guardsmen drawn largely from Protestant cantons. Out of events such as these the distinction between Catholic-royalists and Protestant-patriots emerged and hardened in the popular consciousness.[39]

Closer examination, however, shows a more complex situation than a simple equation of confession with politics. In November 1791, a Société populaire des Amis de la Constitution was founded at Nîmes. Its membership, numbering 760 between 1791 and 1795, came largely from the artisanal class. The records do not provide the confessional composition of the Society, but they do tell us that 58 percent of the members were employed in the textile industry. Given, however, Protestant domination of silk production at all levels, and the hostility among Catholics of all classes in the region to the Revolution, it seems probable that many, if not most, of those in the Société populaire came from the Reformed community.[40]

At first the Société affiliated with the bourgeois Club des Amis de la Constitution, but by June 1793, reflecting the schism at Paris between the Montagnards and Girondins, the two associations were at each others' throats. The Club des Amis de la Constitution joined in the Federalist rebellion, seized control of the city and closed the doors of the Société populaire. Their revolt, however, was not supported by the surrounding towns and villages and was easily suppressed by the armies of the Convention. In the Terror that followed, it was the Société populaire that filled the role of persecutor, helping the *representant en mission*, Borie, purge the city of suspected counter-revolutionaries, as a result of which several members of the Protestant elite were executed.[41]

The failure of the Federalist revolt in the Gard illustrated another division in the ranks of Protestantism. Previously rural Protestants had rushed to the aid of their coreligionists in Nîmes when the Revolution seemed threatened by Catholic-Royalists. In 1793, there was no similar move to rescue the Protestant bourgeoisie from the Montagnards. In fact, in September 1793, the agent of the Ministry of the Interior felt rural Protestants were more trustworthy than their urban counterparts, claiming they "still have the necessary energy to resist the physical and moral attacks of the interior and exterior enemies of the Republic."[42]

As these divisions indicate, social and economic tensions within the Reformed community of the Gard in part accounted for the emergence of the split between Protestant elites and their artisanal and rural coreligionists. Through most of the eighteenth century religious solidarity was reinforced by economic ties in the silk industry, from raising the worms by the farmers of the Cévennes, to the spinning, weaving, and finishing of silk cloth in the cottages and ateliers of the towns and villages, to the organizing and financing of these activities by bourgeois merchant-manufacturers and bankers.[43] Gwynne Lewis has shown, however, that in the late-eighteenth century the closing of the Spanish market, the economic crises that accompanied the Revolution, and the dismantling of the Old Regime's system of social protection, transformed economic relations that had reinforced the Protestant community into the basis of adversarial relationships, especially under the rhetoric of rich versus poor that flavored much revolutionary discourse.[44]

Perhaps these tensions, combined with the affinity the Protestants felt for the Revolution, contributed to the ease with which the Reformed community accepted dechristianization. For the most part Reformed pastors and laity accepted the closing of their temples without resistance. At least forty-two of the seventy to eighty Reformed pastors in the Gard openly renounced their vocation. Many others did not formally abdicate, but simply ceased performing their ministerial functions.[45]

The impact of these abdications on the religious life of the Reformed community is difficult to judge. As already seen, a hundred years earlier Protestants had been similarly deprived of pastors and temples, but many continued to practice their faith. Undoubtedly the institutional structure of the French Reformed Church was severely crippled by dechristianization, but the quick reorganization of congregations in Nîmes, St-Jean-du-Gard and several other locations after freedom of religion was reestablished in 1795, would seem to indicate that at least some continued to worship according to the Reformed religion. In general, however, the French Reformed Church recovered quite slowly, particularly in comparison to the Roman Catholic Church during the same period. For the Reformed Church the number of pastors was far from sufficient, particularly since many churches would not accept a pastor who had abdicated his ministry only a few years earlier.[46]

The end of dechristianization also saw the renewal of confessional violence in Languedoc. Gwynne Lewis and James Hood have shown how the divisions in the Protestant population were evident only because the deeper conflict between Catholics and Protestants had been temporarily submerged due to Protestant victories like the *bagarre de Nîmes*.[47] With the fall of Robespierre, old patterns reemerged as Catholics exacted revenge for past offenses. They focused their attention in particular on the Protestant Jacobins who had earlier so zealously hounded Catholic-Royalists and whom the Protestant elite, remembering their own sufferings during the Terror, were less inclined to protect.[48] These attacks and reprisals continued until Napoleon Bonaparte used the Concordat with the Pope, backed-up by force, to end most open displays of confessional hostility.

The Concordat of 1802 marked a major change in the relationship of the French Reformed Church with the French state and society. It reestablished the Roman Catholic Church, but by way of the Organic Articles also established the French Reformed and Lutheran Churches. Instead of hunting down and executing Calvinist pastors, the state now paid them a regular salary and maintained the buildings in which they preached. This implied a level of inclusion in French society that had been unthinkable, even during the Revolution. In response Protestant elites in the south rallied to the Empire and were rewarded with a dominant voice in the region's administration.[49]

The fall of Napoleon and the restoration of the Bourbon Monarchy in 1815, placed Catholic-Royalists in control. In Bas-Languedoc this was occasion for the White Terror that targeted in particular prosperous Calvinists and their property. Officials did little as Catholic bands killed as many as a thousand Protestants, imprisoned hundreds more with little cause, and looted or destroyed much of their property. Several poorer Protestants, in a gesture recalling a previous era, began going to the Catholic Church where, a pastor observed indignantly, "they rebaptize them as if they were Jews or pagans."[50]

Ultimately Louis XVIII sent General Lagarde to restore order in the region, demonstrating that he intended to enforce the guarantee of freedom of worship accorded by the Charter of 1814. Though the Reformed population welcomed his efforts their sense of vulnerability remained. As descendants of the Huguenots they remembered similar assurances made by other Bourbons. In the White Terror they experienced directly the animosity of the Catholic majority and saw the Catholic authorities' apathy towards, if not complicity in, the attacks against them. With revitalized memories of a century of suffering and the atrocities of the Camisard rebellion and the Wars of Religion, Protestants put aside their differences to reform a solid front against a hostile majority.

The central institution for this Protestant solidarity was again the French Reformed Church. In many ways, however, it was not the same church it had been in previous decades. The Organic Articles provided an undreamed of status, but also made the church dependent on the state for its structure and finances. Politically, Protestants with few exceptions, opposed a return to the Ancien Régime, but the lines of fracture that had become apparent during the Revolution remained below a surface forced smooth by the possibility of oppression. The bourgeoisie was again taking an active part in Church affairs, but in so doing they largely supplanted the leadership of those who had been more faithful, and oftentimes with religious dispositions that contrasted markedly from those steeped in the traditions of the *inspirés* and the *Eglise du désert.*

From the time of the first implantation of Luther's ideas through the French Revolution and the Napoleonic Empire, French Reformed Protestantism had endured civil wars, rebellions, massacres and repression. In the nineteenth century they were well aware of their heritage, and were quite proud of it. In the course of this history, however, differences had developed that threatened community integrity. But above all else history left the Reformed population a self-aware minority confessional community in France, with a need for and tradition of unity in the face of Catholic hostility.

CHAPTER 3

Rebuilding Protestant Institutions

The White Terror that ravaged the Reformed community of southern France from 1815 through 1816 did not necessarily end with the restoration of civil order and the reopening of Reformed churches by General Lagarde. In part, the failure to prosecute some of the more notorious terrorists and the light sentences delivered to others gave the episode life far beyond the events themselves. These events gave renewed vitality to Protestant defensiveness and identity as a select, yet persecuted minority in a Catholic dominated France. The apparent victimization of Protestants in the Terror, combined with the disruption of Reformed worship and the destitution of several pastors accused rightly or wrongly of attempting to organize a Protestant defense all worked to reinforce the place of the Reformed Church as the central organizing institution of the Reformed community. The church, however, had barely begun to recover from its near total collapse in the French Revolution. Though not nearly as disastrous as the dechristianization campaign, the White Terror left the Reformed Church further disorganized and its confidence badly shaken.

In the years after 1816, however, the Reformed Church began to recover. Much of the effort went to restoring and extending its presence within the Protestant community. Churches were built or repaired. The number of pastors increased and their training improved. Worship was restored where it had lapsed, and regularized where it had been sporadic. In addition charitable and educational institutions were established to support and maintain Protestant integrity. Though the church demonstrated considerable vigor in this effort, as an established church much of the recovery was dependent upon and financed by the state.

There is some irony in the fact that the circumstances of the Reformed Church in France improved significantly during the Bourbon Restoration. Not only had earlier Bourbons revoked the Edict of Nantes and presided over the persecution of the Huguenots, by 1830 there was little love between Calvinists and the Restoration regime. Protestants, however, were not inherently opposed to the Bourbons. Several had played a significant role in returning the Bourbon Monarchy to France and two had participated in writing the Constitutional Charter of 1814 that was the basis for the Restoration government.[1] Protestants were pleased by the inclusion in this document of an article guaranteeing freedom of worship, but they were disturbed by the statement in the next article that "the Catholic, apostolic and Roman religion is the religion of the State."

Initial Protestant suspicions about the Bourbons' commitment to religious liberty appeared confirmed by the White Terror, but the government intervened to stop the savagery, and thereafter was cautious to prevent such systematic violence from occurring again. Under the moderate administrations of 1816-1820, Paris even seemed to favor the Protestants. In fact the Reformed Church in Bas-Languedoc was in a better material position in 1830, when the Bourbon Monarchy was overthrown, than it had been at any time since the revocation of the Edict of Nantes. From only fifty churches in 1814, the Reformed Churches in the Gard grew to ninety in 1830, most provided and maintained by the government. A similar trend was evident in the pastorate. At the close of the Empire, for a region with a Protestant population approaching 200,000, the government provided for only seventy-six pastors. Under the Bourbons this number increased 38 percent to 105. Though still less than adequate considering that much of the population was scattered in hundreds of isolated villages and hamlets in the hills and valleys of the Cévennes, it was a significant improvement.[2]

The fact remained that many of the perpetrators of violence during the White Terror were never punished or received light sentences, adding to Protestant anxiety. At the same time, seven Protestants were executed for attacks on Catholics, and in 1816, nearly three-fourths of the prisoners in the *Maison centrale* at Nîmes were Protestants.[3] Less catastrophic, but disturbing for what it might portend, was the ascendancy of the ultra-royalist and fervently Catholic faction to political power following the assassination in 1820, of the duc de Berry, heir of Charles X. Soon after a rumor swept through the Cévennes that Louis XVIII had abdicated in favor of the duc d'Orléans, news Protestants welcomed with choruses of the *Marseillaise*. The rumor proved false and a renewed alliance of

Throne and Altar, symbolized in the Catholic Church's control of education and the reinstitution of the death sentence for sacrilege, dominated the final years of Louis XVIII and the reign of Charles X.

In the south, Protestants feared this would lead to a renewed campaign of terror. Though this was not the case, the administration did seem to regard the Reformed Church much as their predecessors had in the Ancien Regime. An undated policy proposal on non-Catholic religions argued that the Charter's guarantee of liberty and protection to dissident religions "cannot have as its object the favoring of them to the detriment of the religion which the State professes." It went on to state:

> It would not be a departure from the spirit of the Charter for the government of the King to restrict Protestant Churches within the limits of the rights the laws of the realm accord them, and concerns of state seem to require this measure with regards to a sect the doctrines of which are the enemy equally of all spiritual and temporal authority.

On this basis it was claimed Protestants had enough pastors and churches and advised against any additions. Further, the Chief of Staff for the Ministry of Religion suggested the government substitute the phrase "so-called Reformed" for "Reformed" in all legal documents relating to the Reformed Protestants in France.[4]

These proposals do not appear to have been implemented, but their underlying spirit was evident in affairs between Protestants and the civil authorities. For example, the government was slow to investigate complaints of Protestant children being taken from their parents and put into Catholic institutions in order to protect possible conversions. Protestants were also subject to arrest and fines for not decorating their houses for the Fête-Dieu, and it was often difficult for the Reformed Church to obtain adequate places of worship and positions for pastors to serve in them.[5]

The shortage of pastors and church buildings was one of the most obvious needs of the French Reformed Church in the early nineteenth century. During the First Restoration Pastor Jacques Olivier-Desmonts of Nîmes reported that most rural churches lacked a place in which to worship. Five years later the English Methodist, Charles Cook, reported that a large number of Protestants in southern France rarely saw a pastor, and when they did most worship services were held in barns, private buildings, or *au désert* (in open air). After the White Terror the government tried to improve the situation, but after 1822, progress nearly stopped entirely. The national budget for 1824, eliminated all funds for new construction, and reduced by 17 percent the budget for maintaining existing Reformed temples. If funds for temples came from other sources the government claimed the right to authorize their construction, placing a series of conditions that seemed to harken back to the policies of Louis XIV. Construction of a temple in Lasalle (Gard) was forbidden because it faced the Catholic Church. In Parignargues (Gard) and Cournonsac (Hérault) the government claimed there weren't enough Protestants to justify a temple. The congregation at St-Martin-de-Lenscule (Lozère) was told their temple, secured under Napoleon, was being given back to the Catholic Church, and the church at St-Pierreville (Ardèche) was required to change its worship schedule so it would not conflict with the procession for the Fête-Dieu. In the same vein no new positions for pastors were authorized for consistories in the departments of the Ardèche, Gard, Hérault and Lozère between 1822 and 1826.

Towards the end of the decade the government began to moderate its treatment of Protestants, adding two pastors in 1827 and four more in 1829. But by this time Reformed sentiments were thoroughly poisoned. The Nîmois pastor, Samuel Vincent noted that when the Restoration began Protestants "welcomed this venerated family effusively." But the regime's "malevolent endeavors conducted with infernal skill and despicable persistence, uprooted from the hearts of Protestants their ancient love for the Bourbons."[6]

It was not surprising therefore, that most Protestants welcomed Louis-Philippe, formerly duc d'Orléans, as King in the wake of the July Revolution of 1830 that forced Charles X to abdicate. If petty treatment by Bourbon governments and the strength of royalism among the local Catholic population had not been sufficient reason for Protestants to rally to the Orléans Monarchy, their esteem rose considerably with the new regime's altering of the Charter to change Roman Catholicism from "the religion of the State" to the Napoleonic formula, "the religion of the majority of Frenchmen." In addition, the resignation of a large number of local officials, and the dismissal of 473 others in the Gard alone, made it evident the regime would be of a different character than its predecessor.[7] This was confirmed when the government chose Protestants to fill a significant number of the vacancies. Thus the Protestant Chabaud-Latour, led the interim government for the department of the Gard, and another Protestant was named the regional prosecutor. In addition, electoral reforms lowering the tax qualification for voter eligibility worked to the advantage of the middle-bourgeoisie in which Protestants were a majority. Consequently, municipal elections in December 1830, in Nîmes gave Protestants seventeen of thirty-six seats on the town council though they were only a third of the city's population. In towns in which the percentage of Protestants was larger the results were even more favorable.[8]

The Catholic population did not accept this transfer of power passively. In late August and early September it appeared events might follow the paths of 1790 or 1815. In what had become a familiar pattern, a confessional demonstration in Nîmes escalated into mob violence and gunfire. Following the new regime's replacement of the Swiss regiment that had been stationed in Nîmes by the Bourbons with French troops under a Protestant commander, Catholics demonstrated against what they feared would be a pending assault on their church. In response to this Catholic activism, Protestants from the Cévennes and Vaunage took up arms and marched on the departmental capital. Civil authorities scrambled to keep the two sides apart, urged calm and tolerance, and frantically pled for additional troops from Montpellier. Before passions subsided seven were dead, five Protestants and two Catholics, and twenty-three wounded. Despite these casualties most were relieved a worse disaster had been avoided.[9]

The complexion of government in the Gard was not altered by these disturbances. The Marquise de Calavière-Vézénobres noted in her diary:

> No Catholic has been on the municipal council of Vézénobres since 1830. Since the Revolution of July they were excluded from nearly all of the administrations in the entire department. Monsieur Guizot, a Protestant originally from Saint-Géniès-de-Malgoirès, gave the Protestants domination of the Gard, and they are only a small third of the population.[10]

Despite being the demographic majority, Catholics were a minority power in Gardois politics throughout the Orléans Monarchy.

With their new found influence in local and even national politics, (symbolized by François Guizot, Minister of Education after 1830, and virtual prime minister 1840-1848), Protestant institutions continued to expand. The number of pastors grew as eighteen more positions were created for the churches of the Gard. The number of temples also increased as seventy temples were built in the region between 1830 and 1848. With these additions in buildings and personnel the physical presence of the Reformed Church in the Reformed population, and in the region as a whole, was significantly strengthened. This public presence was also a demonstration of the growing legitimacy of Protestantism in France and visible evidence of the religious diversity that was becoming a feature of French society. As Frank Puaux noted at the end of the century, "On every side temples were raised and their inauguration marked for the Protestants the decisive victory of the principles of religious liberty."[11]

The recovery of the Reformed Church was not limited to places of worship and pastors. The church was also concerned to establish schools to educate the community's children. Again this was a case of recovering and extending traditional Reformed institutions. From its origins Calvinism had valued an educated laity and clergy. However, the trials of the seventeenth and eighteenth centuries had destroyed their educational institutions in France. In the more secure environment of the nineteenth century and with the benefits of state support, Reformed leaders began to turn their attention to the educational needs of the community. Pastor Olivier-Desmonts, who oversaw much of the rebuilding of the Reformed Church of Nîmes after the Revolution, told a British correspondent in 1815, that one of the greatest obstacles facing the Reformed Churches of France was "the fact that the children of the peasants and workers do not know how to read." His younger colleague at Nîmes, Samuel Vincent, one of the most celebrated pastors of the first-half of the nineteenth century, praised primary schools for putting "the industrial classes into a condition to draw religious ideas from their true source, that is to say, from the Bible." For the Reformed clerics who gathered at Nîmes to discuss primary schooling a few months after the Revolution of 1830, the value of popular education was not an issue. Instead they focused on how and in what form schools should be founded, how to persuade parents to keep their children in school when for economic reasons they needed them to work, and how they would meet the need for more and better teachers.[12]

In this acceptance of popular schooling Protestantism's theological predisposition for an educated laity was complemented by the usefulness Reformed leaders saw in schools for civilizing the popular classes and advancing society. In fact these ends were often regarded as in essence different aspects of the same thing.

There were those who worried the church might subordinate its spiritual mission to disseminating the fruits of modern science and philosophy. This, they said, was the mistake, if not the apostasy, of the Enlightenment church. Yet, nearly all Reformed leaders, regardless of theological position, saw a close relationship between the advance of *true* Christianity, meaning Protestantism, and social progress. As one pastor stated, "there exists an admirable reciprocity of action of religion upon civilization and civilization on religion." Another remarked, "Christianity has always preceded civilization." Others noted with admiration how missionaries in foreign lands combined spreading the Christian faith with efforts to substitute "the benefits of European civilization for the barbarism of the savages." Putting this approach in action closer to home the Consistory of Nîmes began a nursery school for working-class children, noting it "would allow orderly habits of propriety and discipline to form early in these children, submitting them to a surveillance which can only be favorable to their morals and their health." It would also "accustom them early on to speaking French." Analogously, an evening school for those of working age would "fill a gap which still makes itself felt in the moral development of the poor between the generation already formed and that which is now forming."[13]

The linkage by Reformed leaders of religion and education with civilization differed little in form from their Catholic counterparts. François Furet and Jacques Ozouf have argued that notables of the era saw schools in general, "first and foremost [as] an instrument of control, designed to moralize and discipline the masses." François Guizot, whose roots lay in the Reformed community of the Gard, was "the most systematic exponent of this conception of the school as guarantor of the existing state of society." As Minister of Education his greatest achievement was the Primary School Law of 1833, requiring each commune of sufficient size to establish a primary school, and each department to create a school to train teachers. In an open letter to teachers on this law, Guizot proclaimed, "Universal elementary instruction shall henceforth be the guarantee of order and social stability." Perhaps reflecting the trauma of his father's execution by the Jacobins, Guizot tended to see the turbulence of nineteenth-century Europe as part of a larger struggle in which all Christians must unite to defend "the spirit of Christianity" from the "spirit of Revolution."[14]

The region as a whole was fairly well educated, an exception to the famous north/south division in French society. This success seems to have often resulted as much from confessional competition as from principle. Though Protestant notables and pastors were inclined to agree with their more influential coreligionist about the utility of education, they do not seem to have shared the same conception of civilization as Catholic polemicists. Those of southern France, where religious tolerance was not a highly visible social virtue, certainly did not believe their religious and educational values were the same as their Catholic counterparts. Consequently, education was a hotly contested arena of public policy between the two communities.[15] Though charges of favoritism and oppression followed each change in regime, the rivalry in education extended beyond access and control of the schools to issues of purpose and pedagogical method. Most Reformed leaders were confident that Protestantism was entirely compatible with, if not necessary to, modern civilization. Catholicism they felt encouraged superstition, depended on authority and was the foundation for a society "in which the individual loses himself in the whole, making him relinquish that which is the most intimate part of his individuality, his thoughts and beliefs." More than this, Vincent, who was far from the most crusading of Protestants, charged that the Catholic Church intentionally opposed:

> the progress of human learning, the instruction of the poorer classes, and other establishments appropriate for spreading enlightenment more equally through society. It gives the impression of regarding as directed against it everything that is proposed, all that is done, to extend civilization in every corner of our nation.

Conversely, Protestantism was, "the complement or even the base of the vast system of individualism which constitutes modern civilization." A common assumption among Protestants was that as literacy became general all that would be necessary for the ultimate victory of Protestantism in France was to make the Bible available to the Catholic population "and they will reform themselves." As Vincent stated, education provided the tool with which one could free oneself from "the spiritual tyranny of Rome or of another."[16]

Schools were essential, therefore, but not simply to moralize the population in the sense of inculcating habits of submissiveness to authority. Early nineteenth-century Protestants still preserved some of the Revolution's optimism about the intrinsic moralizing effect of literacy. Education was less threatening than the prospect that, in the words of Samuel Vincent, succeeding generations would come of age "in a state of complete ignorance and brutality," causing civilization to "stand still or reverse itself, and our people to remain the most remote of Europe after those of Spain." The upheavals of the Second Republic mitigated some of this confidence in schooling, but in the early 1850s, Baron Gustave Fornier de Clausonne, a member of the Court of Appeals at Nîmes and Secretary of the Consistory of Nîmes, still confidently advised students at the Protestant Ecole normale des femmes at Nîmes, that the true danger to society was inadequate education, not education itself. By contrast, after the Revolution of 1848, a Catholic lawyer and landowner in the

Cévennes called for the Ecole normale at Nîmes to be closed, saying "instruction alone, instruction that is not guided, moderated by a supreme rule, is a scourge for societies . . . ignorance with its honest rusticity is far better for the happiness of society, better for civilization itself, than an instruction that is corrupted and fueled by evil passions."[17]

Of course there was a tendency to define adequate education as that which leads the pupil to defer to his or her betters. Thus Clausonne told his students at the Protestant Ecole normale for women in Nîmes that education was to impart "habits of respect, obedience, submissiveness, regularity, order, and one might add correctness, cleanliness, industry, attention and thoughtfulness." But for the most part Protestants saw literacy as the primary goal. This was one of the reasons why they favored the mutual or Lancastrian system of teaching. Where previously pupils were taught one-on-one by a single teacher (expensive if classes were small, or boring and ineffective if classes were large), in the Lancastrian system the *instituteur* oversaw a corps of monitors drawn from advanced students who in turn taught students at lower levels. In addition, it introduced the simple yet fundamental innovation of teaching writing at the same time as reading. Thus mutual education promised to provide basic literacy cheaply and quickly. In a society in which children were often pulled out of school in order to work, speed in education could be a virtue. In addition, teaching writing in conjunction with reading assured that more children acquired some facility in both skills than by the customary method of teaching writing only at the upper levels of primary schooling.[18]

Mutual education was introduced into Bas-Languedoc by Pastor Martin fils, who had been trained in the pedagogy in England, and implemented it in a school at St-Hippolyte-du-Fort. In 1817, the Consistory of Nîmes sent one of its teachers to observe this school, and then introduced the system into its free school. A little later, the Consistory opened a free school for girls using the same method. By 1829, there were mutual schools at Nîmes, St-Hippolyte, and Alès in the Gard, and at Ganges and Montpellier in the Hérault. In succeeding years the system continued to spread among the Protestant communes of the Vaunage and Cévennes with most reporting good results.[19]

While Protestants readily adopted the Lancastrian system, French Catholics often battled against it. In the Gard, the Frères des écoles chrétiennes intentionally sought to counter each école mutuel with a school of their own. In part their suspicions were aroused simply by the fact the mutual system originated in England and was favored in France by heretics. With closer inspection critics such as Jean-Marie-Robert de Lamennais found mutual education inherently irreligious and more interested in material progress than order and morality. They objected to its lifting merit over social hierarchy, and claimed it provided literacy too quickly, without allowing sufficient time for proper moral formation. Against this critique, the mutual system's proponents like Vincent replied the method was merely a mechanism that could be applied to teach whatever one wanted. "By itself it is thus no more impious than the ancient method of individual teaching or the method of mixed simultaneous instruction adopted by the Frères de la Doctrine chrétienne." But there was a difference in what Protestants and Catholics wanted taught. Furet and Ozouf have argued that the opposition of the Christian Brothers and Frères des Écoles chrétiennes to teaching reading and writing together was rooted in their attitude towards written culture. Though Tridentine Catholicism encouraged reading, this was principally as an aid to the collective celebration of Church ritual. Reading a common text assisted a corporate culture. The ability to write, whether one's own correspondence, to sign a petition, or to express an interpretation of an event or text, could undermine this collectivity. While Reformed officials often used reading as the gauge for evaluating the successes of their schools, the fact that children were learning to write at the same time can be taken to reflect, intentionally or otherwise, the Protestant doctrine of the priesthood of all believers. Just as freedom of conscience meant little without the right of public worship, freedom to inquire lacked force without the ability of self-expression.[20]

Despite their enthusiasm for primary schooling Reformed leaders were not entirely sanguine about it. On one hand, they sincerely believed in the benefits of popular instruction for religion and society. On the other, they were somewhat uneasy about the impact it could have on the values of the younger generation and the church's place in the community. It was more than coincidental that the Pastoral Conference of the Gard, after discussing primary schooling, devoted the next session to religious education. Pastors frequently stressed the importance of keeping a diligent watch over the schools in their community, both to lend the prestige of the church to the educational endeavor and to use their influence to "direct the teacher and exercise over him a beneficial authority." Not surprisingly, they worried about the detrimental impact of an irreligious teacher on a child's moral and religious attitudes. They also recognized that a teacher could become a rival to the pastor and elders. Even in the best of circumstances, most leaders of the Reformed

Church agreed with Samuel Vincent that without effective religious education as a complement to popular schooling "civilization becomes materialistic and is lost." The greater emphasis the church began to place on catechetical preparation before first communion, the introduction and expansion of Sunday Schools, and other forms of religious education, was at least partially a reflection of anxiety arising from the growing influence of schools.[21]

Despite these concerns Protestants were not convinced popular education should be the preserve of the church. They were willing to contemplate a nationalized and deconfessionalized educational system as a balance against the power and influence wielded by the Catholic Church. It could be a more attractive option than choosing between sending Protestant children to Catholic schools or not educating them at all, since in most areas Protestants lacked the resources to maintain their own primary schools. Even where the Reformed community had the wealth and numbers to operate its own schools, Vincent appears to be correct in claiming Protestants were "nearly unanimous" in feeling that while their own schools "could offer some great advantages . . . they have always found it very repugnant to follow this route." This, he argued, was because "Protestants, upon leaving their temples, want to be and to remain purely, simply and completely French." Confessional schools, he feared, would prolong the segregation of the Huguenots' descendants from the French nation. Because of this and the problems posed by Catholic domination in most of France, Vincent said, "for the mass of Protestants, national education, and not at all clerical, would be an immense benefit."[22]

This did not mean the Reformed community did not have confessional schools. By 1838, there were forty-six communal schools exclusively for Protestants in the department of the Gard, compared to 141 Catholic schools. The Consistory of Nîmes alone had more than eight hundred children in the eight schools it operated during the 1830s. These included a pre-school, three schools for boys, three for girls, and a school for adults. A few years later it added a preparatory for ministerial candidates and a normal school for women. But there were also 125 écoles mixtes, enrolling both Catholics and Protestants. Several communes could not afford separate schools, thus forcing a degree of cooperation upon the two populations. In others, such as St-Hippolyte, Catholic children were encouraged to attend the Reformed school and Catholics and Protestants shared in the administration, a fact Charles Cook felt threatened the entire project.[23]

Protestant opportunities for education beyond the primary level also expanded. Key was the change in the government's attitude after the Revolution of 1830. Under the Restoration students at the royal colleges were required to attend mass and participate in daily prayers regardless of their confession. The situation nearly reversed in the July Monarchy. In 1831, the Consistory of Nîmes was able to bring sufficient political pressure to bear to reverse the expulsion of a Protestant student who refused to take part in the Catholic prayers that were still part of the daily regimen. This case also led to changes in the form of prayer so as to be less offensive to Reformed sensibilities, and a Master of Studies was appointed to serve Protestant students. In 1832, the Consistory of Nîmes noted that Protestants now were nearly half of the students in the college. This over-representation held in the Ecole normale as well where in 1836, 57 percent of the young men training to be primary school teachers were Protestant.[24] The only teacher training school for women in the region was created by the Consistory of Nîmes in 1842. A few years later the consistories in the region joined in establishing the Ecole préparatoire pour le Ministère évangélique to give young Protestant men of modest means the necessary academic preparation to pursue studies at one of the Protestant theological faculties. The Ecole préparatoire, located at Nîmes, soon was so popular as an alternative site for secondary schooling for those unable to get into the royal colleges that it averaged a profit of 2,000 francs a year in its first twenty years of existence.[25]

In education, as in clerical personnel and places of worship, the recovery in the French Reformed community developed through a mixture of local initiative and government support. Once it suppressed the White Terror the State was generally willing to support with funds and legal protection the efforts of the Reformed Church to extend its presence and influence within the Reformed population of France. At Nîmes this went as far as the government funneling through the consistory a portion of funds for public assistance proportionate to the size of the Protestant population.[26] Even the reactionary Villèle ministry sought to restrain the growth of Reformed institutions more than to cut them back. While this respect for the Reformed Church could in part reflect deference to the principle of freedom of worship, the state also found it useful within certain limits to support the Church. Thus, the link to the state entailed restrictions on the Church's freedom of action and mutations in its governing structures and traditions convenient to civil authorities.

The Organic Articles by which Napoleon Bonaparte established the Reformed Church in 1802, created an ecclesiastical system echoing traditional Reformed polity, but with significant deviations designed to moderate consistorial behavior and accord greater government influence in ecclesiastical affairs. Lay participation in church government was maintained by requiring a lay majority in the consistories of pastors and elders administering church affairs. Selection of these elders had never been the democratic process it has often been made out to be, but the Organic Articles even further removed it by requiring that elders be chosen by and from those in the Reformed community who paid the most in taxes.[27] Thus wealth and social status rather than spiritual fitness or even popularity became the first consideration in selecting lay leaders. On this basis the Consistory of Nîmes under the July Monarchy included two members of the Royal Court of Nîmes, the Deputy Prosecuting Attorney for the Gard, the Vice-President of the Tribune of the First Instance, two representatives to the Chamber of Deputies in Paris, the Mayor of Nîmes, the departmental Inspector for Primary Education, a prominent notary, two bankers and several prosperous merchants [négociants]. Another elder resigned in 1842, to become Prefect for the department of the Loire.

While the composition of the Consistory of Nîmes reflected its location at a regional judicial and industrial center, its social composition only differed from others in scale rather than nature. A sampling of five additional consistories in the Gard, reveals among the seventy-three elders serving from 1830 to 1848, seven mayors, six justices of the peace, five assistant mayors, a notary, two members of the General Council of the department, and five négociants. The remainder were overwhelmingly propriétaires living off the rent from their lands. All but six elders qualified to vote under the censitairy regulations that limited the franchise to those who paid at least 200 francs in yearly property taxes. Ten elders paid more than 500 francs and half of these paid upwards of 1,000 francs in yearly taxes. In Nîmes at least eight of the twelve elders paid more than 1,000 francs annually and none paid less than 600 francs. Artisans were completely absent from Church leadership, and only a few manufacturers, usually owners of spinning mills in the Cévennes or fabricants of eau-de-vie in the Vaunage. From the commercial classes only the wealthier négociants tended to make their way into church government, not the more modest marchands or boutiquiers. Professionals were also under represented. There were no teachers, and only two lawyers and four doctors served as elders. Overall, leadership of the established church was firmly in the control of the social and economic elite in the Reformed population, with a marked tendency for a place in the consistory to become a sort of family possession, passing from father to son or uncle to nephew.[28]

Reinforcing ecclesiastical government by the elites was the Organic Articles' establishment of a single consistory for approximately every six thousand Reformed Protestants. Since most towns and communes did not have this large a Protestant population, several congregations were usually gathered into a single consistory associated with an *église consistoriale* at the nearest prominent town. This system compromised traditions of congregational equality and self-government by grouping several churches in a single body and designating one of them as the consistorial seat, lending it a preponderance of influence and often of elders as well. The organization imposed by the government simplified lines of authority, and given the poor economic conditions in many villages, also assured overall a much higher social cast to Reformed leadership than would have been the case if local consistories had been maintained.

Custom, however, was difficult to overcome. Most established consistories allowed *consistoires locales* to oversee much of a local congregation's activities. Sometimes these were an extension of the local diaconate, the body of laymen responsible under a Calvinist polity for care of the Protestant poor and infirm. Though the diaconat was completely ignored by the Law of 18 germinal an X that constituted the structure of the Reformed Church in France, civil authorities recognized and tolerated the fact that most churches had deacons operating in a legally unofficial capacity, but with great local legitimacy. The legally constituted consistory standing above the local congregation often assumed the name *consistoire général*, and would simply ratify the decisions of the local assemblies so as to make them legally binding. Thus, when the local consistory of Mialet voted to dismiss its pastor Jean Buchet for neglect of duty, questionable morality and reputed republicanism, the Consistory of St-Jean-du-Gard ratified the decision, and passed it on to the government. The civil authorities confirmed the move and Buchet lost his position. Similarly, representatives of the deacons at Nîmes joined with the official consistory to choose Olivier de Sardan's successor as pastor. As an elder in the Consistory of Lasalle tried to explain to the sub-prefect of Le Vigan, *consistoires locales* only differed from the *consistoire général* in that the former had a longer history. But as the President of the Consistory of Nîmes informed the Consistory of Marseille, members of the *consistoire local* "are not Elders as they are not among the first rank of notables in their social standing, their fortune, their education, etc., so they are not the equal to Elders; although they are very honorable men." This accommodation to local leadership, however, collapsed as tensions grew between *consistoires générales* and the *consistoires locals*.[29]

A third modification effected by the Organic Articles was the virtual dismantling of the Reformed system of regional and national synods by which the church had established collective priorities, coordinated common action, and enforced ecclesiastical discipline. The system implemented by Napoleon completely ignored the National Synod. Provincial synods were included in the Organic Articles, but all decisions were subject to approval by the state, and, more importantly, the synods themselves could only convene with the government's permission. In practice this permission was never granted.

The absence of synods left the French Reformed Church without an ecclesial organization and authority above that of the consistories. Although religious toleration, commercial expansion, and improved communication and transportation made it easier for Protestants to interact with each other, the Reformed Church did not have any official ties between consistories. This meant, according to Jean-Paul Hugues, pastor at Anduze in 1854, that the Reformed Churches of France were now congregational in polity. Consequently collective decisions and actions could only be arrived at by informal and voluntary means. This made it difficult for the Reformed Church to overcome doctrinal, liturgical and administrative particularism that had developed during the isolation of the previous century. Neither could it respond effectively to new ones emerging in the new century. In addition, though the Reformed Church was an established church of the state, it had no official liaison with the government. Yet for disputes not resolved by a consistory the only course of appeal was to the functionaries of the state, which according to Hugues, thus constituted itself "if not the Pope, at least the Protestant National Synod.[30]

The problems inherent in this system were evident in a dispute within the Consistory of St-Jean-du-Gard. In 1834, when the local Consistory of Mialet voted to dismiss Pastor Jean Buchet, this decision was ratified by the Consistory of St-Jean-du-Gard, and not long after the government formally removed him. The two ecclesiastical bodies, however, clashed when it came to the appointment of Buchet's successor. If custom had reigned Mialet would have chosen its own pastor without interference. Under the Organic Articles, however, the choice rested with an artificial creation of the state, the *consistoire général*, which in this case rejected the congregation's choice in favor of another candidate. In the absence of synods, the church at Mialet appealed to the Minister of Religion in Paris, warning that if the Consistory of St-Jean-du-Gard had its way the local church would be abandoned by the public and the system of charity it maintained would collapse. While civil authorities for reasons of civil order were sensitive to local opinion the government had little choice except to confirm as pastor the nominee favored by the legally established Consistory of St-Jean-du-Gard.[31]

No one would deny that the government acted within its legal authority in deciding such matters. As long as the issues were procedural or legal, there was little problem. Frequently, however, these questions merged with doctrinal and ecclesiastical differences. Though the Law of 18 germinal an X made the state the final court of appeal and required that the government approve all doctrinal or dogmatic decisions in the church, the state was reluctant to involve itself in such matters, and virtually no one in the Reformed community considered it competent to do so. In effect, the Reformed Church of France only existed above the level of consistories in the bureaucrats in the office for Non-Catholic Religions of the Ministry of Worship. Few were comfortable with this situation. From the time of the Articles' promulgation Protestants lobbied for synods or a substitute body standing above the consistories in authority and also acceptable to the government and the church. In 1854, seventy pastors attending the Conférence pastorale du Gard unanimously approved the report prepared by Jean-Paul Hugues charging that the organization imposed on the church by the government had changed its polity from a Reformed system into one that was congregational, and called on the state to restore the church to its traditions by resurrecting synods. Several, including Samuel Vincent, felt the church would be better off without state support rather than suffer the government's restrictions on its organization and freedom of action. Many agreed with a pastor who declared, "Our situation is very embarrassing and cannot remain as it is today. It will soon be necessary to decide between the independence of the consistories and their dependence upon a superior authority."[32]

In the absence of a national ecclesiastical government, voluntary arrangements and societies emerged to partially fill the gap. In 1821, representatives from nearly every consistory in the region of the Gard were present in Ganges (Hérault) for the consecration of several young ministers. They took advantage of the situation to organize a conference of clerical and lay representatives at Nîmes a few months later. In structure the conference mimicked a synod adapted to the civil jurisdictions established during the Revolution. Three delegates, lay or clerical, from each church first met in the capital of their respective arrondissements where they discussed issues of common concern and elected three deputies to a attend a departmental meeting at Nîmes, September 19-20, 1821. This departmental assembly dealt with issues of discipline and organization much as a provincial synod would have done. The first issue it decided was a formal call on the government to restore the synodal structure of the Reformed Church. The assembly then addressed issues such as civil and religious marriages, private baptisms, funeral services, the regularization of worship services for Ascension, Good Friday and New Year's Day, and advised on disputes that had erupted at Anduze and Blauzac.

In trying to set policy for the churches of the region, the conference at Nîmes had to overcome several obstacles, not the least of which was the fact that it had no legal status with either the church or the state. It was hoped that the representational structure and the similarities to Reformed traditions would be sufficient to persuade the consistories to adopt the assembly's resolutions, thereby giving them validity. But here too the conference was hampered by the small number of representatives convened. The assembly at Nîmes did call for an increase from twelve representatives to sixteen, but any number larger than this would have violated restrictions in the Civil Code on the size of public meetings without government authorization. In any event, the ascendancy of the Ultras to political power in Paris seems to have ended the venture as there were no follow-up conferences.[33]

More enduring was the Conférence pastorale du Gard, and others like it in the region and across France. These brought together members of the clergy from various consistories to discuss matters of common interest. The conferences in the Gard were regularly attended by between thirteen and thirty-three pastors from across the region. Overlapping conferences existed for pastors from the Cévennes and the Vaunage.[34] These conferences lacked official status with both the government and the Reformed community, but they quickly became an important means for disseminating information and influencing opinion and practice. Their impact was likely greatest in rural parishes where pastors had a fair degree of freedom due to the fact that their consistories met only a few times each year. In fact, André Encrevé has argued that church leaders at Nîmes intentionally sponsored the Pastoral Conference of the Gard to enhance their influence in the region vis-a-vis the growing importance in French Protestantism of the Consistory of Paris and its pastoral conferences.[35]

While pastoral conferences helped foster links between pastors, the voluntary religious societies that proliferated in the nineteenth century were closer to Reformed traditions in that they usually brought laity and clergy together on an equal basis. For this reason alone their influence is not to be underestimated. Unlike pastoral conferences which were a sort of professional association, the voluntary societies usually formed to address a specific charitable, religious or practical purpose. Usually the presidency of the society was held by a prominent layman, while a pastor often served as secretary, the inverse of the internal organization of consistories dictated by the Organic Articles. The number and variety of these associations multiplied opportunities for leadership and service. In 1830, there were at least three Protestant religious societies active in southern France. By 1860, there were at least sixty Protestant societies registered by the state, and twenty-seven without authorization.[36]

Some of these associations were national or even international in their organization or purpose. The Société biblique was one of the first and most important. It began in Paris in 1818, following a visit by Reverend John Owen, Secretary of the Bible Society of London, to encourage the distribution of Bibles and New Testaments throughout France. Affiliates were founded across the country. Nîmes, for example, had a Bible society in 1820, and by 1829, auxiliary societies were functioning in St-Hippolyte-du-Fort and Le Vigan, each with sub-branches in the surrounding towns and villages.[37] Part of the strength and influence of the Société biblique and other religious societies was their breadth of support. The Société biblique de Nîmes had more than 550 contributors during the year 1832-1833. It included separate supporting organizations for men, women, and children of both sexes, each with their own leadership councils, except those for children which were led by one of the pastors. Though the leadership of the Sociétés bibliques often incorporated members of the local consistory, others from outside the leadership of the church were included as well. At Nîmes, the President of the Société biblique was baron Gustave de Clausonne, Secretary of the Consistory of Nîmes, and a councilor in the Royal Court of Nîmes. The Vice-president was the President of the Consistory of Nîmes, Samuel Vincent, and on his death in 1837, was replaced by David Tachard, his successor as President of the consistory. The directing committee included five of the six pastors in the Reformed Church of Nîmes and six of its twelve elders. But it also embraced six lay members who were not elders in the Reformed Church, as well as a minister independent of the established church.[38]

Most other religious associations were neither so large nor as broadly based as the Société biblique, but all served, in purpose or in structure, to integrate the Reformed community. For example, the Société d'Evangelization chez les protestants disséminées was created out of the Conférence pastorale du Gard for the purpose of seeking out Protestants living in areas without a Protestant church in order to prevent them "from being lost in the mass of Catholics." When such individuals were discovered the society designated a pastor for whom they paid the expenses to provide them with occasional worship services as well as a level of advocacy and encouragement. The Société pour l'Encouragement de l'Instruction primaire sought to encourage the development of primary schools in order to, in the words of one of its supporters, "oppose the plots and passions of the Jesuits" in the Reformed community. Through its collection and disbursement of funds it also helped redistribute resources within the Protestant population of France to that end.[39] In addition, nearly all societies held an open annual meeting that drew together interested persons from the town, region or nation, according to the geographic focus of the association. After 1822, most of the national societies coordinated their annual meetings for the same week in April in Paris. Like its counterpart in London, this *Holy Week* became a major event in the life of the Reformed community, attracting clerics and lay people from across France for an intensive week of reports, debate and worship. The Pastoral Conference of Paris met the same week to take advantage of the large number of pastors in the capital. These conferences became a particularly important forum for disseminating information and ideas, coordinating policies and actions, and for focusing debate on questions of polity or doctrine. Though agreements reached here were not binding, the conferences often led to the initiation of new ventures and set the agenda for national debates in the Reformed Church.[40]

Religious associations also provided men and women alike with a degree of participation and independence in religious affairs unavailable through the consistorial structure. The Comité de la Maison des orphelines, which administered and supported an orphanage for Protestant girls in the Gard, was affiliated with the Consistory of Nîmes, but its president and most of its directing board were women, though several were spouses of members of the Consistory. The Société de Colportage de livres religieux de Nîmes, on the other hand, took most of its lay directors from outside the consistory of the Reformed Church. This organization, which financed and administered the distribution of tracts and other cheap religious writings to Catholics as well as Protestants, formed when the Société biblique de Nîmes, dominated by the Consistory of Nîmes, rejected the project. The new society's directing committee included three pastors from the Reformed Church of Nîmes, two merchants, the owner of a bookstore, and a teacher. At the time of the association's founding, only one of these laymen held a position in the Reformed Church of Nîmes, as a deacon.[41] As a vehicle for common action, and through the interactions they facilitated between regions and social groupings voluntary associations helped integrate the Reformed community across geographic, economic and gender lines.

At the same time these associations further complicated lines of authority in the Reformed Church and by extension within the Reformed community. The societies were an asset to French Protestantism which few could or wanted to surrender, but they operated outside ecclesiastical jurisdiction. The established churches could and often did influence them through its personnel, prestige and funds. Likewise, religious societies, through their broad bases of support, could influence the church on matters falling within their specific focus or theological outlook. Usually, they tried to cooperate with each other or at least find grounds for accommodation, but neither was able to control the other. Church leaders often worried that the activities of these societies, like the insistence of the Société de Colportage on distributing tracts and Bibles outside the Reformed community, would exacerbate relations with the Catholic majority, or engage in actions that discredited all Protestants in the eyes of civil authorities. Equally worrisome in southern France where confessional antagonisms still seethed, was the likelihood debates and contentions raised within and between voluntary associations would spill over into the church. Thus when a schism erupted within the Société biblique of Paris in 1833, over whether to include the Apocrypha in Bibles they distributed, the Consistory of Nîmes and other churches in the region were quick to decry the intolerance and lack of charity demonstrated by the two factions, and were very cautious about aligning with either side for fear of creating a similar division in their own congregations. Likewise, the creation by evangelicals of the Société des Intérets généraux to lobby the government on issues effecting Protestants, elicited a storm of controversy in consistories across France.[42] In a church that already tended to speak with a multiplicity of voices due to the absence of an over-arching organization, the prominence of numerous voluntary religious societies only added to the confusion. In addition, the ease with which voluntary societies could form provided a convenient tool by which minority voices in the established church could pressure the consistories or circumvent its authority altogether.

The most obvious solution was to restore the synodal system, allowing the established church a unified voice. Pastor Hugues complained that as circumstances stood Protestantism in France was more vulnerable than ever to the charge that "the principles of the Reformation are antipathetic to any strong organizational system and of favoring license and anarchy." After the July Revolution of 1830, some in the church felt they should take advantage of the situation to press the government to reestablish the synods. A few even urged that the church act unilaterally in this direction, even if it meant separation from the state. Others, however, were less certain synods would improve the situation all that much. One pastor asked, "With what would synods occupy themselves? Doctrine? Who would not oppose that? Their influence would thus be reduced to the little things."[43] Though on one side were those who felt a national structure was necessary to bring some uniformity to the Reformed Church, for others this diversity was the greatest risk posed by a functioning national ecclesiastical structure. A decentralized church allowed room for a variety of opinions and practices to co-exist. An authoritative National Synod may very well silence these voices and encourage schism.

Separation from the state earned even less support. While most in the church acknowledged the benefits that would be gained by independence from the government in terms of freedom of action and opinion, few were willing to assume the risks that came with it. Their reservations were largely practical in nature, ranging from the state of dependence in which pastors would be placed on the whims of their congregations, to the balance ties to the state offered against the power of the Catholic Church. A majority simply felt the time was not yet right for such a step, particularly given the period of development in which the church found itself. "If our church were to constitute itself in these days, this would be a misfortune," a pastor declared, "for we are in a time of transition." If left to its own devices at this time, another stated, "Our churches would become a republic exposed to anarchy because everything would have to be created new." Most agreed that independence would lead to the closing of many churches that just recently opened, the theological faculties at Strasbourg and Montauban would be forced to disband due to lack of funds, temples would fall into a state of disrepair, the number and quality of pastors would decline, and Protestant charities and schools would suffer greatly.[44]

The Reformed Church benefitted considerably from its link to the state. The number of pastors had increased significantly, and the government had begun almost routinely appointing assistants for ministers who were elderly or suffering from ailments that interfered with their ability to fulfill their responsibilities. Temples had been repaired and restored, and new ones built in places where no church had been for centuries. Protestant security had also improved. Though infractions and hesitations still occurred with disturbing regularity, Protestant access to public services was generally respected and their freedom to worship was broadly recognized even by the ultra-royalist administrations of Charles X. In the anti-clerical atmosphere that followed the Revolution of 1830, public opinion towards Protestantism seemed at an all-time high, and it was widely believed its position would continue to improve into the future. The July Monarchy seemed favorably disposed towards the Reformed community. In the Gard, Protestants actually dominated local politics. And the liberal ideals of individual self-determination, representative government and free inquiry that seemed the wave of the future were regarded as fundamentally Protestant.

In addition, though the institutional recovery of French Protestantism had largely been financed by the state, the church and community had demonstrated initiative and vitality in taking advantage of the opportunities available. The state may have contributed much of the money, but it was the church that initiated the process that led to the building of a new temple or the creation of a new pastoral position, and then used its contacts and resources to see the initiative through. In education, the Guizot Law gave primary schooling a tremendous boost. Yet prior to this a voluntary society had already been created for the purpose, and several churches and communities had taken the lead in founding schools and introduced into France the innovative methods of mutual education. For projects for which state support was not available a network of voluntary associations was created, linking together Protestants from across the country for projects like increasing the public availability of the Bible and other religious works, or even to recruit, train and send French Protestant missionaries to carry Christianity to foreign countries.

This did not mean the recovery of the Reformed Church was complete or without weaknesses. The link with the state from which the church had benefitted came at a price. The dependence of the Reformed Church on the government for its material well-being made it vulnerable to the dispositions of public officials. This was a major reason for the jaundiced view Protestants took towards the Restoration regime following the aggravations of 1821-1828. In addition, the modifications the state made to Reformed traditions of governance undermined some of the legitimacy of local ecclesiastical bodies, while the absence of synods deprived the broader church of an institutional existence. Again, the initiative and vitality of French Protestantism was evident in the efforts to work around these deficiencies. Accommodations were often established at the local level between the customary leaders of the church and the legally recognized consistory. In the broader sphere, various organs, from correspondence committees and pastoral conferences to voluntary religious organizations and religious journals, sought to fill the gap created by the lack of a national ecclesiastical institution. These arrangements were often remarkably effective at helping to restore and maintain the integrity of the French Protestant community. But they only worked by convention and consensus. Under stress they were liable to breakdown.

An increasing number in the Reformed Church, however, were also coming to the realization the community had spiritual needs which the addition of pastors and buildings, or organizational refinements could not necessarily address. The church had recovered remarkably well in terms of physical fabric from the chaos of the Revolution and the White Terror, but some concluded that in terms of depth of religious vitality it had made little progress or was actually in a state of decline. As a pastor declared in speaking against reestablishing synods, "What would synods do? They would make rules. But we need life!"[45] As the Reformed Church recovered institutionally, renewing the spiritual life of the community became a concern of growing importance.

CHAPTER 4

PURSUIT OF SPIRITUAL RENEWAL

On the eve of Napoleon's return to France in 1815, Jacques Olivier-Desmonts, President of the Consistory of Nîmes since its founding in 1802, discussed with an English correspondent the religious condition of the French Reformed Church. Religious zeal, he reported, began to decline as persecution diminished, and in the anarchy of the Revolution, "impiety and immorality" spread through the population. The legacy of these problems persisted, Olivier-Desmonts explained, in large part because of the weakness of the Reformed Church, especially its shortage of pastors, inadequate places of worship, lack of schools, and inability to hold synods. Two decades later, Abraham Borrel (1818-1865), also a pastor in the Consistory of Nîmes, gave a similar description of the religious state of the Reformed population in the late Empire. "[I]f the church had healed in terms of exterior peace," Borrel wrote, "an interior wound, more difficult to heal because it was hidden, was extending its ravages. . . . Incredulity had taken root in the hearts of many. Spirits occupied with battles and glory gave much thought to the enemies of the Empire, but paid very little attention to their own subjugation into a state of slavery to sin."[1] Though both writers agreed on the poor spiritual state of the Reformed community they offered rather different causes for the condition. Where Borrel, looking back from the 1830s was inclined to focus on the individual soul, Olivier-Desmonts centered on the incomplete structures of the Reformed Church.

This contrast represents a theological difference between the two writers, but one each shared with his milieu. Prior to the mid-1820s the quality of spiritual life was not a subject of particular attention. Church leaders were far from indifferent to personal religiosity, but they usually did not consider devotion in terms of depth of personal religious experience. Instead they took a more corporate view of the relation between the Reformed faith and the community in which the church was a medium between the two. If the faith had a feeble hold on the people it was because the frailty of the Reformed Church kept it from providing adequate religious instruction and oversight. A clear conceptual distinction between the spirituality of the faithful apart from the institutions of the Reformed Church did not seem to exist.

In part this was the product of circumstances. As has been seen, coming out of the years of repression the Reformed Church was the central institution of the community and a carrier of an identity intimately bound with the religion which the church administered. To a large extent both church and community in this era concentrated on survival, not the depth of personal spirituality. Moreover, it would have seemed a bit odd to demand a deeper spirituality of the faithful at a time when simply being known as Protestant put one's life and property at risk. In the euphoria of the Revolution many Protestants, including a significant number of the clergy, were ready to abandon their confessional community and its church for the broader fraternity of a French nation composed of free and equal citizens guided by the goddess of reason. As this dream collapsed French Protestants reassumed their confessional identity as they were forcibly reminded of their vulnerability as a religious minority. It was in this climate that the Reformed Church sought to rebuild itself and its place in the Reformed population. As religious toleration seemed to stabilize society, however, Protestants began to feel more secure, and attention in the church began to shift from survival to vitality.

This did not mean the institutional expansion of the Reformed Church stopped, or even slowed. The recovery continued, and with the establishment in 1830 of the more anti-clerical Orléans Monarchy, the pace if anything seemed destined to pick-up. At the same time a felt need for a deeper spiritual commitment to the faith developed alongside that for temples, schools and pastors. Many in the community were left unsatisfied by the formal observances of the faith and sought a more affective experience in the Protestant religion. This desire for spiritual renewal emerged and spread within the context of the Reformed Church's material condition, organization and relations with the government. These arrangements largely regulated the terms by which French Protestantism interacted with the larger society, and set the parameters within which the spiritual awakening in the Reformed community, known as the *Réveil*, developed and spread.

Concern had grown in the 1820s about weak attendance at worship services and other indications of inadequate religious vitality in the Reformed community. But the feeling that French Protestantism was in need of renewal was not entirely new. In the Vaunage a cadre of Protestants apparently descended from the *inspirés* affiliated with the English Quakers in 1788, and reinforced by occasional visitors from England sought to awaken the souls of those around them. In addition, the English cleric Clement Perrot, after making an extended tour of the region, praised several pastors including Olivier-Desmonts, Abraham-Louis Lissingol at Montpellier, André Gachon at St-Hippolyte, for their efforts to recall their communities to their religious duties. For their part, Lissingol and Gachon were influenced by Moravian pietism and propagated this style of affective devotionalism in their own parishes and among the Protestants of the surrounding region. Taking the Methodist missionary Charles Cook on a tour of the Vaunage in 1819, Lissingol introduced him to several pastors and lay people intent on pursuing a deeper spiritual experience, including groups at Sommières and St-Hippolyte organized and led by young women. Cook found similar circles in the Cévennes at Anduze and Générargues. For their part, these individuals welcomed the Methodists in hopes their presence could help revitalize the communities' religious life, and here and there, small awakenings were occurring. These renewals merged into a broader movement across France, which Vincent credited in 1828, with taking society's regard for religion "from profound indifference, and even aversion and hostility, to interest and respect. Life has succeeded death." He noted, however, that this movement accompanying the spread of Romanticism, did not mean society had returned to religion. "The human spirit is in labor, but it has not yet been born. It senses strongly what it lacks, but it has not yet found that which it needs." The strengthening of the Reformed Church can be seen to reflect this broad awakening, but as the Consistory of Nîmes noted in 1832, "the success of Protestant institutions has been due more to a spirit of opposition and the influence of a few men than to any true religious zeal."[2] The Reformed Church was materially and legally more secure in 1832, than in 1815, but there was growing apprehension that the attachment of the Protestant population to the faith, the church, and its services was in decline.

In some cases the problem was a continued shortage of worship space and services, but this was becoming increasingly exceptional. The need for greater religious zeal was perceived as more general and independent of such deficiencies. Vincent attributed the indifference of many

Protestants towards the church to the fact "they themselves have little religion." A few years later several of his colleagues in the Consistory of Nîmes complained of the corruption of the Protestant population and how few were participating in communion. In late spring 1829, the pastors of the region devoted the inaugural meeting of the Pastoral Conference of the Gard to the problem of religious indifference. Concern for the religious condition of the population continued to sharpen in the 1830s, particularly in the wake of the July Revolution as church leaders grew alarmed by an apparent expansion in religious indifference among urban workers.[3]

It is difficult to gauge with confidence the religiosity of the Protestant population. French churches did not keep attendance rolls, and the Reformed religion does not lend itself well to quantifying degrees of piety. It may well have been that the crisis was as much perceived as real. Visitors to France in the early nineteenth century were struck not only by the lack of spiritual fervency in French Protestantism, but also by the absence of concern this elicited among Protestant leaders. On the other hand, though an American attending the Reformed Church of Nîmes on Christmas Day in 1817, was "shocked by the levity of the people" during worship, he contrasted this with the reverent attention of those who stayed for communion. Charles Cook frequently remarked on the general religious lethargy of the Reformed population, but the presence of pastors and laity seeking deeper devotion convinced him to try working for renewal from within the established church.[4]

Given the history of French Calvinists it would have been rather surprising if in the first decades of the nineteenth century rates of participation had been high. The heroism of the Church of the Desert seems a clear demonstration of religious fervor, but for much of its existence regular common worship was impossible in most places due to persecution and the shortage of ministers. In the absence of public worship the *culte domestique*, the regular practice of household devotions, became the mainstay of Protestant religious life. Defacto toleration in the second-half of the eighteenth century allowed greater freedom of worship, but the growing influence of Enlightenment rationalism weakened the obligation for expressions of piety, particularly among the Reformed educated elite, including the clergy. Consequently, though some congregations later showed little sympathy for pastors who abdicated their calling, during the Revolution few church leaders felt public worship was important enough to resist the dechristianization campaign of 1793-1794. When freedom of worship was restored in 1795, the Reformed Church was slower to reconstitute itself than was the Catholic Church. Even in the Huguenot bastion of the Cévennes, public worship did not resume until after Napoleon organized the Reformed Church as a state institution in 1802. Progress was again interrupted by the White Terror which forced the suspension of church services in much of Bas-Languedoc for most of the second-half of 1815.[5]

Despite a degree of ambivalence towards common worship the Protestant community as a whole still seemed firmly attached to the Reformed Church and the religion it represented. The periodic outbursts of confessional violence that punctuated life in the region was one manifestation of this identification with the faith. So too was the emphatic protest of a man denied the church's charity because a pastor did not believe he was a Protestant since he could recite neither the Lord's Prayer nor the Apostle's Creed. "Not a Protestant!" the man cried. "But I would cut myself into little pieces for my faith!" Pastor Frossard observed that while the people seemed "little religious," everyone "says he is ready to die for his religion. . . . Too few seem disposed to live for it."[6]

The church also continued to hold a significant part in individual and community rituals. In most places Easter and Christmas services were very well attended, a point evident in the sermon of a young pastor at St-Jean-du-Gard who remarked in a sermon that many "fancy performing a Christian and Protestant deed at least once a year, and choose for that purpose the days of the great festivals, Christmas or Easter, or sometimes even both." Borrel noted that though poor Protestants in Nîmes seemed to be "Christians in name [only]" and rarely attended church, they "scrupulously inscribed their children among the number of catechumens, and called the ministers to their bedside when they are ill." Likewise, many among the "honorable rank of society" were deemed spiritually "cold," but "never made jokes about religion or offensive remarks about its ministers. They hold it as an honor to contribute with largesse to the care of the poor, to support the existing religious institutions and to give their coreligionists in difficult circumstances proof of their sincere fraternity."[7] A large number of those considered less than fervent in their faith continued to look to the Reformed Church in times of illness and for ceremonies marking the seasons and stages of life. They also supported the church and community with their money and influence, or lacking that, with fists, stones, clubs and guns.

Despite, and in part because of the confessional passion Protestants demonstrated in the streets after the Revolution of 1830, Reformed pastors and lay leaders were much more attentive to religious indifference in their community.[8] Their concern coincided with the emergence of the social question as an issue of intense public discussion throughout France in the aftermath of the July Revolution. The crowds that had demonstrated in the streets of Paris or of Nîmes were largely drawn from workers in the skilled trades, but they received little for their sacrifices. While the revision of electoral laws in 1831 enfranchised much of the bourgeoisie, workers and peasants remained unrepresented. In addition, the new government pursued social and economic policies that earned it the title the *Bourgeois Monarchy*, but disappointed those who remembered the First French Republic sympathetically or who saw in the July Revolution an opportunity for improving their lot in life through better job security, higher wages, improved working conditions, and greater cooperative action. The economic downturn precipitated by the political instability further embittered workers. Among urban workers the sense of betrayal grew to the point many were convinced the cholera epidemic that began in 1831,was the product of a bourgeois plot against them. In the fall of 1831, these frustrations burst into a full-fledged rebellion by the workers of Lyon. In following years working-class action spread across France, climaxing in 1833 when seventy-three strikes occurred in nearly every significant manufacturing center in France, before returning again to Lyon in the insurrection of 1834.[9]

In the Bas-Languedoc the working classes were comparatively quiet but apprehensions remained high. The vast majority of Protestants in both city and countryside welcomed the new regime. Many went into the streets of Nîmes to defend the new order from Catholic Legitimists. Despite the ascendency of Protestant influence in the region under the Orleanist government, Reformed artisans came to share the disenchantment of their counterparts elsewhere in France with the new regime. The rebellion of the Lyon silk workers, or *Canuts*, who battled the National Guard for control of the city for three days in 1831, sent shock waves that echoed powerfully in Bas-Languedoc, the second largest silk producing region in France. Among the Catholic working-class population, discontent strengthened the hand of Legitimist propagandists who contrasted the economic failures of the Orleanist regime with a Bourbon golden age. In the Reformed population this approach was less compelling, but even before the Lyon rebellion, the new prosecuting attorney for the Royal Court of Nîmes, François Viger, a Protestant from Sommières, warned of the danger on the political left posed by opportunists, radical republicans, the poor, and the victims of the White

Terror who were disappointed by the refusal of the new regime to avenge their sufferings. For the Reformed community, which had divided in the federalist revolt of the First Republic, this social polarization was deeply disturbing not just for economic reasons, but also because of the vulnerability of its position before the Catholic majority. In this light the working-class exodus from the pews of the Reformed Church seemed an ominous portent for the future of both church and community.[10]

Though there was an element of social control in the concern of Reformed elites for the religious behavior of the lower classes, their focus was on revitalizing the spiritual life of the whole community. As such, events of the summer of 1830, were a watershed beyond which the discussion and search for means to bring a religious awakening gained urgency and focus. There were those who thought the decline in attendance was an aberration brought on by preoccupation with political events and the economic downturn. Others, however, saw in the changes taking place around them the emergence of a new society with different needs and posing new challenges to which the church had to adjust. Gustave de Clausonne argued that religious indifference was a product of "the new character of our modern civilization which tends more and more to separate religion from the affairs of this world. This is a tendency to watch, which has existed for a long time and to which our last revolution gave a new impetus." Pastor Ferdinand Fontanès agreed, noting the problem was evident in neighboring parishes and departments and throughout France as well. Its causes lay in the "sensualism fostered in the last century . . . the rationalizing turn of spirit, and the exaggeration of individual liberty carried to a repugnance for all dependence."[11]

Fontanès, however, also took the church to task for not adapting to meet these challenges. Despite the demise of the *culte domestique*, the practice of regular family devotions that had been the primary vehicle for grounding the next generation in the faith during the decades of repression, nothing had been done to replace it beyond the customary lessons in the catechism prior to first communion. Preaching continued in the Enlightenment style of philosophical treatises that were beyond the interest and grasp of a large part of the congregation and moved virtually no one. The way in which the faith was thought of and presented was out of date. Sacred music, for example, was based on sixteenth-century adaptations of the Psalms of David which Fontanès said were more appropriate to Judaism than Christianity. Prayers were long, formal and sometimes obscure. Consequently, services were dry and irrelevant, understanding of the faith was limited, the faith itself appealed little to the sentiments, and the need for common worship was being lost.[12]

Fontanès was not alone in finding fault with the practices of the established church. A French seminary student at the close of the Second Empire categorized preaching between 1800 and 1820 as the era of "Slumber" due to the dry academic style and heavily philosophical content of the sermons. The pastors of the Gard in 1829, advised that "Scientific discussions are not a proper means for reviving piety. It is necessary to preach to the heart and occasionally homiletically." Some felt preaching should be de-emphasized or eliminated altogether in favor of liturgical services promoting adoration of the divine. Others thought preaching should be instructional to combat religious ignorance. It was suggested that the pastor lead all aspects of worship to de-emphasize his role as preacher. Conversely, several felt the laity should be more involved in the service. Other aspects of worship, from the reading of scripture to the manner of prayer and the formal ambiance of the service were also critiqued, but with little consensus about what should be changed or how. Even those who defended the traditions of the church admitted that the way they were being conducted was failing to keep the people in the pews.[13]

To address the problem numerous ideas were exchanged and discussed in a variety of forums. As already seen, many of these proposals centered on the form of worship itself, with a view to give it more meaning and emotion. Another focus was enhancing pastoral effectiveness. It is not surprising that clergy were given much of the responsibility for bringing about religious renewal. They were the most publically identifiable representatives of the faith. In the course of the nineteenth century, however, expectations for their role began to change. An earlier generation had been inclined to view the ministry as an occupation and means of advancement. Several pastors, like Samuel Bruguier at Mont Mamert and Daniel Encontre of Anduze, were directed into the ministry by their parents for economic and social reasons. Once installed, Bruguier found the occupation attractive because it "favored in a certain manner my love of letters . . . furnishing me with the means to develop my limited talents and to make myself useful to my fellow citizens in preaching to them virtue, good habits, and patriotism."[14]

In the nineteenth century this utilitarian and moralistic model of ministry still existed, but it was being replaced by one in which a good pastor was one who had a demonstrably positive impact on the religious lives and sentiments of his parishioners. To accomplish this, pastors were exhorted to be better examples of the spirituality they were charged with promoting. A contributor to *Archives Evangéliques*, a journal edited by Pastors Frossard and Borrel of Nîmes, solemnly cautioned the young against lowering "your noble vocation to that of a simple occupation, casting a justifiable doubt upon your faith." The Conférence pastorale du Gard advised its members that before a renewal of their congregations could be expected, "[t]he pastor must first consider himself as a believer and put his own salvation in the forefront." The pastor must also "read the Bible as it relates to himself before he can later do so for others." In addition "visits to various members of his flock are good for augmenting the piety of the pastor himself."[15] Of course not all ministers had to be told to perform such seemingly basic duties. That it was believed necessary to mention them indicates the degree of functionalism with which some pastors approached their duties.

An important spokesman for refashioning the Reformed pastorate was Samuel Vincent. He spoke contemptuously of pastors "who do not see in their ministry anything other than a means by which to earn their livelihood and only fill their duties in form." He warned his colleagues that in modern society they could not simply rely on their position as pastor to gain them a hearing in their communities. "It is necessary that one respect [the pastor] as a person, much more than his position."[16]

The son and grandson of pastors *du désert* and head of a family with extensive property holdings in the region, Vincent was widely respected nationally and locally both as a Protestant religious thinker and citizen. After completing seminary at Geneva in 1809, he was called by his home church at Nîmes to serve as Pastor/Catechist. Four and one-half years later he was raised to full pastor. The retirement of Olivier-Desmonts in 1824, made him the pastor with the longest tenure in the consistory, but he did not become President of the consistory until the 1830 Revolution overthrew the Bourbon Monarchy.[17] Despite an active presence in civic life, Vincent was a sincere minister of the Gospel, and it was in this capacity that much of his reputation was made.[18] He first gained notice in 1817, with the publication of a small catechism for local use, but which by 1861, was in its ninth printing. He also translated several German and English theological works into French, and in 1819, published a new edition of Antoine Court's account of the War of the Camisards, *L'Histoire des troubles des Cévennes*. In 1820, he defended Protestantism against Félicité de Lamennais' attack in his *Essai sur l'indifférence*. Later that year Vincent began publishing *Les Mélanges de religion, de morale et de critique sacrée*. He wrote and produced this journal, of which ten issues were printed between 1820 and 1824, nearly without assistance, using it as a vehicle to further introduce the ideas of English and German theologians, especially Friedrich Schleiermacher, to French Protestants. Finally, on the eve of the July Monarchy, his two principal works appeared, *Vues sur le Protestantisme* and *Méditations Religieuses*. Upon his untimely death in 1837, the Venerable Company of Pastors in Geneva formally conveyed its regrets to the Consistory of Nîmes over the loss of "one of its own."[19]

Although Samuel Vincent was not alone in calling for reform of the pastorate as a necessary preparation for renewal in the church, most of these other voices did so from a perspective largely informed in one form or another by the pietistic or evangelical awakening occurring in the rest of Protestant Europe and America. Theologically Vincent's position has been described by Daniel Robert as *preliberal*. This is to distinguish him from the theological liberals of the second-half of the century who were more positivist in their philosophy and influenced by the biblical scholarship of David Strauss. Vincent followed Schleiermacher in the effort to merge modern philosophy and biblical revelation in understanding Christianity. In a sense he embodied the unlikely reconciliation of the Enlightenment with the prophetic and mystical traditions of the *Eglise du désert*. He did not hesitate to use philosophy and higher criticism in the study of Christianity, insisting that the results, while reasonable, harmonize with the "sentiments of the soul." He was not comfortable with either the rationalizing religion of the eighteenth century, which was too cold and impersonal to lend comfort to the heart, or the simple devotion of the persecuted Huguenots, which too easily sank into intolerance and fanaticism.[20] Though his effort to blend rational philosophy with divine revelation was not universally representative of French Protestantism, in southern France where many shared Vincent's roots in the Enlightenment and the *Eglise du désert*, his thought was particularly influential. As the Reformed community began to move out from under the shadow of repression, Vincent tried to establish a bridge between the simple and prophetic piety of the *désert* and the Enlightenment influenced pastors and lay leaders of the French Reformed Church.

Implementing reform was more difficult than recognizing its need. Without synods there was little mechanism beyond mutual exhortation by which to enforce pastoral discipline. The government would remove a minister at the request of a consistory for immorality or negligence. These instances, however, were relatively rare. On less tangible issues of spiritual fitness the civil authorities lacked interest and competency, while the consistories were without a mandate to act.

Attempts to alter the character of worship also raised obstacles. Custom alone was often a formidable barrier, especially in a church for which the formal act of worship was the principal religious experience of many in the community. A pastor noted, "among the people the worship service is entirely confused with the religion. To change it is to provoke the religion itself."[21] Tradition was not the only obstacle to reforming the structures and services of the Reformed Church. Fear of compromising Protestant confessional solidarity was perhaps an even more potent deterrent to ecclesiastical innovation. This was clear in the discussion in the Consistory of Nîmes of a proposal from one of its pastors for reorganizing the system of pastoral care in order to create more meaningful contact between clergy and laity. According to the procedure that was in use pastors rotated weekly between the various worship services and all other pastoral duties. Thus a minister never presided at the same worship service two weeks in a row, and one week in four was responsible for all home and hospital visits, weddings, and baptisms for the entire church. Excepted from this rotation was the pastor-catechist who was responsible for preparing most of the church's youth for first communion.

The advantage of this system was that it essentially treated the 13,000 members of the Reformed community in Nîmes as a single, and in many ways, undifferentiated congregation. Though parishioners lived in different quarters of the city and worshiped at several services conducted in two separate temples they were served equally by all of the pastors. Similarly, all of the catechumens, except those of wealthy families who contracted with a pastor for private lessons, were taught in common under the direction of the same minister regardless of where they lived or which worship service their families may or may not have attended. In the words of Borrel, this organization "accustomed the flock to set aside personal considerations . . . precious advantage for fraternal peace and union since it excludes all preferences."[22]

The benefits of this arrangement for community integration, however, came at the cost of distancing ministers from parishioners. In essence pastors were set up as public figures, much like the mayor and town counselors. They were readily identifiable by all, but few had much meaningful interaction with them. As the emphasis in religion shifted from public affiliation to quality of experience, the adequacy of the model of a pastor as public functionary came into question. Instead, it was suggested that each of the church's five pastors be assigned to a specific neighborhood for which they would be responsible for such duties as home visits, baptisms, marriages and preparation for first communion. In addition, pastors would have a monthly rotation in the hospitals and prisons, and each would take a turn of several weeks leading the Thursday evening and the 8:00 A.M. Sunday worship services.

Though the plan was supported by the pastors, the lay elders ultimately rejected it. They acknowledged "the church could be better in relation to its exterior zeal," and even believed the new organization could help. But fears the plan might fragment the community overrode these benefits. Dividing the city's Protestants into parishes might create competition and rivalries between the pastors to attract followers from each others. Moreover, doctrinal differences could further separate the faithful as each pastor imprinted his own theological views onto his assigned quarter. The net result, as one elder explained, would be to weaken "the unity of which the Protestants of Nîmes, more than elsewhere, have need because of their political position."[23]

The likelihood of such a result had been demonstrated several years earlier in Anduze. This cevenol town of 5,500 people was 85 percent Protestant, and had three pastors serving it and its hinterlands. In 1821, a dispute erupted between two of them, Alexandre Soulier and Orange Massot, over succession to the position left vacant by the retirement of the President of the consistory. The conflict was particularly volatile because Soulier, the senior of the two contenders, was sympathetic to Methodism and on occasion had invited Charles Cook to assist him. A few years previously he had been chastised by the consistory for not including it in a meeting held in his home at which about a hundred people had gathered to hear Cook speak. The President of the consistory explained that the absence of the other pastors and most of the consistory could "lead the people to think there was a difference of opinion among the pastors." A short time later, the consistory refused to sanction any such private worship services feeling they were "unnecessary." Because of this earlier confrontation the consistory was inclined to side with Massot, though he was Soulier's junior and at that time not even a full pastor. Soulier's partisans saw this favoritism as an assault on their religious interests and protested vehemently, creating a crisis that disrupted the life of the entire town. Eventually passions cooled, but not before the government had to intervene, and Pastor Massot conveniently left for a position outside the region.[24]

Concern to prevent similar disputes hindered other attempts at innovation as well. At Nîmes, the suggestion that pastors give courses on religion for the educated classes was rejected because the content of the courses could commit the church to a particular theological position, alienating those not sharing it. A request to allow pastors to hold reunions of their former catechumens was also denied. These meetings would provide an opportunity to "recall in simple terms the moral and religious instructions which have perhaps been forgotten," and thereby "to bring back to communion a rather considerable number of young persons who are not assiduous in their attendance." Several elders, however, questioned the effectiveness of these meetings noting that though they have been used elsewhere for years, "everyone still complains of the progress of corruption and of seeing the Holy Supper neglected." Given the uncertain results and the peril that such meetings would solidify relations between segments of the population and a particular pastor at the expense of his colleagues, church leaders decided the reunions weren't worth the risk.[25]

Questions such as these were most pressing in urban centers, such as Nîmes, Alès and Lyon, with a large differentiated Protestant population. Elsewhere the dispersed character of the population reduced organizational options and there was little overlapping of responsibilities since pastors worked in relative isolation from each other. Issues of confessional solidarity, however, penetrated even small towns and villages, particularly where Protestants lived side-by-side with a large Catholic population. In addition, as communication and commerce increased, differences and nuances in religious belief and practice that may have been obscured by geographic isolation, now became more apparent. The disruption such divergences could create is what made the question of synods so pertinent. It is also one of the reasons their surrogates, pastoral conferences and voluntary societies, were so attractive.

Concern for Protestant integrity was also evident in the increasing competition that developed between the established church and foreign missionaries. The Reformed community had been the object of missionary activity before. Prior to the nineteenth century these had usually been Catholic missions, which though unsettling, had limited lasting effect against the animosity and disdain in which the vast majority of French Protestants held the Roman Church. More disruptive were Protestant missionaries from Switzerland, England, and later the United States. A product of the evangelical awakening that had been underway since the 1740s, Protestant mission organizations turned their attention to France following the collapse of Napoleon's Empire. Using the guarantees of religious freedom under the Charter they hoped to redress French impiety and superstition which they felt lay behind the barbarity and anarchy of the French Revolution. "Ignorance of the book of God, with the immorality and infidelity consequent on that ignorance, was the principle cause of the French Revolution," charged a contributor to the *Methodist Magazine*. Jabez Bunting, soon to be the head of the Wesleyan Methodists in England, declared at a meeting of the Methodist Missionary Society at George-Yard Chapel, "Did not every British heart triumph in the victories recently obtained over French tyranny; and would not every Christian heart triumph in the success of those Missions over French infidelity and wickedness?"[26] As such, the missions' ultimate interest was conversion of France's Catholic population, but for political and religious reasons many Protestant missionaries found they had better success among the Huguenot's descendants.

Particularly important in southern France were the Methodist missions conducted out of London. They began with Charles Cook's first trip through the Midi in 1819. Pastor Lissingol of Montpellier introduced him to sympathetic pastors and laity throughout the Vaunage and lower Cévennes. In Nîmes, Cook spent time with Pastor Tachard, whom he felt held Methodist opinions, and Vincent, who though he had been told Vincent was opposed to evangelical doctrines, Cook found to be quite sympathetic.[27] In fact Vincent helped ease French suspicions towards Cook, making it easier for the English missionary to gain access to Reformed pulpits. A few years later Vincent wrote of the Methodists:

> Whether by the nature of their doctrine, or by the superiority of their lights, or by their personal character, they have shown themselves much more adept [than other missionaries]. They carefully avoided all that could harm or wound the pastors. They were more patient and made a greater effort to justify themselves, to make themselves understood, to dissolve the prejudices that could form against them, and to profit from all favorable circumstances which could be offered to their zeal.[28]

On the basis of his reception in the region Cook advised his superiors in London that rather than attempting to establish an independent Methodist Church the better strategy for political and practical reasons would be to cooperate with the established church in trying to effect spiritual renewal. For the Reformed Church, short of trained pastors, exhausted by a generation of political and social upheaval, burdened by the legacy of persecution and rationalism, and uncertain of its position under an apparently inhospitable Bourbon regime, the assistance of these missionaries from abroad was welcome relief. At Nyons in the Drôme, a pastor begged Cook to come and help him counter the visit of three Catholic missionaries to the region. In other areas, especially in the Vaunage, where Cook met his wife and served for a time as an assistant to the Reformed pastor at Congénies, the Methodists made a significant impact.[29]

Leaders of the Reformed community were also uncomfortable with the aggressive evangelism practiced by the Methodists and other missionaries. They feared the insistence of the missionaries on proselytizing among the Catholic population would exacerbate relations between the two confessions and jeopardize the good will of civil authorities. French Protestants were also becoming suspicious of Methodist devotional practices and the independent spirit they seemed to encourage in the population. Particularly unsettling were the evening prayer meetings and occasional fasts Methodists held in private homes, away from the view of established authorities. The prominence of women as participants in these meetings (many of whom were known to suffer emotional or physical abuse from their husbands or other male relatives) raised suspicions even more. In Le Caylar, fasts organized by a Methodist minister were twice forcibly broken-up by men from the village, and threats were made against the missionary's life. That the wives and daughters of two elders in the local consistory took part in these meetings against the will of their husbands and fathers further poisoned relations between the established church and the Methodists. In his investigation of the incidents, the Procureur Général explained the assailants hoped "the Methodists would experience enough difficulty to force them to leave the region."[30]

By 1830, those Methodists who had taken positions in the Reformed Church had surrendered them. Exploiting the more liberal disposition of the Orléans Monarchy, they continued to evangelize aggressively, but now often as competitors rather than partners with the established church. Consequently, many in the Reformed Church became increasingly disillusioned with the Methodists and other missionaries active in the region. One pastor observed that religious separatism only appeared with the arrival of "foreigners who claimed to preach the Gospel with more purity than the national pastors. . . . Some of these strangers have used reprehensible means in order to achieve their goal, and have attacked the reputation of some estimable pastors."[31] This cry of betrayal echoed across the Protestant Midi. They had welcomed the Methodists into their churches and community only to have them try to lure away those on whom their preaching and spirituality had an effect. The number who formally affiliated with Methodism was quite small. After forty years of effort the Methodist Conference of France in 1857, had only 1,272 members. The influence of Methodism on French Protestantism, however, was much greater than its membership. Many did not break with the established church, but participated in Methodist meetings and were deeply influenced by its theology and style of spirituality.[32] In this way, the Methodists operated much like a voluntary religious association within the Reformed community. Unlike most of these societies which operated parallel to the established church, Methodists were becoming the church's competitor. With the close connection that existed between the Reformed Church and the community, the Methodists and other independent missions were increasingly regarded by Reformed leaders and people alike as a threat to the integrity of church and community. As such they provoked a response.

At a popular level this response could be rather direct and sometimes violent. Beyond the incidents surrounding the fasts at Le Caylar, Charles Cook reported being pelted with stones as he traveled from one place to another in the Cévennes. Cook's younger colleague, Mattheiu Gallienne avowed "the vicious insults with which we are unmercifully assaulted in these parts give me a case of nerves. I dread, for example, the long road from St-Jean-du-Gard along which at each door cries of 'Goat!' assail us. At Tornac, four-footed dogs are set on us, and I do not like the two-footed ones in the valley of Mialet any better."[33]

Less dramatic but perhaps more deliberate was the decision of consistories to simply cut-off relations with the missionaries. A Reformed pastor declared, "The foreigners who carried separatism into our churches began by preaching in them. They abused our confidence. Do they offer us their pulpits? We will no longer allow them to enter ours." The Consistory of Nîmes formally forbade, "under any circumstances," the use of its churches to anyone not of the established church. It then sent copies of this decision to other consistories in the region urging them to adopt similar measures.[34] Reformed authorities could also take advantage of their connection to civil authorities to bring governmental pressure to bear against Methodists. This option, however, raised uncomfortable comparisons to the Reformed community's own experience of repression. It also contradicted the freedom of inquiry that many Calvinists proudly hailed as the great contribution of Protestantism to modern society. Thus, a pastor told the Prefect of the Gard, "I have no love for separatism, but I respect as an act of religious liberty all faiths that do not trouble public order."[35]

Rather than pursue government intervention against the dissidents, a more positive strategy entered into by Reformed leaders was to counter the attraction of Methodism and other dissident movements by paying greater attention to the unfulfilled religious needs of their congregations. Several pastors began introducing some of the practices of the Methodists such as extemporaneous prayer, hymns and small prayer groups. Others initiated Sunday schools and night worship services when they saw the popularity of these services as introduced by Methodists.

Next to Sunday schools, night services were one of the most common, but also one of the more controversial reforms implemented in French Protestantism. Though night meetings were not unknown in French Protestantism, their systematic use was an innovation introduced particularly by English Methodists. Some of the resistance to them derived simply from this association with foreign missionaries. But these night services also raised suspicions among church leaders and civil authorities alike by the very fact that they took place at night, and therefore seemed inherently subversive. Three of the men arrested for assault for their part in breaking-up the Methodist meeting in Le Caylar defended themselves by protesting the disruptive nature of these night meetings. The Consistory of Privas [Ardèche] spelled the case out more explicitly, invoking the potential for moral and civil disorder in the working classes. Against its instructions, Pastor Bosc of Fonts-du-Pouzin had organized night services, which was taken not only as evidence of his latent Methodism, but was "the occasion for the downfall of many, above all among the working class." The many workers, the consistory explained, "who leave their workshops scattered across the countryside, in order to attend, or under pretext of attending, these meetings and finding themselves sheltered from the master's eye, at night and alone in the mountains, are safely able to surrender to their wickedness, satisfy their passions, and even commit crimes."[36]

Another pastor, however, claimed it was exactly because of the potential for misdeeds at this hour that these services were useful. "Evenings are the most dangerous time of day," he argued. "This is a time of laziness and dissipation. There are spectacles at this hour for the worldly; there should be some temples open for the pious!" Perhaps more persuasive was the fact that evening services seemed to work. Part of this success was simply that they offered an opportunity to worship for those whose occupations did not allow them to attend on Sunday mornings. These services were also believed more appropriate for poorer Protestants who were too ashamed of their meager clothing to attend church on

Sundays. Some even attributed the effectiveness of night services to a mystical effect of the lights used to dispel the darkness. It seems more likely that after the initial novelty it was the nature of the services that accounted for their popularity more than the hour at which they were held. Night services were not simply the transplanting of regular worship to a different time, but constituted an entirely different genre of worship. They tended to be simpler and less formal than those of Sunday mornings. As one pastor observed, at these meetings the "pastor is less a functionary, and more a man." Others agreed, noting the extra services were more instructive in content, and easier to experiment with and adjust according to events and desires.[37]

It was this type of service that the Consistory of Nîmes initiated in response to the opening of a Methodist chapel in the city. The Sunday school the Methodists began there grew from thirty-two to one hundred-sixty members in six weeks. Similarly, the worship services were so popular all the seats were filled, with many standing in the aisles and along the walls. This success, however, alarmed leaders of the established Church. Matthew Gallienne, leader of the Methodist mission at Nîmes, remarked that their presence "excited the wrath of our Reformed brethren . . . so that quite alarmed for the safety of the French Church and of the progress of that marked and troublesome creature, Methodism, they blow the trumpet and sound the alarm and (pity!) take on the armor of strife." Feeling itself challenged by the Methodists the Consistory of Nîmes resuscitated its own Sunday school that had been allowed to lapse for want of attention, rented a building on the same street as the Methodist chapel, and began holding services there of a similar nature and scheduled for the same time.[38]

The *culte de l'Oratoire*, as these services were called, was designed to be less formal and more intimate than worship in the Reformed Church on Sunday mornings. The consistory directed that it be "appropriate, as much as possible, to manifested needs, and by consequence efficacious for maintaining union." The message was to be short, biblically based and to "expose, in a practical manner, the truths holding the closest to the saving of souls by Jesus Christ." The pastor would officiate "without robe or the gravity of the pulpit," and was to encourage participation by the congregation, particularly in hymn singing. There would be no designated reader or cantor, and liturgical prayers were not to be employed. Neither would there be a pulpit or parquet, but only a few chairs reserved for those members of the consistory who chose to attend. The pastor was not to be robed, but dressed in dark clothing, and would speak seated or standing before the stage.[39]

The new services were an immediate success. Soon after they began the consistory received two petitions thanking it for meeting a need which "for a long time was felt in our Church of Nîmes; that of a religious service where the word of God was explained in a simple manner and to the level of persons of all classes." At the same time, however, the petitioners pointed out that the building was not convenient to where the bulk of Protestants lived, particularly Protestant workers. Despite this, the room also was not big enough for the four to five-hundred people who attended each evening, and in order to find a seat it was necessary to arrive an hour early, and others were being turned-away for lack of room. To address these problems the Consistory, somewhat surprisingly, immediately decided to build a third temple in the working-class neighborhood of the Placette to house the *culte de l'Oratoire*. The cost of the new building was estimated at 25,000 francs. Ten thousand francs were already in hand from a bequest for this purpose received earlier from a wealthy Protestant woman. Additional funds were believed available from the government, with the balance to be raised in a door-to-door solicitation among the city's Protestants.[40]

A few weeks later, however, the President of the Consistory announced that the fund drive was not well received by wealthier members of the community. They felt the existing temples were adequate for the church's needs, and if they weren't it was the city that should take responsibility for providing a new one. But several in this class were also concerned that opening a temple in a working-class neighborhood, combined with the informal type of worship that was to be celebrated in it, risked "constituting a division in the body of the church by isolating those who frequent it." In other words, providing the working classes with their own building with services distinct in form from those in the other temples might encourage an independence in this class that would further loosen the social bonds holding together the city's Protestants. This was a concern similar to that which led the consistory to put aside plans for reorganizing its system of pastoral care, but in this case with a more overt class complexion.

This opposition to a new temple placed church leaders in a dilemma. They could not go forward with the project without the support of the Protestant elite of which many neither believed the new building was needed nor agreed with the principles behind it. The consistory's initial discussions of the *culte de l'Oratoire* showed that some of its own members shared these hesitations. Yet they had felt compelled to go ahead with the project because of the popularity of the Methodist services and Sunday school. Though it was possible the new temple and services might encourage division in the Protestant population, if the *culte de l'Oratoire* was suspended it seemed likely those who favored it would end up with the Methodists. In the end church leaders split the difference by continuing the new services, but moving Sunday night services to the Petit Temple and holding the others in the rented building. It was hoped this would satisfy those who had gone to the Methodist chapel while also appeasing "those who saw with pain a religious service conducted away from the temples." Plans for a new temple, consequently remained dormant until the mid-1850s.[41]

This episode was an early indicator of the dilemma and divisions which religious awakening could raise for the Reformed community. Church leaders had been disturbed by the religious indifference of the Protestant population but reforms to address the problem proved difficult to balance against the traditions, class interests and security needs of the community. As at Nîmes, changes might only be implemented when faced with competition or crisis. Yet the fact foreign missionaries attracted enough attention to prod the church into action, even if only in half-measures, was evidence of the dissatisfaction in another portion of the community with the established church. Rather than indifferent towards the faith these were people whose faith had been enlivened as part of the Réveil in French Protestantism. Often, however, they longed for a deeper religious experience than they found in the customary practices of the Reformed Church. It was not among those spiritually "asleep" that foreign evangelists were gaining followers, a pastor observed, but among "souls reawakened."[42] The Reformed Church wanted renewal, but those giving evidence of awakening could prove difficult to satisfy in the church as it was then constituted.

Though many in the Reformed Church had worked for this renewal, the spiritual awakening that developed exceeded the Church's ability to control or contain. It was a religious movement that transcended institutional structures and conventions. At St-Hippolyte-du-Fort a "great religious movement" to which "the pastors were foreign" developed around a pious cloth dyer with Moravian roots. Elsewhere, as at Lyon with Adolphe Monod or at Privas with Pastor Bosc, the pastor was awakened while much of his congregation remained unaffected.[43] In the Vaunage a pastor had to deal with a group that emphasized the spiritual at the expense of the temporal manifestations of the faith in the church and communion. Conversely, other pastors had parishioners who declined communion because they felt unworthy to partake in the remembrance of Christ's sacrifice. In the first case individuals pursued a mystical union with God that superseded temporal acts and institutions. In the second they were so aware of personal sin they shunned the sacraments. Though coming from different perspectives both behaviors resulted from a heightened concern for the spiritual that diminished the pertinence of religious rites celebrated in the established church. Others were more conventional in their devotion. Laymen and women at Nîmes for example, met on their own in the days prior to celebrating communion to prepare themselves in common for this event. Here and elsewhere this practice, rooted in Calvinist devotionalism reaching back to the Reformation, grew into regular meetings of private citizens for prayer and spiritual encouragement. Several church leaders were uneasy with these meetings, but like the pastors of the Gard in the 1830s, admitted they were "too generally established not to be considered an indication of a real need."[44] Such examples were evidence of religious renewal, but they also demonstrated a degree of independence from church structures and personnel that could be just as disturbing as religious indifference.

Thus the Réveil, rather than building unity and reinforcing authority in the Reformed community, instead became another force that tended to sow difference. In practical terms most of these distinctions were rooted in differences in religious sentiment and practice resulting from the awakening. The Réveil in French Protestantism was part of the wider evangelical renewal that swept through much of the Protestant world in the eighteenth and first-half of the nineteenth century. It shared with this Great Awakening what W. R. Ward has identified as a "combination of theological conservatism and practical innovation." Though in specific and institutional terms there was little commonality among evangelicals, nearly all looked back to the Reformation doctrines of justification by faith alone, the priesthood of all believers and the authority of scripture. Evangelists like John and Charles Wesley, George Whitefield and Howell Harris and their followers added to this dogmatic foundation an intense personal devotionalism rooted in the direct experience of the divine, often beginning with a dramatic conversion experience.[45]

From this broader perspective the evangelical awakening arrived relatively late in France. It first appeared in the early 1820s, to be followed by a longer and more powerful wave of revival after the Revolution of 1830. The coincidence of the renewal with the arrival of foreign missionaries after the collapse of the Napoleonic Empire has led some historians to portray it as a foreign import to France. This is to ignore, however, the themes current in the Reformed community that were tapped by the Réveil. In its reaffirmation of Reformation theology and moral rigor it easily blurred with remnants of dogmatic and devotional traditions stemming from orthodox Calvinism. In addition the revival's emphasis on the believer's empowerment by the divine and call to action echoed the spiritual mysticism and prophetism still present in popular religion from the *inspirés*. But the Réveil also introduced newer emphases on experiential and affective spirituality that echoed the romantic mood sweeping Europe and came from abroad with foreign missionaries. With this variety of dispositions, the possible combinations of theology and spiritual nuances alone would make the movement difficult to contain in a single ecclesiastical institution. Thus it is perhaps not surprising that institutional fragmentation was a characteristic feature of the evangelical Protestant renewal of the eighteenth and nineteenth centuries wherever it occurred.

For all its variety and differences, however, the Réveil did have a certain unity. For those under its influence the basic distinction came to be between the awakened and the unawakened. It was a distinction that operated, not between Reformed and Methodist, Swiss and French, or rich and poor, but within the Reformed church and its congregations. Though they often differed over doctrinal particulars and ecclesiastical polity, those effected by the renewal generally recognized each other as kindred spirits. Those who were not awakened, including many with whom they lived and worshiped, were the *other*.

In practical terms most in the Reformed community were made aware of this distinction through the worship and devotional practices and attitudes advanced by evangelicals. But the religious division also assumed a theological expression that justified and perpetuated this partitioning. Before the Réveil and even as part of its early expression, a generation of church leaders intent on rebuilding the Reformed Church had tried to distance themselves from the natural theology of the eighteenth century which they felt had led the church into the disasters of the Revolution. For the most part this was a relatively narrow dispute operating largely among the clergy, and tended to obscure other theological divisions that were still ill-defined and only vaguely perceived. The interest raised by the awakening brought these theological issues to light. Partisans of the Réveil, convinced of the leading of the Holy Spirit within them, sought to overcome all obstacles to the complete revival of the Reformed population. As resistance was encountered they were inclined to interpret it in theological terms that prompted their opponents to defend themselves on a similar basis. Thus the renewal tended to clarify and harden doctrinal positions giving rise to a self-conscious theological division between proponents of the *théologie du Réveil* and their more liberal opponents.

In terms of broad doctrinal categories it was difficult to distinguish between these two groups in the first-half of the nineteenth century. Positions later became more distinct as liberals moved from a theology based on Kant and Schleiermacher to one that owed more to the biblical criticism of David Strauss and the philosophical positivism of Auguste Comte. But where these later liberals were naturalistic if not materialists, the generation represented by Samuel Vincent, Ferdinand Fontanès, Gustave de Clausonne, and Jean-Paul Hugues in the south, and at Paris by Athanase Coquerel (père), were supernaturalists who allowed for direct revelation and divine action in the natural world and emphasized the affective in Christian faith. The catechism of Samuel Vincent, used widely in Nîmes and other churches in Bas-Languedoc, may have been too moralistic in tone for evangelical tastes, but it did not shy away from doctrines held dear by the orthodox faction like the trinity, the atoning sacrifice of Jesus, and the resurrection. As Fontanès observed, for all the debate between orthodox and liberals, "There is in our churches rather extensive religious unity."[46]

Though in a broad sense this was true, liberals allowed considerably more room than evangelicals for interpreting these doctrines. The orthodox accepted explicitly dogmas like original sin and the divinity of Jesus. Liberals, on the other hand, adhered to what they termed the *Protestant principle*. This principle, derived from the priesthood of all believers and the inscrutable nature of God, was freedom of inquiry in all areas of knowledge, spiritual and temporal. Every individual should have the freedom to come to their own understanding of Christian truth. For example, liberals and orthodox agreed on humanity's need for regeneration from sin, and that this came from Jesus Christ, the Son of God who was one with the Father. But if one went beyond this, Fontanès explained, "to ask how the Son of God, who was in heaven, became human you approach an abyss to which the doctor in theology might have the temerity to expose himself, but where the simple faithful dare not descend." Similarly on the question of salvation, "The entire church responds with a single voice, 'The believer and the believer alone'" will be saved. Evangelicals, however, insisted on justification "by faith alone, without works." Liberals provided more room for human action in the form of proper behavior, arguing "Faith, repentance and sanctification, those are the conditions for salvation."[47]

Partisans of the Réveil demanded more rigor and clarity. Emilien Frossard, who as pastor/catechist and later full pastor at Nîmes, was a regional leader of renewal, counseled a newly ordained pastor, "He who embraces a pastoral career is not in the least a man who searches for the truth. He is a man who has found it." This truth was:

> *Christ and Christ crucified.* Christ! Not a being of the imagination, but a real being whose life is a historic fact, whose preaching was heard by men, who's blood was actually poured out in ransom for the sins of those who repent. A precious savior who *died for our sins and rose from the dead for our justification.* Without this idea it is impossible to conceive of Christianity. [emphases in text][48]

Christian faith was unqualified acceptance of these essential doctrines. This consent was more than intellectual assent to abstract principles. It was expressed in a deeper personal change in purpose and behavior. A correct understanding of the *Grand Facts* of Christianity demanded a personal response. The individual's life had to change, and this change was the product of unqualified acceptance in Jesus Christ as Savior.

This did not mean the followers of the Réveil were anti-intellectual. The emphasis they placed on human depravity led them to qualify much of the optimism in human progress expressed by some of their contemporaries, but many were quite learned, were firm advocates of popular instruction, and did their part to disseminate the benefits of modern science and technology.[49]   When it came to theological knowledge, however, they parted company with their more liberal colleagues on the value of modern learning and methods. For them the Bible was the only reliable foundation for Christian dogma, and its truths were readily accessible to all who read or heard them.   The critical methods and theologies pioneered in Germany were unreliable and misleading at best. Reason was of little use for understanding the truth and significance of the life of Jesus Christ, as the intellect suffered the consequences of sin and would likely lead one astray or induce complacency about the state of one's soul.

Scripture was the only reliable foundation for Christian truth, and it was understood through the heart not the intellect. Timoléon Béziés told the congregation of St-Jean-du-Gard one Easter morning that if they had trouble believing these truths they should not assume it was because the doctrines were wrong, or their proofs too weak to affirm them. The problem was "singularly due to your heart, and your assumption that religion is only dogmas and facts which have no effect on the ordinary course of your life." Accepting the truth of Jesus' life was not the assent of the mind to a set of principles. It was the assent of the heart to Jesus as Savior. Evangelicals did not seek to persuade one of the intellectual validity of Christianity. They sought to convert him.[50]

The emphasis was on the individual, who had to recognize his or her own depravity, humble him or herself before God and transfer their affections to their divine master. Though evangelicals claimed the doctrinal mantle of the Reformation, in preaching conversion they modified Calvinist teaching on divine election in favor of individual initiative and the role of the affections. Reformed revivalists insisted upon salvation by grace alone, but where Jean Calvin interpreted this as predestination of the elect by an inscrutable and omnipotent God, evangelicals stressed the responsibility of the individual to act in her or his own salvation by submitting to Jesus Christ as Lord and Savior. Theologically the vehicle of conversion was the Holy Spirit, but revivalists urged their listeners to prepare the way for divine action, implying they had some part in God's bestowal of grace.[51]

Assurance of salvation came from the individual's inner sense of the divine and their response to this presence in a life devoted to God. This devotion involved the commitment of the entire person - possessions, actions, and affections - "towards that which will please his divine master." Theologically it was an expression of gratitude to God for salvation, but in practical terms it was a "demonstration of faith revealing that one is following it in all its stages; that he reflects all its characteristics." Piety was a manifestation of the strength of one's faith. Conversely, failure to live piously indicated the absence of true faith. As one evangelical writer put it, "Much faith, much devotion. Little faith, little devotion. No faith, no devotion." Without faith Christianity had little significance or satisfaction, and one's efforts at devotion were inherently corrupt.[52] Fontanès was close to the truth when he complained that the orthodox faction "assimilated the indifferent members of our churches with pagans and Jews as enemies of the Gospel." For evangelicals faith was rooted in a private relation with God, but it was quite public in their expectation that it could be identified in one's demeanor, conversation and actions. The title *Protestant* was only correctly applied to those who had a spiritual conversion resulting in a change in behavior. Claiming the name of Protestant or Christian (the two terms were often used synonymously) without living like one was to degrade a noble calling and thereby little different from actively opposing the faith itself.[53]

Personal conversions and perseverance in a pious life were outward signs of divine grace, and inwardly offered the believer assurance that his or her ultimate fate was secure. This assurance of God's grace was one of the defining and most powerful features of the evangelical renewal. It was the source of their confidence and enthusiasm that motivated and sustained their numerous evangelistic and charitable activities. This certainty of God's calling, however, did not well tolerate ambiguity in its theological foundations. If the core doctrines of Christianity, such as the divinity of Jesus and his resurrection, were subject to interpretation, then so too was the promise of salvation. In this respect orthodox insistence on Christian fundamentals was as much an object of devotion as its cause. Faulty doctrine led to insincere devotion, and insincere devotion was an indication of faulty doctrine.

The linkage in the theology of the Réveil of doctrine, conversion, and devotion was the source of a divergence between liberals and evangelicals on ecclesiology. Since this difference involved who belonged in the church it was one of the most visible and emotion-laden in the French Reformed community. The nature of the church was a persistent issue in Protestantism. Reformation theologians separated salvation from the action of the church and placed it instead in the relation of the individual with God. This created a distinction between the temporal church and the mystical church that was the true communion of the faithful. Though it was hoped that the visible and invisible church would coincide, Reformed theology generally taught that the mystical and temporal churches did not fully correspond. This ambiguity provided a convenient platform for malcontents and prophets (the difference often being one of perspective) to challenge the institutional church throughout the history of Protestantism.

The French Reformed Church was not exempted from this critique. Originally it had required allegiance to the Confession of La Rochelle adopted by the first National Synod of the French Reformed Church in 1559, and scrupulous moral surveillance by pastors and elders to bring the assembly of communicants into as close alignment as possible with the mystical communion of the saints. Over time the rigor of this surveillance subsided so that coming out of the eighteenth century the Reformed Church was essentially coextensive with the community. In the nineteenth century Ferdinand Fontanès noted that the common definition of a Christian was one "baptized and admitted to the Eucharist by the public profession of faith in the Savior." As the Reformed Church recovered its institutional structure this included nearly everyone, particularly since popular understanding tended to regard communion like baptism, "holding it necessary to do only once."[54]

In the religious enthusiasm of the Réveil this laxity was evidence of the corrupting influence of human depravity on a sacred institution. From the perspective of their conversion experiences and devotional fervency, revivalists saw a clear distinction between the multitudinous French Reformed Church and the spiritual body of Christ. They criticized the church for compromising its integrity by its ties to the state, its emphasis on formal observance of religious rituals without taking to heart their meaning, and for making these rituals available to the religiously indifferent and theologically heterodox.[55] Not surprisingly their solution was to purify the church of its unfaithful members. With standards of piety and belief reflecting the experiential emphases of the renewal, evangelicals felt it was possible to discern who was and who was not part of the Kingdom of God. A Christian was one who accepted on faith certain basic doctrines and lived a life of personal devotion. Therefore, evangelicals felt moral discipline, acts of piety and submission to the Confession of La Rochelle, or another confession yet to be written, should be required for full participation in the life of the church.[56]

Evangelicals wanted to make the French Reformed Church into a believers' church. Being born and baptized a Protestant was no longer sufficient. Acceptance into the church required evidence of conversion in heart and mind. Without this there could be no genuine communion in worship or effective cooperative action to further God's kingdom. Including the unfaithful would only compromise the church and her mission. It also risked breeding complacency in the unconverted about the true condition of their souls. If they were allowed full membership in Christ's church while in God's eyes they still stood outside the kingdom, the unawakened may never recognize their need for grace. Even worse was the presence of heterodox beliefs among the church's pastors and leaders. Not only would they encourage complacency among the unfaithful, they would lead these lost souls to regard their unbelief as belief.[57] For the good of the church and the ultimate well-being of the unconverted, evangelicals sought to separate out those who did not meet the necessary standards for admission. In this way the Réveil not only was excluding many French Protestants from heaven, it also threatened to exclude them from what was the unifying institution of their community. In effect they sought to transform the French Reformed Church into a voluntary association.

Reformed liberals, who dominated most of the consistories in the region, vehemently opposed such exclusivism. It was not that they explicitly rejected the doctrines professed by the orthodox faction. They objected to the restriction of free inquiry implied by their dogmatism. Confessions of faith, they argued, were historical documents bound to a specific time, place and understanding. As such they could never capture the infinite possibilities of God's truth. For Reformed liberals faith was variable and deeply personal.

This can be seen in the writings of Ferdinand Fontanès, a pastor in the Consistory of Nîmes. Influenced by Samuel Vincent, whose niece he married, he became a leader of the liberal wing of the Reformed Church after Vincent's sudden death in 1837. Fontanès argued that the Gospel centered on the life of Jesus of Nazareth, not the ideas or principles devised about that life. Doctrines were nothing more than "a compilation of ideas for the spirit, a collection well or poorly made, a system more or less true, but that is all." The church was not based on doctrine, but on identification with the life of Christianity's founder. "Instead of gathering around a word, a tortured phrase or some textual subtlety, we go straight to the facts, to the person. Instead of an abstract notion we have a being, a reality. Alone, ideas form a skeleton, while history is a living body." The Bible was the chronicle of this history, "the authority after which there is no other. What it teaches, we believe. What it prescribes, we must put into practice." But unlike evangelicals, liberals regarded the Bible as a complex document and difficult to interpret. As a historical document, written within specific cultural settings, understanding the scriptures required special training and study. Even then the ambiguous nature of its content meant conclusions were far from certain. Some things remained "hidden to mortal eyes until God removed the veil with which he covered them, or remain hidden today because it has pleased God to reserve to himself alone their comprehension."[58]

Therefore it was to be expected that different people might arrive at varying conclusions about the significance of the life of Jesus as each arrived at his or her own understanding with God, but all were united in a focus on the life of Jesus. Christianity was no more controlled by dogma than were personal relationships. In this respect liberals shared the Réveil's emphasis on a personal relationship between the individual and God, but for them this was not necessarily reflected in uniformity of belief. Christians came together in the church, but in a way similar to a circle of individuals gathered together in the presence of a common close friend. They associated within vaguely defined parameters, but not all relationships were governed by the same terms. Thus, Fontanès hailed two acquaintances who were devotes of the utopian-socialist Saint-Simon as "*organic Christians.* . . that is to say, Christians like the apostles, Christians according to Jesus-Christ." [emphasis in text][59] Though in terms of doctrine they were unorthodox, in spirit they were faithful followers of the Gospel.

It was important for liberals that the Reformed Church not be defined to exclude such individuals. Unlike their evangelical opponents they were reluctant to set the boundaries of Christianity too sharply. They criticized evangelicals for "claiming to be the only Christians," and for branding as "enemies of the Gospel" the indifferent members of the Reformed Church. Liberals did expect certain standards of behavior, but even then there is no evidence a consistory intentionally excluded anyone from taking part in the practices of the faith so long as they were baptized and confirmed.[60] It was ridiculous, Fontanès said, to think one "needed to have the same beliefs in order to live together in the same church. . . God calls and attracts all men to him through his Spirit." Rather than requiring a confession of faith, Fontanès thought Christianity would be better served by a church that encouraged "a spirit of inquiry and liberty to penetrate everywhere."[61] This was the true value of the Reformation for modern society.

Neither Reformed liberals nor evangelicals were indifferent about participation in the church. In a culture in which church and community were closely identified they both sincerely believed all should join fully in the church's worship and, as already seen, earnestly sought to accomplish this end. For evangelicals, however, worship could only occur among those who had experienced a personal spiritual conversion and consequently shared a common core of beliefs and similar spiritual dedication. Liberals refused to restrict access to the church according to modes of belief or regularity of attendance. They rejected the notion that one should be denied the right to worship simply because they did not meet the standards of doctrine and pious behavior dictated by another. Though they saw religion as deeply personal in its particulars, they believed the entire community in all its diversity should unite in common worship within the structures and rituals of the Reformed Church. In this way they continued to defend the linkage between the Reformed Church and the community.

As the French Reformed Church rebuilt its institutional structure in the early nineteenth century, it also began to experience a renewal in its spiritual life. Such an awakening was sincerely desired by many in the church. They were troubled by the widespread indifference towards religion in the Protestant community and struggled to restore meaning and purpose to the Reformed faith in the wake of the dry rationalism that had characterized the Reformed Church leading into the Revolutionary era. The Réveil, however, placed church leaders in a dilemma. Samuel Vincent warned pastors to put themselves at the fore of any religious renewal in their churches or their congregations would abandon them. Many tried to follow his advice, but the awakening that developed exceeded their ability to control or harness. Now as they tried to combat the religious indifference that threatened their relevancy, they were also confronted by a growing number who earnestly sought a deeper spiritual experience but threatened to take control of the church and exclude from it the indifferent and doctrinally suspect. In the background was the possibility that if the established church did not adequately respond to the needs of these awakened souls they would slip into religious separatism with the Methodists or other independent churches forming on the community's margins.

CHAPTER 5

CONFLICT AND CRISIS

In mid-November 1836, nineteen pastors from the Gard and the surrounding region gathered in the Petit Temple at Nîmes to discuss "The Réveil and the strengthening of the national churches of France." No sooner had they finished with the opening prayer and a few announcements than someone asked that the topic be split into two separate issues, arguing there was no direct connection between "the Réveil" and "strengthening the national churches." His motion failed and the assembly went on to discuss the religious awakening as a means of fortifying the church. It was clear from the ensuing debate, however, that many pastors remained ambivalent towards the benefits of the Réveil. Several persisted in addressing the renewal and the church's well-being as unrelated. A few noted that some groups associated with the Réveil were of "doubtful tendencies, at least in terms of the question of strengthening the national church." One minister declared, "As for the question of strengthening the church, it is necessary to be very sure it will in fact be strengthened by being awakened." Another insisted that confusing the Réveil with fortifying the church was a mistake. "These two points of view," he argued, "are so different that those who focus only on the Réveil have undoubtedly caused a great deal of unease for those trying to strengthen the church."[1]

A few years before many of these same ministers were earnestly searching for ways to revive their congregations. Their later suspicion of religious awakening grew out of the confusion and disruptions in the religious life of the Reformed community that followed the awakening. As with Protestant churches in America, Great Britain, Switzerland and elsewhere, the Reformed Churches of France found that religious renewal, though seemingly desirable and even needed, was a very divisive force.   Historians have often remarked the activism that was part of nineteenth-century evangelicalism.   David Bebbington has even cited it as one of the movement's defining characteristics.   French evangelicals were no exception.[2]   Not content to demand greater fervency of themselves, they felt those around them should also be awakened to a life of spiritual devotion.   Such evangelism often forced a response, either positively or negatively.   For evangelicals there was little room for ambiguity.   Refusal to convert was evidence of an unrepentant heart. Their willingness to categorize their neighbors as either saved or damned could   understandably   be   invested   with   considerable   emotion. Consequently, as a growing number of French Protestants experienced spiritual awakening, rather than reinforcing confessional bonds, religion instead became a source of tension and division.

Formally, much of the controversy surrounding the Réveil involved theological differences.   But since in practical terms the issue involved the nature of the church and who was legitimately a part of it, the dispute transcended the relatively limited circle of those versed in the doctrinal particulars to involve the broader community.   Thus only a few months after the debate over the Réveil at the Pastoral Conference of the Gard, Gustave de Clausonne felt compelled to devote his presidential address to the annual meeting of the Société biblique de Nîmes to an impassioned appeal for restraint and mutual respect.   Such pleas were fairly common in the region, but on this occasion Clausonne was asking for tolerance among Protestants, not between confessions.

His address began by invoking the broad-spiritedness of Samuel Vincent, recently deceased.   Vincent, Clausonne argued, had felt that liberals and orthodox differed not so much in the essentials of the Christian faith than in temperament and emphases.   Where one stressed "wisdom" the other emphasized "fervency."   Both, Clausonne said, were essential for the health of the church.   The absence of fervency led to neglect and indifference, while fervency without wisdom risked error and intolerance.   "The most desirable state would be that the two tendencies, instead of excluding each other, would share equally in the influence and the direction of spirits."   This, he said, was not currently the case.   "The second of these tendencies [fervency] is about to surpass the first in a noticeable manner.   Not content with giving progress and direction, there are churches it aspires to take-over completely."   Consequently, "clashes and internal ruptures have developed.   The peace has been troubled."[3]

Such conflict, Clausonne claimed, was not necessary.   Citing Nîmes as an example he argued that theological differences did not have to lead to schism. Here Vincent, though personally favoring the philosophical to the zealous, had led the church to respect all legitimate religious needs. As a result, Clausonne boasted, Nîmes avoided the dissension marring other places while at the same time advancing in its religious life. "We have had movement without tumult, heat without conflagration."

The key, Clausonne said, was to "reject neither of these two tendencies that exist among us as elsewhere." Instead the churches needed to "put them in a state not of struggle, but of contact, making of them not two enemies, but friendly competitors [émules] towards a higher good; working to balance, clarify, and temper one by the other; allowing each to have its representatives in place for discussion and debate."[4] In practical terms this meant supporting a variety of religious services and practices and choosing pastors and lay leaders so that a doctrinal equilibrium was maintained in governing ecclesiastical bodies.

Clausonne's address may have been more a symptom of the growing crisis than proclamation of a successful strategy for others to follow. To a certain extent the presbyterian system of church government, with its reliance on lay leadership and representative institutions, seems to assure a degree of quarrelsomeness in ecclesiastical affairs. In the middle-third of the nineteenth century they became particularly contentious in French Protestantism. Selecting new pastors proved particularly touchy. It was not just a matter of choosing the best candidate for the needs of a particular congregation. Though the Reformed pastor's spiritual and ecclesiastical power was substantially less than that of his Catholic counterpart, he was still an important public figure. In rural parishes and small towns they could be the most educated member of the community, with valuable contacts and knowledge of the outside world. Accordingly choosing a new pastor could raise a variety of competing interests and agendas. Thus in the best of times the choice of a new minister was of great interest to the Reformed community and those who hoped to influence it.

The process was further complicated by the fact that the Organic Articles took the power of appointment away from local congregations and vested it in consistories overseeing several churches. The state hoped this would result in a socially and politically moderate pastoral corps, but it also increased the probability of conflicts in the selection process. Consistorial jurisdictions were too large to be strictly local, yet not far enough removed to offer the aura of disinterestedness. Though contested appointments were not unheard of, prior to the 1830s their number was lessened by the deference shown by most consistories to the will of the congregations involved. The development and spread of the Réveil, however, interjected additional concerns for spiritual fitness and doctrinal purity. Evangelicals saw a faithful pastor as vital both for the spiritual renewal of the community and for maintaining a pure and effective church. Confronted by evangelical enthusiasts, consistories countered by taking a more active role in the choosing of new ministers. Not surprisingly, the number of disputed appointments increased dramatically. In Nîmes, at the very time Clausonne was preparing his address to the Société biblique, the consistory was battling with its deacons for a consensus on a new pastor/catechist as it shuffled its personnel to fill the vacancy left by Vincent's death.[5] Eventually they abandoned consensus and named Aristide Fermaud on a majority of one, and the matter ended there. Other appointments could not be settled internally and ended up on the desk of the Minister of Religion in Paris. Between 1837 and 1842, eight of fourteen appointments made in the Gard were appealed to Paris. In 1837 alone, three of the five positions filled were contested and civil authorities were called upon to resolve them.[6]

Much of the problem pitted the desires of the local congregations against the authority of the legal consistory. In the Consistory of Lasalle a candidate sponsored by an influential member of the consistory was chosen by a single vote over the person favored by the congregations composing the sectional church of Soudorgues. Though the church in question had only a single representative on the consistory, three elders were so disturbed by the result they refused to sign the minutes of the deliberation, and joined local leaders in an appeal to the Garde des Sceaux who also served as Minister of Religion. The Sub-Prefect for Le Vigan backed the appeal noting "the desire of the faithful should have some influence on the decision of the General Consistory." The Garde des Sceaux did not agree, and confirmed the choice of the legally constituted consistory.[7]

A similar result met an appeal from the sectional Church of Ribaute against the Consistory of Anduze. In this case the consistory consulted the congregation on the choice of the new pastor, but then split evenly between Louis Ribard, a recent graduate of the evangelical dominated seminary at Montauban, and Jacques-David Bastide, who had studied at the more liberal seminary in Geneva. As President of the Consistory, Alexandre Soulier, long a promoter of the Réveil, cast the deciding vote for Ribard, claiming he did so in deference to the local church.[8] Bastide's supporters immediately protested to the Minister of Religion arguing the deliberation was invalid since the consistory had not been renewed as required by the Organic Articles. Every two years half the elders of a consistory were to stand for reelection by the consistory and an equal number of prosperous laymen. This had not been done in Anduze since 1831. Consequently the Minister of Religion annulled Ribard's nomination and ordered all the lay members of the consistory to stand for reelection.[9]

The issue then shifted to how the twenty-five *plus imposés* Protestant notables required to join with the consistory for the renewal should be chosen. Were they the twenty-five heads of households who paid the most taxes or could they be selected from among the richest Protestants? Soulier favored the latter as this would allow some consideration to be given to spiritual fitness in choosing the men responsible for appointing the next pastor.[10] The Minister of Religion decided otherwise. He determined that the law required convening the twenty-five Protestants who paid the most property tax. As a result, five of the nine incumbents lost the ensuing election. In addition, all the elders now came from Anduze, depriving the other congregations in the consistory of lay representation. This body then voted 12 - 0 for Bastide, with Soulier and another pastor abstaining. Though these two wrote the government pleading the unfairness of imposing a pastor on congregations that were not represented in the decision, the letter of the law had been met and Bastide's appointment was confirmed.[11]

Differences between evangelicals and liberals were less a factor in the controversy that developed in the Consistory of Le Vigan over the choice of a pastor for Avèze and Molières. Deacons for these congregations were actually allowed to vote in the election. When the majority went against them, however, they circulated a petition signed by most of the residents of the two communes asking the government to rescind the consistory's choice. Though the elected pastor, Paul Laune, was known for his ardent orthodoxy in his prior position as pastor at Mialet in the nearby Consistory of St-Jean-du-Gard, it does not appear the complaint involved him directly so much as it did the disregard shown by the consistory for the wishes of the congregations. As the Prefect observed, "The struggle is not between the nominated pastor and the population. It is between the *Deacons* and the *Consistory*." [emphasis in text][12]

The religious diversity of this mountainous region did, however, complicate matters. In addition to Reformed liberals and orthodox, independent revivalists were also active in the area and helped create conditions in which it was easier for leaders at Avèze and Molières to rally support for their rebellion against the consistory.[13] The independent missionaries themselves were widely disliked and their followers represented only a tiny minority, but they were known for their attacks on the legitimacy of the Reformed Church. One of these revivalists, a follower of John Nelson Darby of the English pre-millennialist sect the Plymouth Brethren, had even gone so far as to declare that a devil stood behind the pulpit whenever a pastor of the Reformed Church of Le Vigan preached. This nearly cost him a beating from an angry mob, but attacks such as this, together with the implicit critique of those worshiping outside the established church, could resonate in the Reformed population in its dispute with the Consistory of Le Vigan. An informant reported to the sub-prefect that the temples of Avèze and Boissières were nearly empty in protest of the consistory's decision, with many boycotting the church and attending private religious meetings. He warned that if the controversy persisted they may never return to the national church.[14] The Prefect, however, insisted on supporting the consistory. Annulling the election would reward the congregations for rebelling and "destroy the consistory by depriving it of all influence." He further counseled the Minister of Religion to take measures to keep deacons from meddling in consistorial affairs.[15]

In the end Laune decided to stay at Mialet rather than face the animosity of his new parishioners. His decision saved the government from having to judge the issue, but not long afterwards the Minister of Religion issued a circular letter forbidding all Reformed consistories from allowing any involvement by local deacons in pastoral appointments. This directive only asserted existing regulations, but it formally ended conventions followed in many consistories respecting customs of congregational self-government. Enforcement of the regulation reduced the number of pastoral appointments appealed to civil authorities, but conflicts remained. For example, the Consistory of St-Chaptes refused to appoint a pastor despite the near unanimous support of the involved communes, because he would not condemn the recently established evangelical Société des Intérets généraux du Protestantisme français. The government rejected a bid by the sectional Church of St-Martin-de-Corconac, in the Consistory of Lasalle, and St-André-de-Valborgne, in the Consistory of Valleraugue, to form themselves into a separate consistory in hopes of gaining more control over their affairs. In Valleraugue itself, tensions between the town council and local farmers over tax rates coalesced around the consistory's attempt to remove a popular young pastor on allegations of an illicit liaison with a woman of a prominent family. A series of public disorders ensued resulting in several arrests and occupation of the town by the gendarmes. The country party then boycotted the local church, and built a temple of its own which it intended to open as a dissident congregation. When the structure was completed, however, the government refused to authorize its use for this purpose. Except for a clandestine worship service the building ended up first a factory for the manufacture of silk thread, and then a warehouse.[16]

Religion was more directly involved at Sauve where strains between liberals and evangelicals prevented the consistory from renewing itself for nearly a year. The issues were similar to those at Anduze a few years before except a pastoral appointment did not hang in the balance and it was the orthodox faction, not the liberals, that was trying to consolidate power in the consistory. Under the pastorate of Charles Fraissinet, Sauve became an evangelical stronghold and the consistory centered on this town was one of the few in which evangelicals were a majority. They hoped to protect their position by choosing notables for the renewal from a list of the sixty wealthiest Protestants, rather than convening the twelve top tax-payers. Since it was only a simple renewal and not the total reconstitution of the consistory the government felt the law could accommodate this request. The orthodox faction was thereby able to control the election. Their victory did not last long. An orthodox elder died soon after, giving liberals a working majority. At the next renewal none of the previous notables were convened, the son of the deceased elder failed to win his father's place, and another evangelical elder lost his bid for reelection thereby giving liberals a comfortable majority.[17]

The frequency and intensity of intra-confessional strife evident in episodes such as these raised considerable anxiety among Reformed leaders. In part their concern reflected genuine differences in religious disposition, but also at work were fears that the chaos overtaking the Reformed Church would compromise the community's security. Living in a region where confessional violence was a real possibility Protestant leaders were sensitive to anything that might indicate weakness to Protestantism's enemies. The tendency of evangelicals to distinguish between true and false Christians was particularly disruptive in this regard as it called into question the religious foundation of the community's identity. Closely related were fears the disorder in the Reformed community, signaled by the frequency with which Protestant affairs ended up on the desks of civil authorities, would try the good will of the state. History had demonstrated the extent to which the welfare of French Protestantism depended on this good will. Protestant leaders were aware that much of their current good fortune was a function of the July Monarchy's suspicion of Catholic clerical power. For a regime that made the golden mean a policy objective and placed a high value on public order, the turbulence in French Protestantism might feed residual prejudices associating Calvinism with disorder and rebellion.

Efforts by consistories to impose order, however, fed a cycle in which the extension of consistorial authority fostered resistance if not rebellion against consistorial control. Despite enjoying the state's sanction the legitimacy of the leadership of the established church was problematic for part of the community. Tensions resulting from alterations under the Organic Articles to the structures of church government had remained largely latent since many established consistories tried to accommodate themselves to customs of local initiative. With the injection of doctrinal and devotional differences that accompanied the spread of the Réveil, stresses between local and official church leaders grew in number and stridency. Lacking a mechanism to settle such conflicts internally they often ended up in the Ministry of Religions. Civil administrators tried to limit the number of these appeals and to resolve those which persisted by strict enforcement of the Organic Articles. This entailed further reliance on the consistories at the expense of congregational independence. Though the legal consistories tried to claim the function and authority of the old Huguenot consistories, the local diaconate was closer to this institution in form and history. Lacking a foundation in Reformed tradition, the consistories were uncomfortably dependent on civil power for their authority in a confessional community known for its independence and resistance to the state in matters of religion.

The heightened spiritual sensibilities that came with the Réveil further undermined the position of legal consistories. This was particularly true in Bas-Languedoc where, unlike Paris and other regions where the orthodox faction gradually gained control in the 1840s and 1850s, most consistories remained liberal in sympathy. Orthodox influence therefore was greatest in local settings where their activism, concentrated numbers and religious assiduity increased their impact, especially when seconded by a sympathetic pastor. As these evangelicals saw official consistories extend their power over church affairs and then pursue policies they felt hindered the Réveil they became increasingly restless. An orthodox member of the Consistory of Nîmes was not alone in questioning whether consistories constituted according to the Organic Articles could claim jurisdiction in questions of religious practice and belief. In current conditions, he said, consistories only possessed "the budget, administration [of church business], and venerable memories of times past."[18]   Predisposed towards distinguishing between true and false Christians, evangelicals could easily conclude that compromises in Reformed principles that were the price for state support had put the church in the hands of apostates.

Suspicious of the legitimacy of the consistories, partisans of the Réveil pursued activities independent of official ecclesiastical authority. Private prayer meetings and Bible studies were the oldest and most common example. Others were local and national religious societies that were too aggressively evangelical for the liking of many southern consistories. When the Consistory of Montpellier refused to take up the cause of missions, Pastor Lissingol and several lay people created on their own one of the first mission societies in France. The Société des Traités religieux was formed by Nîmois evangelicals in similar circumstances.[19]   The popularity of these and other organizations with a significant part of the most active members of their congregations, combined with a liberal commitment to the principle of freedom of worship, prevented church leaders from opposing them too hastily. Some consistories even tried to tap into their success by establishing less formal services like those of the Oratoire in Nîmes or by championing and even founding more moderate parallel societies such as the Société d'évangélisation des protestantes désséminées.

Eventually, however, evangelical activism independent of consistories convinced many Reformed leaders to take a more aggressive line. A catalyst was the creation in spring 1842, of the Société des Intérets généraux du protestantisme by a group of orthodox pastors. The idea for the society developed out of a series of articles in the Protestant journal L'Esperance detailing the condition and needs of French Protestantism. In particular the series' author, Agénor de Gasparin, Master of Requests to the Conseil d'Etat and a leader of the orthodox faction in Paris, resurrected discussion of the National Synod or another agency to coordinate Protestant activities and to serve as an advocate with the government on Protestant affairs. Sentiment for such an institution was becoming particularly strong given the renewal taking place in French Catholicism. For Protestants, Catholicism's recovery in strength and confidence was manifested in a number of energetic and sometimes malicious attacks leveled against them by Catholic commentators such as Louis Veuillot, who began his tenure as editor of L'Univers in 1842. Adding to Protestantism's sense of insecurity were indications the government's favor towards it was softening vis-a-vis a revivified Roman

Catholicism. It was a paradox of the era that while the royal family entered into several marriages with Protestants and the King's government was led by the Calvinist, François Guizot, French Protestants continued to suffer from the hostility and limitations of an earlier age.[20] Defending Protestantism, therefore, became the topic of discussion for the Pastoral Conferences of Paris that May, meeting in conjunction with the annual gathering of the major religious societies.

As usual the *Holy Week* conferences attracted a large number of pastors from across France, including Abraham Borrel of Nîmes. They agreed on the utility of an agency to coordinate Protestant actions, but in four sessions of sometimes passionate debate the pastors were unable to resolve the issue of how or even if doctrinal standards should apply to the institution's structure. Frustrated by this failure twenty-one orthodox pastors, in a meeting chaired by Borrel launched the Société des Intérets généraux du protestantisme français. Though they promised the agency would work in the interests of all Protestants for greater religious liberty, equality of religions, and the advancement of works not addressed by an existing religious society, the directing committee would come from the established churches and would be limited to those professing the "vital doctrines designated in all ages by the name of *orthodoxy*."[21]

Announcement of the society's creation released, in the words of the independent revivalist Jean Pédézert, "a storm the likes of which had never before been seen" in French Protestantism.[22] Liberals used words such as "exclusivist," "fanatical" and "schismatic" to denounce the association, and quickly mobilized a national campaign to repudiate it. The Consistory of Nîmes, in one of the first actions that would make it a leader of the liberal cause in the French Reformed Church throughout the century, took an immediate role in this campaign. Following the line of attack set forth in Paris by Athanase Coquerel (père), it charged the society with violating the "principles of liberty which form the honor of Protestantism." But reflecting southern Protestants' sensitivity to security concerns, Nîmes also claimed the society "risked the greatest evil by introducing division and anarchy into the church" and weakening it by including the interests of dissident churches under its umbrella. One Nîmois elder declared application of the principles behind the new society would not strengthen French Protestantism, but would "inevitably lead to the dissolution of the Protestant Church."[23]

Though this view may seem overly alarmist the Consistory of Nîmes perceived itself sufficiently threatened by the new association to do more than just deny it support. The Société des Intérets généraux received extensive coverage in the Protestant press, and the directing committee followed this up with a letter to every Protestant Church in France asking for assistance. In Nîmes, one pastor had participated in the association's birth and two others, Jean-Paul Gardes and Emilien Frossard, proclaimed their approval soon after. Twenty other pastors in the Gard, and the sectional Consistory of Sauve, went on record in favor of the project.[24] With this publicity church leaders worried that the new agency would be well received in their community, particularly given Protestants' sense of besiegement by a hostile majority. Fearing the society's evangelical bias and potential for bypassing consistorial authority, Pastor Tachard, President of the Consistory of Nîmes, urged the consistory to "break the silence by publicly demonstrating the impression the new society produced on it."[25]

A majority in the consistory agreed, and drafted an open letter describing how the consistory "far from supporting the Société des Intérets généraux du protestantisme français, saw itself obligated to oppose its influence." It explained that the Société not only would promote evangelical interests to the detriment of all others, its commitment to religious freedom for all Protestants would weaken the national church by protecting the interests of *schismatics*. In fact the consistory's letter lumped supporters of the new society with foreign missionaries and religious dissidents having similar doctrinal views but hostile to the Reformed Church of France.[26] It also challenged evangelicals' claim to orthodoxy, asserting the Société des Intérets généraux in its narrow dogmatism was "neither really Protestant, nor truly Christian" as "Protestantism rests on the Gospel and Free Inquiry." The letter concluded with an appeal of its own to the Huguenot heritage, urging Protestants to honor the memory of their ancestors by seeking a more enlightened expression of Christian zeal than that offered by the Société. "Conserve in yourselves a holy respect for the honorable memories of your Fathers, their faith in the Gospel, their attachment to the great principles of the Reformation, their love for peace, their zeal for good, their attachment to the divine chief of the church. Be sincere Protestants, enlightened and pious Christians."[27] The consistory then announced that salaried members of the church were forbidden to collect funds for the new society.

In publicly renouncing the Société des Intérets généraux the Consistory of Nîmes understood it risked exacerbating tensions in the Reformed population. Borrel warned the consistory that publicizing its opposition would endanger the harmony of the Protestant community they earlier were so concerned to preserve. A colleague agreed, noting those who supported the society were already suspicious of the consistory. The consistory's disavowal would make them even less likely "to submit to the authority of the consistory." At the same time, those in the community unaware of a division in the church "will be mortally wounded" in learning of it. Neither would it make the religiously indifferent any more likely to come back to the church. Finally, he warned, "the Catholics, who will read this letter, will not fail to concern themselves with it in their journals."[28]

A majority, however, agreed with Pastor Tachard that the consistory could not "allow itself to be stopped by the inconveniences or the pain" action against the society could entail. If it did not act now to oppose orthodox actions the consistory's own position would erode by default. To prevent this the Consistory of Nîmes drew a clear line between itself and the supporters of the Société des Intérets généraux and called on other consistories to do likewise. Several in the region did. The Consistory of St-Chaptes drafted a letter charging the Société des Intérets généraux with endangering Protestantism by dividing the church into two distinct camps. The Consistory of Vézénobres was harsher, publicly characterizing the society as "exclusivist in principle and vicious in its organization."[29]

The action of the Consistory of Nîmes also put three of its own pastors in a difficult spot. Borrel's part in the founding of the society and the early support given it by pastors Gardes and Frossard was well known. Now the ecclesiastical body to which they were responsible had condemned the society and prohibited its employees from acting in its behalf. Frossard later said that he felt the consistory had effectively declared them "innovators and bad Protestants."[30] Despite this, they did not want to leave the national church. "To leave," Frossard explained, "would be to leave our own house. The church was our home. Intruders are not the caretakers of traditional beliefs." Neither did they want to engage in a polemical battle which would "put us into a struggle with a body of which we were part and which, no matter how it misunderstood our intentions and our rights, claimed our respect."[31] It would also confirm the charge against them that they did not respect consistorial authority and were a threat to Protestant unity. Instead Frossard felt they needed to:

> justify our ministry, affirm our faith, and consolidate our pastoral labors with a work that was practical and at the same time essentially Protestant and officially evangelical; a work whose success would be a testimony to

the approval of our mission and a judgement on the men of our age. It should be a work of charity and faith, which if blessed by God would last long after our sad and sterile contentions had ceased.[32]

The night after Pentecost Frossard believed God blessed him with a concept for a response. He shared the idea the next day with Gardes and Borrel, both of whom gave their wholehearted support. They then brought in eight laymen, "well known for their attachment to the doctrine of the Gospel." Together they formed the Directing Committee of the Maison de Santé protestante de Nîmes to oversee creation of a hospital for poor Protestant women, which if successful they hoped one day to expand to include men. This institution, which survives to this day, would be based upon "inviolable attachment to the pure doctrine of the Gospel, filial attachment to the historic and traditional church, and fraternal affection and cordial hospitality for the ill of all denominations."[33]

An integral part of the hospital would be a chapel in which simple prayer and preaching services would be held for the patients and all others who cared to attend. The Directing Committee was careful to stress that these services were not intended to rival those in the national church. They would not be held at the same time as those in the Reformed Church of Nîmes, and communion would never be celebrated at the Maison de Santé. But though national pastors from the Directing Committee would preside over all religious activities in the hospital they "would be happy to profit from the passage of Evangelical Christians of all denominations, pastors or laity, and invite them to take part."

Whether the result of divine inspiration or simple insight, the Maison de Santé was a shrewd maneuver on the part of Nîmois evangelicals. It met a felt need in the community. It did not break with the established church. It was practical and faithful to the Reformed heritage, and founding a hospital fit evangelical perspectives on the believer's duty in the world. A frequent criticism of the Réveil was that it advanced a religion devoid of good works. Evangelicals adamantly rejected the charge arguing that instead of making salvation depend on good works they saw works as a proof of faith. But they were sensitive to the fact that the Réveil's emphasis on salvation by faith alone could be misconstrued by critics and followers alike. Thus, in the *Archives Evangéliques* Frossard urged the faithful to take personal responsibility for fulfilling "this merciful prophecy: 'the Gospel is announced to the poor.'" This would be accomplished by their testimony to their own spiritual experience, "but above all through your Christian compassion. . . . The poor suffer. Give! The poor are sick. Give! The poor lack work. Give! The poor have many children to feed, to cloth, to raise. Give! They are cold. Give, and give quickly!"[34]

Making medical care available to the poor at the Maison de Santé would demonstrate evangelical concern for the physical as well as spiritual well-being of the poor. Evangelical faith, the project's creators explained, inspired "a profound Christian affection for their suffering brothers," and led them to offer "healing care for the perishable body and for the immortal soul." Caring for the physical needs of the poor thus merged into their vision for ministering to the spiritual needs of the community. In this way they would have "the assurance that the care of God is acquired by all who implore him with a sincere heart." The Maison de Santé was to be a physical and spiritual refuge for the Reformed populace of Nîmes.

The hospital also recalled similar institutions from the seventeenth and eighteenth centuries. Frossard noted that founding "a Protestant hospital was at its base to recover a Huguenot tradition." These earlier hospitals had been founded and run by the Consistory of Nîmes as part of its duty towards the Protestant poor and sick. In the fraternal euphoria of the Revolution, however, the Protestant hospital merged into its public counterparts. Since then the consistory had not undertaken to establish another despite the deterioration of inter-confessional relations. Instead, the Consistory of Nîmes arranged to have a number of beds set aside in municipal institutions for the Protestant population.

Theoretically this was a viable alternative, but like most French towns, Nîmes depended on Catholic religious orders to staff its institutions. Not surprisingly there were occasional incidents in which Protestants were refused admission, or were separated from their coreligionists, denied the right to pray or to receive the services of Reformed clergy, were forced to attend mass, and were pressured to convert. Despite the consistory's immediate and usually effective intervention to redress this discrimination, the reputation of municipal hospitals was such that most ill Protestants refused to go to them.[35] Recognizing this, the consistory helped make it easier for them to stay at home by underwriting the services of several doctors and arranging with a Protestant pharmacist to provide the necessary medications. But home care still exposed a working-class family to considerable hardship. The prospectus for the Maison de Santé chronicled their dilemma.

Who has not been sadly affected by the complete state of destitution in which [the poor] immediately fall when illness comes to strike a member of their family? . . . The sick worker, unable to gain care from his coreligionists, obstinately continues, despite all our insistence, to live in his narrow and incommodious dwelling. There, his resources are exhausted, his family is kept from the work that is necessary for its subsistence and death comes in all haste to put an end to this accumulation of misery.[36]

Lacking an acceptable alternative, ill Protestants stayed at home, forcing their families to take time away from their livelihood in order to care for them. Illness was a serious threat to the family's economic viability, even if the sick member recovered. It is no surprise that most families on the consistory's dole were there either because of illness or widowhood.[37]

Compounding matters were cuts made by the consistory to its budget for charity. In 1839, the Church of Nîmes overran its budget and faced a shortfall in the next year of more than 8,000 francs. Blame for the deficit was placed on spending for the poor. The Reformed Church of Nîmes had an endowment that would allow it to absorb such an overrun for several years, but the consistory decided instead to restructure the system of charity in order to cut costs. This included disqualifying families of sick Protestants from all other forms of consistorial assistance unless the ill person was in one of the municipal hospitals. With the reforms in place the church spent less on charity in 1840 and 1841 than at any time since 1829. Overall the budget for charity declined 14 percent for 1840-1845 from the level of 1835-1839. Though a fiscal success the cutbacks were quite unpopular with many in the community, and one consistory doctor resigned in protest.[38]

Consequently, announcement that a Protestant hospital would be opened was widely acclaimed by the Reformed population. Within a few weeks the organizing committee received nearly 10,000 francs, much of it in small contributions.[39] Its popularity also forced the Consistory of Nîmes into a difficult position not unlike that in which the three evangelical pastors had been a few weeks before. While much of the population applauded the new institution, Pastor Tachard opened the consistory's next meeting by solemnly announcing, "A grave deed has suddenly occurred in the church." The problem was the ambiguity of the consistory's relation to the Maison de Santé. The fact that the three pastors marginalized by the consistory over the Société des Intérets généraux were the only members of the consistory named in the prospectus for the Maison de Santé led the public to ask, "why in an institution intended for the good of all, the others are not named?" Their conclusion, Tachard explained, was "the other pastors are opposed to it, as is the consistory, and consequently that they are not friends of the poor." Confirming this, some pastors had received anonymous letters in which they were "represented in a most ignoble manner."[40]

To "clarify public opinion and stop the slander," the Consistory of Nîmes drafted yet another open letter to the Protestant community. The consistory did not directly attack the Maison de Santé which, given its enthusiastic reception, would have likely only further tainted the consistory's reputation. Instead the consistory explained it was not included in the project because the Directing Committee of the Maison de Santé had deliberately disregarded it even though the hospital was something which naturally lay within the church's purview. In this way, the letter charged, the hospital's founders were trying to subvert the consistory and thereby were endangering the integrity of the Reformed community.

The orthodox members of the consistory insisted they did not intend the consistory any harm and, perhaps disingenuously, instead claimed they had hoped the project was of such obvious worth everyone could look past their differences and unite behind it. As for the assertion that they had violated the consistory's rights, the three pastors argued the hospital was "not an affair of the church but a civil and private affair" over which the consistory had no legitimate claim or prerogative. This was a telling argument to advance considering the structure of the Reformed community. Prior to this the church had filled a variety of what could be considered public roles and there was no clear differentiation between religion and society. Even in the late eighteenth century when many Protestants hoped to elevate the bonds of citizenship above confessionalism and even to dechristianize society they were not necessarily trying to isolate religion from civil life, but hoped to free it of what they saw as fanaticism and doctrinal incidentals in favor of the universals of natural religion. Now, in justifying founding a hospital without involving the consistory, evangelicals put forward a distinction between public and ecclesiastical spheres. They still granted the consistory rights over the ecclesiastical affairs of the Reformed community, but they were no longer willing to recognize that privilege in the realm of charity. Evangelicals may have regarded the Maison de Santé as an expression of their religious duty towards the poor, but it functioned in the civic world of charity. As such, in the liberalizing society of nineteenth-century France, the decision whether to support it or not was a matter of personal conscience. "The Consistory," a Nîmois evangelical declared, "cannot claim to arrogate to itself a monopoly on charitable works."[41]

From the energetic response it elicited the majority of church leaders seemed to find this an extraordinary argument. In a personal letter Gustave de Clausonne professed to Frossard the difficulty he had believing the founders of the hospital had not intended to hurt the consistory. For Clausonne and most of his colleagues the Maison de Santé was not a neutral act, but part of a calculated effort by evangelicals to undermine the consistories and advance their own position in the community.   Frustrated that their aggressive preaching and rigid dogmatism had not won them the influence they desired, partisans of the Réveil were now trying to cover themselves "with a character of practical utility to win the people over by good works."

At the national level the Société des Intérets sought to do this through its efforts to expand Protestant rights in society. Success in this area would win the orthodox faction influence in the Reformed population and a favorable hearing for "the religious doctrines that are dear to it." The same tactic was being used locally in projects like the recently created reform farm for boys at Saverdun in the Ariège, or the Maison de Santé at Nîmes. Though these works were of widely recognized utility in the Reformed community, Clausonne charged they were framed to cast:

> blame against the Consistory and other pastors. By this as much harm was done as it was possible to do. It is easy to see that soon the Directing Committee of this Maison would acquire more strength and importance than the Consistory, would substitute itself for the other, and would seize influence for itself in the religious point of view.[42]

The organizations' founders claimed they were private associations and as such did not need to involve the national church, but liberals saw them as a ploy to win the favor of the Protestant population through charity and deprive the consistory of its influence and authority. Thus Clausonne told Frossard that on learning of the Maison de Santé "the cry that left the mouth of all our colleagues was, 'So, it is to be war! [Eh bien; C'est la guerre!]'"[43] This was perhaps an extreme view, but it did capture the sense of crisis that gripped much of the Reformed Church.

Charity was not the only arena in which the position of the consistory in the Reformed community was under assault. They were also being challenged, bypassed or ignored in their role as mediators with civil authorities. This was the other side of the consistories' primary religious responsibility to assure regular worship, and for many in the Reformed community it may have been their most important duty. As the carrier of the Reformed community's collective voice the church's consistories, as long as there were pastors or lay leaders available, had interceded with officers of the state to explain, justify and defend Protestant interests. The voluntarization of religion that was a by product of the Réveil tended, however, to breakdown traditional hierarchies of authority in the Reformed community. The Société des Intérets généraux was an obvious example of this tendency, but in the debate that developed in French Protestantism over freedom of worship consistories found they were being outflanked with the government by a variety of independent associations and even private individuals claiming to speak in behalf of the interests of the Reformed faith.

In early 1842, the preaching of the independent evangelist and anti-Catholic polemicist Napoleon Roussel sparked a mass conversion to Protestantism among the Catholic residents of Senneville [Seine-et-Oise]. Civil authorities, however, refused to allow public Protestant worship and Roussel was arrested. Despite an impassioned defense by Odilon Barrot he was convicted of violating the Penal Code's requirement for authorization of meetings of more than twenty people. On appeal this verdict was upheld by the Court of Cassation and the fine increased from sixteen to one hundred-fifty francs. The following year pastors under duly constituted consistories [Mas d'Azil and Meaux] ran into similar obstacles in their efforts to minister to Protestants living at Foix [Ariège] and Joinville [Haute-Marne] where no Reformed Church existed. For French Protestants, still sensitive to their earlier persecution, these violations of the free exercise of religion were deeply disturbing. They were exactly the sort of thing the Société des Intérets généraux was intended to address, which it apparently did, especially through the auspices of Agénor de Gasparin, elected Corsica's representative to the Chamber of Deputies. In addition the Chamber of Deputies was flooded with protests and petitions, nearly half of which came not from consistories but from private associations and persons. The consistories of Bas-Languedoc, hesitant both to provoke the Catholic Church or to support evangelists outside the national church, stayed largely on the sidelines, especially in the case of Roussel at Senneville.[44]

The incidents at Foix and Joinville were more troubling as they involved activities of the established church. Intervening, however, in the cases of Foix and Joinville when they had not for Senneville would put the consistories in a delicate spot. For most Protestants the episodes were essentially identical. Protestants had been denied the right to worship. It made little difference whether they were part of the French Reformed Church or not, the consistories should come to their defense. The fact that some had converted from Catholicism made it all the more pressing, since such conversions were seen as confirmation of the superiority of the Protestant faith. On the other hand, the Consistory of Nîmes worried that if it remained entirely uninvolved the government would consider the private appeals "as the expression of Protestant thought," a circumstance "the consistories cannot accept."[45]

Worried in particular by the risk posed for consistorial authority Ferdinand Fontanès urged the Consistory of Nîmes to "repair the ill done by the petitions addressed to the chambers and recall the government to its obligation to recognize the opinion of national Protestantism." But he warned that it would be unwise to "criticize individuals who by virtue of their personal rights addressed petitions to the chambers in support of religious freedom." By this he essentially conceded the point made by evangelicals in Nîmes the year before regarding the Maison de Santé, that consistories could no longer claim an exclusive right to act in behalf of the Reformed community. Others in the Consistory of Nîmes worried, however, that if they did not challenge the private petitioners the standing of all consistories with the government would be weakened by drawing attention to the fact that they did not speak for all in the Reformed community. Thus the consistory faced the delicate task of asserting its prerogatives as a corporate body without seeming to impinge the individual rights of members of the community, yet maintain an aura of Protestant solidarity.

Its approach was to assert the consistory's privileges as the governing body of a state church in a letter to the Minister of Religion, but with a narrow interpretation of the consistory's jurisdictional responsibilities. It argued that since neither Roussel nor the converts of Senneville were part of the national church there was no reason for consistories to interfere in their behalf. Conversely, at Foix and Joinville the rights of persons of Protestant heritage had been compromised. In this case, the Consistory of Nîmes argued that those involved had a right to worship according to their beliefs even though there was not a Reformed Church in the area. Accommodating this right was "as much in the interest of order as of liberty, for if the religious needs of our brothers are not satisfied in a regular manner it is possible they will try to meet them by means under which the church and public order could suffer." The Church of Nîmes proposed that Protestants in such circumstances be put under the authority of the closest consistory. This would legalize their worship and put them under the supervision of an officially recognized body.[46]

The Consistory of Nîmes did not explicitly oppose the right of Protestants to practice their religion independent of the national church. Instead it emphasized the advantages for public order offered by the established church compared to the risks involved in the activities of religious dissidents. The consistories were composed of men of order drawn from the upper-classes of the Reformed community and defenders of the regime. They had found "justice and benevolence" under the King's government which "aided in establishing the prosperity of our churches." Unlike the independents, the consistories respected government officials and would not try to circumvent them by taking their grievances directly to legislators in the Chamber of Deputies. The dissidents, on the other hand, had no ties to the regime and did not offer the same guarantees of order and stability. Neither did their leaders, many of whom were foreigners, fully appreciate the particularities of French society and, therefore, were prone to irresponsible actions. The established church, the Consistory of Nîmes avowed, would never attempt anything like what had happened at Senneville.[47]

This argument seemed to have had some success in that the Minister instructed Prefects that they should interpret "the principle of religious liberty in a large sense. One should not, without very grave motives, restrain its application when it is claimed in good faith by citizens practicing one of the forms of worship recognized in France." These forms of course were Roman Catholic, Jewish, Lutheran and Reformed. Worship outside these traditions was not necessarily forbidden as Prefects were told when Protestants asked "to meet together in a private house for prayer" permission should be granted as long as the petitioners "show themselves animated by the most benevolent of dispositions." This distinction, however, allowed a fair degree of administrative latitude to judge the "benevolent disposition" of Protestant dissidents. Overall, this directive must have been close to the best the Consistory of Nîmes could have desired.[48]

If the Consistory of Nîmes hoped its intervention would reinforce consistorial authority by forestalling private individuals and groups from interjecting themselves into the controversy, its letter was a failure. Not content simply to write the Minister of Religion, the consistory circulated its response among the Reformed churches of France. Not surprisingly it provoked a response. Some were positive, as Consistories like Aiguesvives and Sauve sent letters of their own seconding that of Nîmes. Others were opposed. Most consistories liked the idea of attaching dispersed Protestants to the nearest consistory, but were less willing to adopt Nîmes' approach to religious liberty.

The real storm came from outside the hierarchy of the national church. The *Archives du Christianisme* reported that the Consistory of Nîmes, "faithful to the sad path it has followed for several years, . . . has placed itself against the freedom of worship 'for all'." A flood of petitions from a variety of private groups and individuals were sent to the government and legislature on the issue. Eight petitions to the Chamber of Deputies originated in the Gard, one of which came from more than fifty heads of households in the Church of Nîmes. Their appeals went beyond Senneville, Foix and Joinville, to list a series of offenses against freedom of worship, leading them to ask, "Are we really in France and in the nineteenth century?!" None of the orthodox pastors signed the document, perhaps made cautious by preceding events, but seven of the eight lay directors of the Maison de Santé and at least three deacons in the Church of Nîmes did. This appeal and most others like it did not mention the Consistory of Nîmes' letter. By calling, however, for the full application of "Article 5 of the Charter, which guarantees equal freedom for all forms of worship," they were rejecting Nîmes' discrimination against Protestant clerics and congregations not included in the Concordat of 1802.[49]

The apparent willingness of the Consistory of Nîmes to accept such a limited place for Protestantism in French society seems to go beyond the reluctance of southern church leaders to risk offending French Catholics. Its disavowal of Roussel's efforts to proselytize and refusal to serve as advocate for the recent converts certainly was at odds with the evangelistic enthusiasm of the Réveil. It also seemed to contradict the confidence of liberals and orthodox alike that Protestantism's advance was closely linked to France's progress into the modern age. The Consistory of Nîmes may have gone farther than most in its retreat from absolute freedom of worship, but it did reflect a liberal tendency to shun activities that seemed to approach too closely what the previous century described as fanatical. For Reformed liberals, Protestantism's contribution to modern society was its commitment to individual freedom within a strong sense of personal and social morality, not in a rigorous adherence to prescribed doctrinal formulas.

This compromise on religious freedom could prove difficult to accept for many of the Huguenots' descendants. Their ancestors had struggled centuries for this freedom, and had suffered greatly because of its absence. They had rallied to the philosophes and then to the French Revolution in large part on this issue. More recently they welcomed and even defended the July Monarchy because they believed their rights would be safer with it than they had been under the Bourbons. Throughout the consistories had been at the forefront of the crusade, and few as effectively as the Consistory of Nîmes. Now this same body openly accepted and even advocated restrictions on its rivals' right to worship as they saw fit.

For Reformed evangelicals this was only further evidence of the apostasy that infected the national church. Not only were they the ones most often suffering discrimination, but the evangelistic imperative to "Preach the gospel to every creature" was being obstructed. Claiming a firmer commitment to both the gospel and freedom of worship than the Consistory of Nîmes and its allies, they felt empowered to take the rather extraordinary step of breaking with the church's established leaders and went to the government directly as private citizens. Their way may have been prepared by the Société des Intérets généraux or their own experiences in religious associations and private prayer groups. Their response could also reflect the spread of principles of an open and representative society. Perhaps this is why they sent their appeals to the elected legislators of the Chamber of Deputies where they were debated openly and followed in the press, rather than to government functionaries making decisions behind closed doors with little public involvement. Whatever the inspiration, it was becoming evident that with the spread of religious awakening Protestants no longer deferred as a matter of course to their recognized leaders even in matters involving the state.

For the consistories of the established church these demonstrations of autonomy were disturbing. In the same way they tried to lessen opposition from sectional churches by stripping local consistories of their power, liberal consistories like Nîmes did not shy away from restricting evangelicals' access to positions in the Reformed Church and to regulate more tightly the behavior of its clergy. Evangelicals did not miss the irony of such behavior from those who so frequently claimed free inquiry was the essence of Protestantism. In response, liberals said they were acting to protect free inquiry in the church from the ecclesiastical intolerance of the orthodox party. Unlike the partisans of the Réveil, they would not close the doors of the church on anyone because she or he did not understand the faith in a manner defined by others. Thus they would not tolerate religious dissidence for the sake of tolerance.

The Consistory of Nîmes was not alone in its concern about dissension in the Reformed Church. The letter of Jean-Paul Hugues, pastor at Gallargues in the Vaunage, to the Prefect of the Gard seems to contain more than a note of exasperation in his chronicle of confrontations between the Consistory of Aiguesvives and deacons of some of its sectional churches. Though the Consistory of Aiguesvives was liberal in its sympathies the region was a known hot bed of the Réveil, with three of its six pastors, including the consistory's president, and several parishes openly sympathetic to the Réveil. Consequently, when the consistory voiced its disapproval of private religious meetings, deacons in these churches openly supported, attended and even led such meetings. The consistory would call for a special collection only to have some deacons refuse to participate because they did not approve of the cause. When the consistory wrote the government to disavow the petitions calling for absolute freedom of worship, these deacons signed the petitions, circulated them, and then sent them to the President of the Chamber of Deputies. Similarly, the same day the consistory, following the lead of Nîmes, publicly disavowed the Société des Intérets généraux, several deacons declared their support for the organization.[50]

As embarrassing and annoying as these episodes were it was only after these deacons, "[who] decorate themselves with the title of Evangelicals," opposed the appointment of an elder that the consistory decided it had enough. The elder, Hugues reported, was "one of the most qualified members of the congregation due to his attachment to the national church, his personal position, and his municipal functions." But he told the consistory he could not reach an understanding with the deacons of his church, was tired of fighting with them and wanted to quit. Instead of losing a colleague, the Consistory of Aiguesvives decided to remove the troublesome deacons. Since the Reformed diaconate had no official standing with the state, there was little but tradition to protect it. As already seen, this tradition was powerful and few consistories were willing to challenge its claims unnecessarily.[51]

Hugues told the Prefect that the health of the church and the stability of the community required an end to diaconal independence. The Réveil had created so much religious confusion the consistories had to be more vigilant than ever to preserve and defend order in the Protestant community. Most rural consistories, however, only met a few times a year and therefore could not act in an effective or timely manner. Instead, he explained to the Prefect, they had to depend on local leaders who could "perceive the least menace and check it with their resistance and assume the shock until the consistory can take action."[52] The Réveil's ability to create conversions, however, meant it was not enough for consistories to appoint loyal deacons. Later they might have a change of heart. "Does not one count today among the dissidents' ranks," Hugues asked, "brothers who yesterday carried, and who carry still, the titles of deacon or elder!" To protect against such changes Hugues declared, "We are nominating deacons known for their devotion to the national church, and we reserve the right of reelection for the purpose of removing those who allow themselves to defect."[53]

The Consistory of Aiguesvives was not alone in taking action to restrict the independence of its personnel. The Consistory of Nîmes had already begun nominating new members of the diaconate itself. It also took over from its pastors the power to appoint suffragans for those pastors who needed them. It did this after Jean-Paul Gardes, eldest of the three evangelical pastors at Nîmes, put forward the name of a recent graduate of the seminary at Montauban to serve as his assistant. The consistory felt the young man was tainted by an "unenlightened zeal." It chose instead, Athanase Coquerel (fils), the son of the Réveil's leading critic at Paris, and who would go on to become one of the century's leading theological liberals. As such, he was hardly compatible theologically with the pastor he was designated to assist.[54]

The Consistory of Nîmes also placed limits on the activities of its pastors. After instituting the worship services of the *Oratoire* the consistory forbade its pastors from participating in any services other than those of the Reformed Churches of France. When the Consistory of St-Hippolyte-du-Fort complained that Emilien Frossard had led a prayer meeting in this town without its consent, the Consistory of Nîmes expanded this prohibition to include any ministerial activity without the permission of the appropriate consistory. In addition it required its pastors to obtain consistorial consent before allowing anyone outside the Church of Nîmes to use their pulpits. The Consistory then published these regulations and sent them to other consistories for emulation.[55]

In a similar vein the Consistory of Privas, in the Ardèche, required one of its pastors to swear he was not a Methodist and submit an undated letter of resignation as a condition of his call to one of its parishes. When a few years later this minister began holding unsanctioned prayer meetings the consistory activated the letter and sent the government notice of his dismissal. The Ministry of Religions rejected this "voluntary" resignation, but approved the pastor's removal anyway due to the consistory's obvious hostility towards him.[56] Elsewhere, Jean-Antoine Rabaud, pastor/president of the Consistory of Castre [Tarn], informed Hugues that in 1828, they ran into a similar problem as Aiguesvives with its deacons and dismissed them. The Consistories of Montpellier and of

Bordeaux reported that they had begun appointing deacons themselves for similar reasons. In the department of the Gard, the Consistories of Sommières and Vézénobres had done the same, as did the Consistory of Sauve. The latter consistory also on one occasion took the extraordinary measure of cashiering the entire sectional Consistory of Sauve and chose one-hundred heads of households to choose its replacement.[57]

Hugues, in an effort to explain to the Prefect of the Gard why such measures were being pursued by the Reformed Churches of the region, repeated the observation made earlier by Samuel Vincent and Gustave de Clausonne about "two great nuances" in the Reformed Church. But where Vincent and Clausonne said this in a call to include both sides in the structures of the church, Hugues used it to justify removing partisans of the Réveil. It is worth remembering at this point that his concern was not about the influence of heretics or religious skeptics. Evangelicals were accused of being too orthodox, not of lacking orthodoxy. They were not considered non-Christian or even non-Protestant. They were resisted because they were challenging the practices of the established church, undermining the position of its leaders and raising the specter of religious division in the Reformed community.[58]

Certainly evangelicals objected to what they saw as the spiritual poverty of many church leaders and the laxity in devotion and doctrine they permitted within the Reformed Church as a whole. Consequently they had greater confidence in the dictates of their own consciences than in the leadership of the consistories. When the two conflicted they ignored, bypassed or circumvented the established leaders of the church. Though its partisans did not necessarily see it as such, the Réveil thereby assumed an aspect of rebellion against traditional hierarchies of authority in the Reformed community.

Henri Dubief and Emile Léonard have argued that the awakening represented an alliance between "urban oligarches, rural nobles and the popular classes against the liberal middle classes" that dominated both the Reformed Church and the community. This view depends largely on the public face of the Réveil, particularly as seen at Paris and in the major religious societies, bolstered by occasional reports of popular support for revivalists in confrontations with church leaders. The documentation, however, does not allow so clear a sociology of the Réveil. The leaders of the movement, such as comte Agénor de Gasparin, Frédéric and Adolphe Monod, and Admiral Verhuel at Paris or Emilien Frossard, Abraham Borrel, and Abraham Lissignol at Nîmes and Montpellier, are well known because of their public exposure. It is a stretch, however, to take the leadership of the Réveil, particularly in Paris, as representative of the movement as a whole. As for popular support of evangelicals, there are also examples of the Protestant populace rallying to theological liberals. This was the case at Gallargues where demonstrations and a charivari occurred in behalf of Jean-Paul Hugues, or at Valleraugue after the consistory dismissed Jean-Alexandre Sarradon for his alleged illicit liaison.[59]

At least for Bas-Languedoc the argument of Léonard and Dubief needs to be nuanced. Though again the evidence is uncomfortably sketchy, that which exists presents a complex picture. While elsewhere in the course of the 1840s and 1850s evangelicals came to dominate the Reformed Church, in Bas-Languedoc they stayed an influential minority. Under the financial requirements for church leaders imposed by the Organic Articles this fact would seem to support an association between religious liberalism, the urban bourgeoisie and rural *proprietaires*. Thus the Minister of Religion's directive to convene the twenty notables paying the most taxes to reconstitute the Consistory of Anduze resulted in a liberal majority where evangelicals had previously held a slim advantage. This linkage between wealth and theological liberalism, however, should not be pushed too far. At Anduze and again in Sauve the orthodox party believed it would win a majority if allowed to choose electors from among the fifty or so richest Protestants. At Sauve this proved to be the case. Evangelicals did not dominate the Reformed elite, but they were not without representatives among it.[60]

In addition, in Bas-Languedoc liberal dominance of the consistories seemed to reflect the sentiments of the Reformed community. Consequently, the democratizing changes in church structure instituted in March 1852, by the regime of Louis-Napoleon, had little effect on the theological character of southern consistories. This reform established presbyterial councils for each congregation, in effect legitimizing local consistories, and opened the election of elders to all adult male members of the church. Though many consistories were reluctant to accept the changes, and the Consistory of Nîmes openly opposed them, in practice they had little to fear. The reforms gave some power back to the congregations, but the democratic election of lay leaders returned most of the same men who had held office before the vote. Even where personnel changed the theological composition remained liberal. If anything the democratization of church structures worked against evangelicals in Bas-Languedoc. At Nîmes they lost votes throughout the 1850s, culminating in a wholesale change in 1859, in which even moderate liberals like

Gustave de Clausonne and Félix de Lafarelle, who had been elders for decades, were branded orthodox sympathizers and lost to a younger, more radical brand of liberal.[61]

Though they remained a minority in southern France adherents of the Réveil can be found virtually everywhere and in every class. The awakening was particularly strong in parts of the Vaunage like Le Caylar, Calvisson and Congénies, but this may have been as much the result of earlier Moravian influences as of material preconditions. In addition, though Methodist evangelists encountered greater resistance in the mountainous Cévennes than in the Vaunage, Calvinist dissident churches formed fairly early in cévennol towns and villages like Bréau, Ganges, Le Vigan and St-Hippolyte, not to mention influential cadres within the national church in these locations as well as Mialet, Sauve and Lasalle, to mention a few.[62]

The situation was no different in the major cities of Nîmes and Montpellier. As seen earlier the consistories of both these communities drew from the urban oligarchy and academic elite. Evangelicals, however, had little difficulty organizing, funding and maintaining their own projects. Mission societies, societies for tracts and Bibles, hospitals; none of these seemed to broach the limits of orthodox resources. When a group of evangelicals left the Reformed Church of Nîmes after their defeat in a consistorial election, they quickly built a building of their own in the exclusive neighborhood of La Fontaine. At the dedication of this church in 1865, the police reported an attendance of five to six hundred "appertaining to the rich or comfortable class of society." This evaluation was supported by the composition of the directing boards of evangelical organizations such as the Société des traités religieuses and the Maison de Santé. Léon Noguier retired as a *négociant* in the silk industry at an early age to devote himself to charitable works towards which he and his brother often provided a good deal of the funds. Heimpel-Boissier paid 430 francs in taxes each year on his property in Nîmes. Bianquis-Gignoux, a publisher had an annual income of about 10,000 francs.[63]

Though in terms of wealth these men were the peers of the lay members of the Consistory of Nîmes, with the exception of Bianquis-Gignoux who was a deacon, they were outside the church's leadership until after 1848, when Noguier became an elder. In addition, none were part of the urban oligarchy of Nîmes. The consistory contained judges in the Royal Court, the city's mayor and other public officials, as well as bankers, the oligarches of the region's economy. By comparison the most visible of the evangelical elite were relative parvenus.

From this perspective the Réveil can assume an aspect of status rebellion. For the leaders of the Réveil at Nîmes at least, it seems the Réveil not only provided them a more profound religious experience but perhaps relatedly, it also gave them a sense of purpose and an outlet for public action and respect to which they otherwise did not have access.

Admittedly this is a tentative evaluation and rests on a narrow foundation, but a similar process may help account for the prominence of women in the awakening. Nineteenth-century France was not a time of significant empowerment for women. The Napoleonic Code that was the foundation of French domestic law placed the female gender under the authority of males and the courts regularly affirmed the duty of wives and daughters to obey their husbands or fathers. Though women found ways to carve out realms of action for themselves, it was rather surprising to see them take a visible place in public life. Yet, as was the case in the evangelical awakening in eighteenth-century England and nineteenth-century America, women appear frequently, though usually secondarily, in accounts of the Réveil. Charles Cook, in his first tour of southern France, frequently noted the part women played in awakening religious life in the Reformed community. Later Methodists commented on the over-representation of poor women and those known to be physically or psychologically abused in their societies. Petitions for government authorization required of all independent religious societies by the Second Empire provide a similar picture. For example, the petition for the Réunion Salvagnac at Valleraugue, contained the signatures of eleven men and twenty-four women, with all but nine of the women signing their own name, while nine of the men signed theirs. The Réunion Gui at Anduze, was composed of ten men (eight signed for themselves) and eighteen women (eleven signed for themselves). At St-André-de-Valborgne thirty women asked for authorization of a *Société religieuse des dames.* At St-Mamert, Marie Coulorgues wrote under her own name in behalf of a meeting in her home. Her request was supported by the local Commisar de Police who wrote, "This woman, who is of a perfect morality, very pious and charitable, only asks to gather in her home with some others each Sunday, for the sole purpose of worshiping with more fervor and tranquility than at the Protestant temple." The meetings, he reported, were composed "in general of women." In most of these societies women were a clear majority. In addition, the significance should not be underestimated of the fact that as a result of their participation in these organizations they were called upon to ascribe their names as individuals on a public document, often without the involvement of their fathers or husbands, and many went on record as having leading roles in their direction.[64]

Marguerite-Coraly Hinsch-Armengaud is particularly noteworthy in this regard. Daughter of a wine merchant at Sète she gradually became convinced of her need for a more serious commitment to her faith until, she later wrote, "I received the blessing of the Holy Spirit, life of Christ, plenitude of God . . . I abandoned innocent pleasures in which even our pastors participated, I bought a Bible and read it assiduously."[65] At the age of thirty-one, she committed herself to work for the salvation of others. She began by focusing on her own family. She assumed the role her father, who died when she was nine, had once filled by organizing morning and evening devotions for her family, and taking responsibility for the religious education of the children of her eldest sister, Elisabeth Hinsch-Kruger. Expanding her concern to the small Reformed community in Sète, she helped establish a Sunday school for the children and evening religious classes for adults. Still, though the husband of another of her sisters was the pastor of the local church, she complained that "death the most complete reigned in the Church of Sète."

At this point she attracted the attention of Abraham Lissingol, pastor at Montpellier. He supplied her with Bibles, religious tracts, and encouragement. She was uncomfortable, however, with Lissingol's insistence on the doctrine of predestination. She found more amenable Methodist teachings on sanctification, having been introduced to them by Charles Cook. She allied herself to this movement, writing a letter in 1839, to "Wesleyan Christians of England and America who desire the advance of the Kingdom of God" through which she appealed for funds for her fledgling mission in southern France. Eventually, however, she was put-off by what she perceived as the Methodists' excessive sectarianism. Meanwhile Hinsch's critical attitude towards the national church and the tepid piety of many Protestants, combined with her relations with evangelicals and dissidents, offended many in the Reformed community including her brother-in-law, the local pastor, and her mother who considered her an ingrate and a fool.

For the next three decades she itinerated throughout the region, sharing in a number of small revivals and gathering a small following from Sète to the Tarn. It was during this time that she also met a young colporteur and evangelist from the Tarn, Jean-Etienne Armengaud, whom she married, though he was fourteen years her junior. Mme. Hinsch-Armengaud remained, however, the guiding spirit and director behind the work. By her constant travels and frequent letters, the style of which mimicked that of the Apostle Paul's epistles, Mme. Hinsch-Armengaud wove this cadre of followers into a highly integrated and disciplined church. In addition she founded as part of her mission a spa at Sète for poor Protestants in need of the healing effects of salt baths, and a refuge for fallen women and young orphans at Nîmes. The latter association at one point ran afoul of civil authorities for taking-in a minor against the will of her father, but it survived the inquiry and continued to operate through World War II, as did a small independent Hinschist Church.[66]

By nearly every measure, Mme. Hinsch-Armengaud was an exceptional example of the room the Réveil created for experimentation and expansion in women's roles within the Reformed community. More typical was the part taken by women in the voluntary associations of the Réveil. At first, most of these organizations perpetuated the gender exclusivity that characterized much of French society. The Société biblique and the Société des Missions évangéliques of Montpellier were among the first to break with this pattern and include both men and women in the same organization from the very beginning, though the leadership was exclusively male. Later, in 1825, several prominent women in Paris formed a Société auxiliaire des femmes to the Société des Missions évangéliques in 1825. Their inspiration apparently owed more to the example of associations in Geneva and Bristol than to Montpellier, but the Parisian society then became the catalyst for the formation of women's societies throughout the departments. Thus a woman from St-Hippolyte-du-Fort wrote the women's auxiliary in Paris, recounting how, "an association at one sou a week" had existed "for ten months, unperceived in the breast of the church. Formed spontaneously, without noise, without apparatus, even without a committee. Jesus our great God and Savior is its only witness, its councillor and protector." Soon women's societies were common in French Protestantism, most often as adjuncts to the male society. Usually, however, they had their own leadership and enjoyed a fair amount of autonomy in their own affairs. By 1830, approximately thirty women's auxiliaries existed in France for the Société des Missions alone, seventeen of which were in Bas-Languedoc. Others worked in favor of the Sociétés bibliques as well as more localized societies for an array of pious and charitable causes from sewing circles in villages to the directing committees of orphanages and schools for girls.[67] It is perhaps significant in this regard that in the struggle between liberals and evangelicals dividing the French Reformed community, though men took the organizational and polemical lead, there existed on the evangelical side a large supporting cast of women that provided most of the numbers, did much of the work and on occasion spoke out in favor of their beliefs. A similar women's movement is not readily evident among theologically liberal Protestants.

The orthodox faction did not necessarily condone the challenges to the social order that seemed to follow in the wake of the Réveil. For the most part its leaders were men of order. Few followed the example of Edmond de Pressensé who carried ecclesiastical radicalism into the social and political sphere during the Second Republic. In fact, most evangelicals seemed almost defiantly apolitical, regarding politics as a temporal distraction from the eternal cause that was their focus. Similarly, evangelicals tended to be quite conventional in their approach to social relations. Pastor Frossard wrote, "it enters into the plans of God that fortunes and conditions should be and will remain unequally distributed ... Thus each fills his vocation, each occupies his place." Masters were warned not to be too familiar with their servants as it "inspires insolence among the domestics." In fact, "Ignorant servants must be treated like children who imitate everything they see their parents do." On issues of gender Frossard advised young women to separate themselves from the world's affairs. They should do so "less out of formality or legal duty than out of a deep and definitive distaste for things of the world," but the result was still to exclude women from public life. Young men, on the other hand, were told to shun worldly pleasures, but urged to develop their understanding of the world for "God has delivered all the treasures of his creation and all the mysteries of his moral works for your study." Similarly, Frossard's advice for young women leads ultimately to deciding on a spouse, which "could be called the supreme event of her life in that it will determine its direction entirely and definitively." In entering into marriage a woman should put aside romantic fantasies, but "not forget for a single instant the legitimate importance that must be given to rank, social position and even fortune." For young men, Frossard included directions on choosing one's friends but nothing about choosing a wife. On another occasion he complained, "Who would have imagined that anything else was necessary for a husband than to be honest and good, sober and blameless? No, now Monsieur must also understand Madame!"[68]

Evangelicals largely upheld conventional forms of social relations, but the primacy they placed on the individual's relation to God spiritualized the basis on which these interactions took place. This could have the effect of further internalizing social norms, or conversely it could clear the way for transcending these norms. The Réveil emphasized the individual's direct experience of the divine and made it central to their existence. It could override all human constraints and dictates. Thus women were encouraged not to mix themselves in worldly matters, but propriety and duty were subordinated to moral distaste as the reason for this withdrawal. Rejecting the world on moral grounds, however, could feed into a call to minister to the world's need, to transform it. Frossard told women to devote themselves to the care of the home, but then seemed to expand the domestic sphere outward, calling on them to care for the unfortunate, visit the sick and educate the children. He concludes by charging them to commit themselves "to an entire future of activity and true joys promised to the disciples by Him who traveled day by day, and whose food and drink was doing the will of his Father." It is understandable how one could get the message confused and, like Mme. Hinsch-Armengaud, spend thirty years wandering the countryside preaching, and end up founding a religious sect of her own.

In the same way a young woman was advised to put aside romantic fantasies and remember social rank and standing when deciding on a marriage. Yet, these considerations shrank before her duty to seek a husband whose "conduct is habitually directed by the fear of God." This could allow a woman greater room to choose her spouse than otherwise may have been the case, or, again Mme. Hinsch-Armengaud is an example, to delay marriage for some time and then, though part of a prominent merchant family, to marry a simple but pious colporteur from the Tarn. Young men were to develop their intelligence and abilities, not to acquire "a lofty position or gain more money," but out of "love for God, admiration of his work, and respect for his own soul of which he is directed to develop all his talents." How many young men, under this commission, became pastors, missionaries or followed another vocation than that which was intended for them by their fathers? Finally, the master may have the duty to correct the behavior of his servants, but he should also "respect them as men, as equals who hope in the same salvation as you." It was not unheard of in the Réveil, for a servant to end up spiritual mentor to his master. This spiritual egalitarianism made it difficult for evangelicals to enforce the social conventions they often seemed to espouse. Even if they did not entirely approve of the behavior they had difficulty condemning the results if it led to the conversion of souls and greater spiritual devotion.

For their opponents, however, such disregard of established authority only confirmed that evangelicals were schismatics in the church and dissidents in the community. This was a common theme of the liberal polemic against followers of the Réveil. It was a sub-text to the letters of the Consistory of Nîmes against the Société des Intérets généraux and the Maison de Santé, and numerous other comments made in a variety of contexts. Hugues was more explicit in justifying the actions of the Consistory of Aiguesvives against its deacons. Perhaps the clearest elaboration of the argument was Ferdinand Fontanès' pamphlet, *De la Lutte engagé dans les Eglises protestantes de France*. This document, drafted in the tumultuous summer of 1842, was remarkable for its willingness to lay bare the division within the Reformed Church, a bold and disturbing public acknowledgment in a minority confessional community obsessively concerned about its security. Fontanès made it clear that evangelicals were responsible for this division. Though they "call themselves the true Church and the true Protestants," he wrote, "they hardly submit at all to ecclesiastical authority, or to the consistories in whose hands it is concentrated." But the orthodox went beyond rebelliousness. "[T]hey are completely prepared to fraternize with dissidents sharing their theological opinions. They open their pulpits to them and live in better understanding with sectarians than with many pastors of the national church, and even members of their own consistory." For evangelicals the true church was defined by a common set of beliefs, not by historical-confessional bonds. By insisting on a believing church, Fontanès charged, they were more comfortable worshiping with foreigners and schismatics than with their own compatriots in the Reformed community.[69]

In contrast to these exclusivist rebels Fontanès elevated the "tolerant" part of the church which "follows an entirely different rule of conduct." Where evangelicals disregarded the authority of the established church and were imperious in their insistence on following what they saw as a higher authority, liberals were satisfied with "those rights with which the church has consecrated them, and they regard themselves as obligated to respect the deliberations of these consistories as our sole legal power." Where the orthodox made common cause with Methodists and other sectarians, the liberals ignored these dissidents "unless it is to push away from our population their sectarian spirit and their maxim that it is necessary to have the same beliefs in order to live together in the same church." Where the evangelicals were exclusionary and fractious, liberals were "resolved to remain united in one body, desiring that all our Protestants form one compact mass. . . . They do not want French Protestantism to fracture into small sects without strength and without means of existence."

Playing further on fears of Protestant vulnerability, Fontanès described revivalists' efforts to proselytize among the Catholics. "Religious tracts, polemical brochures, evangelical colporteurs and preachers, they use them all in the holy war, and the first fruit of their efforts has been to sow divisions between the Protestant and Catholic populations." Evangelicals committed the double sin of dividing Protestant strength, while exacerbating tensions with the Catholics, thereby putting the community at risk.

Nearly all southern Protestants worried about the precariousness of their position, and were likely to respect that which strengthened their situation and reject what might weaken it. This was one of the reasons liberals were so concerned by the Société des Intérets généraux and the Maison de Santé. If they succeeded in improving the position of French Protestantism it seemed likely the community would accord the organizations considerable influence over the internal affairs of the church. Similarly, confessional solidarity was one asset few Protestants in Bas-Languedoc were willing to risk. Protestant leaders in Nîmes had refused to divide the church into parishes, despite the potential benefits for spiritual care, because it too easily could lead to social and religious differences. Unable to regulate the Réveil, however, consistories set aside fears of devotional diversity and founded Sunday schools, sponsored Bible studies and prayer groups, and introduced less formal forms of worship to counter the incursions of Methodists and other outsiders.[70] Prominent liberal spokesmen like Samuel Vincent and Gustave de Clausonne exhorted the Reformed community to adopt a tolerant attitude towards differing beliefs and advocated a system of equal representation in the church in an effort to preserve unity. But as evangelicals emerged as an independent force, ignored consistorial authority, assumed functions traditionally the province of the consistories, and seemed to foster a spirit of rebellion against established hierarchies in the Reformed community, accommodation seemed impossible.   Consequently, many echoed Clausonne's cry when he learned of the founding of the Maison de Santé. "*Eh bien; C'est la guerre!*"

CHAPTER 6

COMPETITION, ADAPTATION AND ASSOCIATION

Against the backdrop of nineteenth-century France the cohesion of French Reformed Protestantism seemed yet another aspect of traditional society giving way to a new order. Racked by social tensions pitting manufacturer and worker, rural laborer and urban artisan, small farmer and propriétaire, urban oligarch and commercial entrepreneur, the Reformed Church could appear as the only strand holding Protestants together. Despite the recovery from the disasters of the Revolution, here too lines of fracture were evident. Confessional identification remained strong, but devotion to the faith itself seemed on the decline, especially among workers and elements of the urban elite. Even among those most committed to Protestantism as a faith system the spread of the Réveil seemed destined to divide the Reformed Church itself.

The danger of schism was real and the disputes that erupted between orthodox and liberal were frequent and bitter. Yet while the Réveil seemed to be tearing French Protestantism apart it also facilitated the development of a new sense of religious community. The foundations of association, however, were narrower, more voluntaristic, and redefined the relationship between religion and the Protestant population in ways that reflected a break with hereditary and paternalistic structures and the ascendancy of liberal society.

The religious renewal demanded the individual to be more directly involved in the practice of the faith. In this way it shared some of the concern for individual responsibility that was part of the natural theology of the eighteenth century. The faith of the Enlightenment, however, was based on an optimistic view of the mind's ability to penetrate rationally the mysteries of the universe and govern human passion. Its acolytes were proportionately few and came largely from the elite. It was assumed the masses would depend on the enlightenment of their betters for right understanding and direction. This theme continued among liberals in the nineteenth century. Thus Coquerel (fils), noted that while Nîmois Protestantism did not compare to the university town of Montpellier in terms of intellectual resources, the influence of some "old families belonging to the nobility of land or office" provided an enlightened theological influence. Most Protestants, however, were more ardently pious than informed. "There is no shortage," Coquerel wrote his father, "of peasants in the countryside of the Gardonneque and the Vaunage who, furious towards the Catholics and Methodists, mistake their anger for religion. Of religion itself they have little other trace."[1]

The Réveil called upon the mass of Protestants thus bound dogmatically or culturally to the religion of their Huguenot forebears to make their own spiritual decisions. In this sense it reasserted the Protestant doctrine of the priesthood of all believers. Taking seriously the power to act as one's own priest, however, could risk dissolving the church into a confusion of personalized beliefs and nuances or a rejection of religion altogether. Evangelicals, however, insisted that spiritual conversion was based upon the acceptance of a common theological core and demonstrating a higher level of devotional behavior. These standards became the foundation on which a consensual association developed that ideally would supersede all other temporal identifications.

In addition, with the exception of the Darbyites and a few other fringe groups, the Réveil did not create sectarians in the sense of withdrawing from society into a closed community of like-believers. For those not caught up in the fervor of the revival perhaps its most annoying characteristic was the enthusiasm with which the awakened sought to bring those around them into the community of the saved. Their goal was a believers' church, but one that would reestablish and broaden a religious community that seemed in the process of dissolution. For this reason they preached aggressively, handed out Bibles and religious tracts, adopted rituals of worship that were accessible, egalitarian and personally involving, and sponsored charitable projects to ease the pain of disease, old age and poverty. These works of charity, it was hoped, would also enhance the effectiveness of their efforts at evangelization. Regardless of their success in this latter regard sociologists of religion such as Karel Dobbelaere, have shown how these types of charitable foundations could become effective supports of a confessional identity amidst an increasingly complex society. In Belgium and the Netherlands, this *pillarization*, or the development of a "conglomeration of organizations founded and run by committed church members . . . to serve church members with respect to various secular functions," helped brace religious identifications in a religiously neutral state and highly differentiated society.[2] French Protestantism did not pillarize as thoroughly as did the Low Countries, equivocating as it did on church-related schools and failing to find a coherent confessional political party, but the impetus evangelicals gave to the development of Protestant hospitals, relief agencies, orphanages, and publishing did much to keep the religion a part of daily existence. More importantly, the success and influence of these projects, along with evangelical forms of worship and types of organization, prompted their opponents to establish similar institutions and adopt many of the same strategies. In this way the impact of the religious restructuring of the Reformed community extended far beyond those embracing the Réveil.

The communitarian aspect of the Réveil, however, was not readily apparent in the battles of 1842, and following years. The Reformed Churches seemed trapped in a cycle of act and counter-act, confrontation and recrimination, destined to lead to irreparable division. Neither the orthodox nor liberal faction, however, wanted this result. While the fact that they feared schism as a real possibility was evidence of Protestants' increasing confidence in the confessionally tolerant society that was emerging, the urge for Reformed solidarity remained a compelling force. This was particularly true in the south where security concerns continued, especially as Catholicism recovered in strength and vigor. As already mentioned, the resurgence of anti-Protestantism in public discourse and the apparent violations of Protestant religious rights were the catalyst for the creation of the Société des Intérets généraux. At the same time Catholic missions were conducted in Protestant towns and villages while Catholic orders expanded into schools, hospitals and other public institutions. Even in Nîmes, where the mayor and several municipal and departmental councillors were Protestant, the Reformed Church could not prevent the Frères de la Doctrine chrétienne from establishing themselves in the regional penitentiary. The same order had charge of the public hospitals and was believed responsible for several violations of confessional decorum, including isolating one Protestant patient from his coreligionists and pressuring him to convert. Meanwhile Catholic schools opened in neighborhoods with large Reformed populations and the students given polemical works to read that attacked Protestant doctrines and forms of worship.[3]

Protestants were less likely to be harassed for their unwillingness to observe Catholic religious processions, but new controversies emerged in their place, particularly regarding access to cemeteries. Under the Ancien Regime the Huguenots had responded to their exclusion from consecrated ground by interring their loved ones on family land. In the nineteenth century the migration of Protestants into towns and cities, as well as increasing government regulation of burial practices, made this option less available. The state required that grave sites be available for all recognized faiths, but this did little to relieve Catholic scruples about desecrating holy ground. Where Protestants were few in number or had recently located, such as Beaucaire where the body of a Protestant was dug-up on orders from the local priest, they could find themselves barred from public cemeteries or relegated to the sepulchral company of suicides, libertines and the un-baptized.[4]

Perhaps most jarring to Protestant sensibilities in southern France was the reported kidnaping of Maria Vidal, a fourteen-year-old girl from Sommières. For Protestants this incident seemed to replicate one of the worst aspects of the era of repression. The case was complicated by the fact the girl was the product of a mixed marriage and had been baptized Catholic. After the death of her mother, Maria's maternal aunt placed her in a convent to protect her from the influence of her Calvinist father. Maria's father protested this transgression of his paternal rights bitterly, and the Protestant community quickly rallied behind him. Both the Consistory of Sommières and Nîmes took-up his cause, and pursued the case through the civil courts since the authorities had refused to intervene. Ultimately, despite the presence of several Protestants on the Royal Court at Nîmes, they were unable to win a favorable decision.

The Consistory of Sommières wanted to pursue the case further, seeing in the court's decision "the victory of the anti-Protestant party. . . . For Louis XIV it was with *lettres de cachet* that one sought to dissolve our families. Today it is with intrigue and impunity."[5] The Consistory of Nîmes shared their disappointment, but cautioned against pressing the matter too far. In a letter to the Protestants of Sommières, Tachard advised, "We should be both firm and prudent. We should defend our rights, but we should not compromise the interests of our churches uselessly." For all they had gained since the collapse of the Ancien Regime, French Protestants continued to feel themselves in an ambiguous position in French society. Their status had improved considerably, but they hesitated to assert their rights too aggressively for fear of provoking a backlash from still skeptical public officials or the Catholic majority with which they lived in daily contact.[6]

Security issues, therefore, continued to play an important role in the dynamics of the Reformed community. Protestant elites and laity alike were predisposed to favor what seemed to strengthen the community and reject whatever appeared to put it at risk. It was a defense of community that lay behind popular harassment of Methodists and informed the liberal polemic against the orthodox faction. Evangelicals in turn blamed their opponents for abandoning Reformed principles and for trying to exclude partisans of the Réveil from church leadership. But the defense of Reformed community was not strictly negative. The Société des Intérets généraux was explicitly created to defend Protestant interests and to coordinate projects for its advance. Other evangelical foundations such as the reform farm at Saverdun, the home for the deaf and mute at St-Hippolyte or the Maison de Santé at Nîmes were welcomed for their contributions to the welfare of the Reformed community. Though suspicious of the motives behind these projects, leaders of the established church in southern France could not easily criticize such manifestly useful endeavors. Neither could they rely entirely upon their power to hinder if not suppress religious dissidence in their communities. Instead they gradually undertook many of the same type of projects and practices characteristic of the Réveil.

An example was the Consistory of Nîmes' creation of a mutual aid society for the city's Protestant workers. At the close of the debate over the Maison de Santé the consistory had charged a special committee, composed entirely of theological liberals, with forming a strategy to address the perturbed state of affairs in the Church of Nîmes. This committee introduced plans at the consistory's next meeting for a mutual aid society called the Société de prévoyance et de secours mutuels. This project they felt, "was a work for the true benefit of all and would become a new proof of the consistory's solicitude for the most numerous part of the Protestant population." As a result "the populace, which has drawn some false conclusions from a recent event, will know they can count the consistory and the three pastors they have ridiculed among their greatest friends."[7] The point was further emphasized in the formal announcement of the project read from the pulpit by the pastors at Sunday's services. The opening paragraph declared:

> The diverse classes of workers which make part of the Protestant population have always occupied [the consistory's] solicitude. The true

means of showing the interest of which they are worthy consists as much in preventing the ills to which they are exposed as in helping them when malady and misery have stricken them. One of the best ways to assist them is by inspiring them with confidence in the future, convincing them that with the aid of God and the assistance of their brothers, they can be reassured with regards to the most pressing needs of life.[8]

The consistory promised to endow the two divisions of the society, one for men and another for women, with 6,000 francs. In addition wealthier Protestants were called upon to support the work as honorary members for a minimum yearly fee of 9 francs for the Société des hommes and 6 francs for the Société des femmes. Those actually benefitting from the society had to pay an initiation fee of 6 francs for men (roughly the equivalent of two and-a-half days' wages for a silk weaver), and 3 francs for women. Subsequent monthly payments ran from 75 centimes to 1 franc for men, and 50 to 75 centimes for women. In return they were promised 5 to 6 francs per week, plus doctor's visits and medicine, in case of illness or injury. Further, if a participant died, funeral expenses were covered and a small stipend provided to the surviving spouse and dependent children. This aid, it was hoped, would help protect working-class families from destitution in case of illness or an untimely death.

Evangelicals could not easily oppose such laudable ends, especially since they complemented their own stated purpose in creating the Maison de Santé. A member of the consistory did question the mixed motives for the project, saying, "When one performs a good work it should be done for itself, independent of all other circumstances." But he quickly acknowledged the project was too important to oppose as it rested "upon a principle of great importance, that of association." His concern for association, however, was less for healing the religious wound in the Reformed Church than it was with the widening social division in the Protestant population between the working class and their wealthier coreligionists. Thus the elder observed, the project "should lead to some good results by furnishing the unfortunate worker, who becomes discouraged when isolated, with a means of strength and perseverance in misery." Others agreed, noting the consistory's sponsorship gave "the cause more strength than if it had first formed among the workers." A consistorial association could mobilize support in all sectors of the Protestant population, something that was far less likely if the initiative had originated with the working-class alone.[9]

The concern among Reformed leaders for association between classes was one shared by many in the leading sectors of French society. In general they welcomed trends freeing the individual from corporate constraints and responsibilities, but they were disturbed by the cultural and geographic separation this was creating between rich and poor, professional and worker. With the lower classes increasingly left to their own devices, bourgeois unease and suspicions of them grew, inclining them to equate, in the formulation of Louis Chevalier, "laboring class" with "dangerous class."[10] For church leaders at Nîmes, part of the promise of the Société de prévoyance was its potential for redressing this situation.

Related to the *sociétés de compagnonages* abolished during the French Revolution, mutual aid societies became increasingly common during the Bourbon Restoration. In 1837, the July Monarchy legalized their existence provided they registered with the government, and Napoleon III sought to manipulate them as a support for his regime with the promise of subsidies derived from the confiscated Orléans estates to those recognized by the government for their public utility. Unlike the *sociétés de compagnonages* of the Ancien Regime, which had included all in an industry, masters, journeymen and apprentices, the newer associations often were composed only of workers. In addition, they frequently moved beyond a single industry to include a broad spectrum of the working-class in a single association, a fact William Sewell argues helped working-class identity to form in place of craft exclusivism.[11]

In some ways the mutual aid society created by the Consistory of Nîmes recalled the older form of association. It substituted confession for craft boundaries and intentionally included the upper classes, both for financial support and administration. All heads of household "interested in the relief of our estimable workers" were asked to second the consistory's efforts in behalf of workers, "so often miserable in being abandoned to themselves, to disease and to destitution." Compassion played a genuine role in the project, particularly since working-class misery was believed to derive as much from its isolation from the rest of society as from the deprivations of disease and poverty. Its prospectus promised the Société de prévoyance would provide the "diverse classes of workers" with confidence in the future, showing them "that with the aid of God and the assistance of their brothers, they can be reassured as to the most pressing needs of life."[12]

Concern for workers' social circumstances also bore on what was seen as their tendency towards inappropriate behavior. In another context Frossard observed, "[the poor] are ignorant which leads them into the worst sorts of prejudices, the most disastrous errors, and in turn into incredulity, superstition and fanaticism." To cure poverty, therefore, the poor needed to be educated in their best interests. Consequently, charity assumed an educational role. Thus the regulations of the Société de prévoyance expressly excluded workers who were "scandalous in their conduct, or chronically insubordinate." Members of the society not only had to pay a substantial initiation fee, but also had to furnish four written assurances of morality, two from the general membership and two from society officials. Though there was some concern cost would keep many workers from joining, and the most needy would be excluded entirely, most felt this "light sacrifice [was] a means of attaching the members to the society." Besides, "the society [did] not need to include the indigent, but only the laboring and orderly workers." It was observed that at Lyons, where a similar institution had begun several years earlier, "no member of the society took part in the troubles" in the insurrection of 1834.[13]

This interest in using charity to shape working-class behavior was a product of a certain ambivalence towards the breakdown of the corporate structure of society. It allowed the individual greater freedom, but also made the individual, or class of individuals, increasingly vulnerable to the whims of nature and economics. This insecurity in turn made the working class a potential threat to the stability of society. In response the consistory sponsored an institution that brought together the various parts of the Reformed community in a common work geared towards its worthy, but vulnerable members. It fostered association not just across classes, but also across theological divisions. Theological liberals and evangelicals alike held important positions in the organization's administrative structure. Tachard, senior pastor and President of the Consistory, presided over the organizing committee for the foundation and was made President of the Société des hommes. His colleague, Ferdinand Fontanès was named President of the Société des Femmes. But the evangelical Frossard was one of the vice-presidents of the organizing committee. Gardes became Vice-President of the directing committee for the Société des hommes, and Borrel held the same position in the Société des femmes. Neither did the consistory monopolize the entire direction of the Société de prévoyance. Though church leaders controlled the top administrative positions each of the directing committees included twelve members from the societies' general membership, six chosen by the consistory and six elected by the society, including working-class women.

The resemblance of the Société de prévoyance in its organizational assumptions and structure with evangelical notions of the church is worth noting. In both, emphasis was placed on personal decision and responsibility. One had to choose to participate in the organization and alter behavior accordingly, whether in terms of financial investment, moral behavior, or spiritual devotion. Once the commitment was made, however, the individual was less isolated as he or she became part of an association, with broader rights of participation and reason to expect a certain level of mutual recognition and support. This is not to say the consistory was mimicking the forms of the Réveil in a temporal organization. If anything it was the other way around. Voluntary societies were forming throughout France during the period, as well as other forms of elective sociability as identified by Maurice Agulhon. In addition to workers' associations studied in detail by William Sewell and William Reddy, devotional societies, literary and scientific circles, drinking clubs and other organizations, were becoming a familiar feature of French society. The structure of the Société de prévoyance et de secours mutuels was part of this broader pattern in voluntary forms of sociability. The evangelical interpretation of the church, from this perspective, merely transferred this pattern of sociability to the realm of religion.[14]

In terms of attracting Protestant workers the Société de prévoyance was a marginal success. Four years after it began the association had 254 men and 260 women as active members, with the women's society operating at a slight deficit. This was a respectable degree of association, but far from extraordinary for a Reformed population of more than 14,000.[15] It was perhaps more successful in bringing the various factions of the Reformed community together. Pastors Frossard, Borrel and Gardes, the three ministers behind the Maison de Santé, quickly subscribed as honorary members and assumed important positions on the association's directing committees. Many others in the community also signed on to support the work, and the consistory received two letters, one from the general membership of the society, the other from the inspectors, collectors and several members of the women's society, thanking the consistory for "the good deed it has rendered the working-class by founding this society." Even the *Archives du Christianisme*, which seldom said anything positive about the Consistory of Nîmes, while noting this was a consistorial project and "not a work of individual zeal," expressed its desire that "so useful and excellent a work spread among our churches."[16]

Using charity to reinforce the consistory's position and bolster the integrity of the Reformed community did not stop with the Société de prévoyance. A few months later church leaders at Nîmes fulfilled a promise they had made in their letter against the Maison de Santé to improve the church's system of medical assistance. As noted earlier the consistory had largely depended on the public hospitals despite their poor reputation in the Protestant community. The founders of the Maison de Santé thereby appeared "more indulgent and better able to perform a good the consistory would not." Rather than persist in an approach that elevated the prestige of the evangelical institution the consistory softened its restrictions on in-home medical care. It also hired more nurses and bought several beds that were lent complete with sheets and blankets, to poor families struck by illness.[17]

The consistory was not entirely comfortable with the increased costs this leniency required. By August 1843, the entire year's budget for medicine was already spent, and a month later the Committee for Charities had to ask for an additional 1,000 francs. Reluctantly the consistory approved the extra money, but with a warning to increase surveillance in order to prevent any further overruns. Later, however, Borrel still reported that bouillon was being given-out "at an alarming rate." Ultimately, the budget for charity, which ended 1842 in the black, finished 1843 with a 1,300 franc deficit. The consistory covered the overrun, but again instituted controls to restrain costs. The budget for medicine still ran over its allotment for the first quarter of 1844, before finally coming under control. The difference Borrel reported, however, was less an effective reduction in expenditures than an unexpected increase in receipts.[18]

This increased giving to the Reformed Church of Nîmes may have been the greater success of the consistory's Société de prévoyance and its liberalization of medical assistance to the Protestant poor. In general the figures for Protestant charity in Nîmes support Borrel's claim that while Nîmois Protestants were not always as assiduous in church attendance as desired, they were generally willing to come to the aid of their coreligionists in need. The consistory was the customary conduit by which this aid was collected and distributed. From even before the July Monarchy, civil authorities had funneled through the Consistory of Nîmes a share of public funds for poor relief proportional to the city's Protestant population. In the 1840s, however, the consistory's near monopoly on Protestant charity was challenged. Revenue from church offerings and the consistory's door-to-door annual collection, both of which were dedicated to assisting needy Protestants, grew steadily until the early 1840s when the consistory cut-back on aid to the poor. The founders of the Maison de Santé took advantage of these cuts to launch their own

Figure 6.1
Charitable Giving in the Reformed Community of Nîmes, 1829-1859

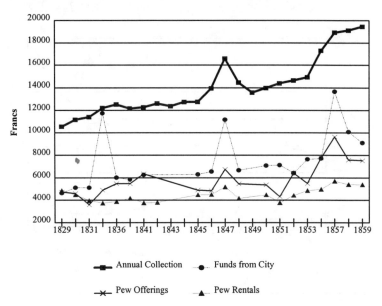

Annual Collection   Funds from City

Pew Offerings   Pew Rentals

venture in religious patronage and quickly raised more than 10,000 francs.

At the same time the consistory's funds for charity declined. The amount received in the annual collection stagnated and even fell slightly [Figure 6.1].[19] Church offerings, which had averaged 5,908 francs in 1840 and 1841, fell more than a 1,000 francs to an average of 4,860 francs for 1845 and 1846. Except for two extraordinarily large gifts in 1842, memorials and gifts to the consistory were unusually flat in the early 1840s. Conversely, income from pew rentals was growing, indicating a rise in church attendance, or at least that more people were reserving places at worship services. In other ways, however, they were giving less to the church.

As the consistory liberalized its spending on charity, its income recovered [Figure 6.2].[20] At the start of 1844, the level of giving was such that the budget for charity began out of balance and more than 100 francs had to be transferred from cash reserves to cover the expected shortfall. By the end of the year, however, additional gifts covered this deficit and even provided a slight surplus, though this was not allowed to carry over

Figure 6.2
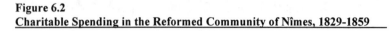
Charitable Spending in the Reformed Community of Nîmes, 1829-1859

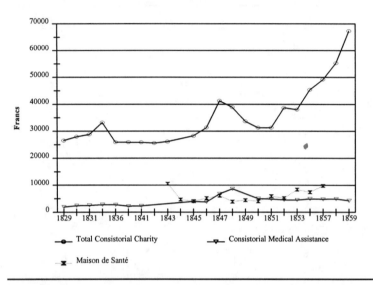

into the next year.[21] In following years income and spending for charity continued to grow, reaching a new peak in the economic crisis that preceded the Revolution of 1848. It declined somewhat in the uncertain climate of the Second Republic, but expanded rapidly through the first decade of the Second Empire.

Surprisingly, charitable giving generally was in inverse relation to the health of the local economy. For example, 1846-1847 and 1856-1857 were periods of considerable hardship in southern France, yet they were also times of the greatest charitable giving. There was a more direct relationship with political uncertainty. Church offerings and pew rentals alike were significantly lower immediately following the July Revolution of 1830, and during the Second Republic. On the other hand, both sources of income recovered quickly after Louis-Napoleon's coup d'état on December 2, 1851, as did the annual collection, and generally remained at this level or higher.

To an extent this generosity reflected need. Economic pressures continued to mount in the late 1840s and 1850s as the failure of the regional textile industry to modernize, compounded in Nîmes by an inadequate water supply, made it difficult for it to compete with increasing foreign and domestic competitors. The onset of the pébrine parasite in the mid 1850s, which devastated silkworm cultivation, only accelerated the decline. Meanwhile, expansion of wine production in the Vaunage encouraged consolidation of landholding, forcing many peasant farmers into the ranks of wage labor. In response the number of those abandoning the countryside for towns and cities increased at a time of tight regional urban employment. Eventually many would migrate on to larger cities like Marseille, Toulon, Lyon and Paris. In the meantime civil and ecclesiastical leaders in Montpellier and Nîmes had to deal with the immediate suffering at their doorstep. Even when migrants moved on in hope of brighter prospects elsewhere they left their parents behind, sometimes without family members to care for them in their declining years.

Reformed leaders were also perhaps more responsive to these social problems because of the popular discontent manifested during the turbulent years of the Second Republic and its collapse. Social elites and government officials alike were quite disturbed by the support the democratic and social republic received throughout much of southern France. They looked at the democ-soc agenda of political democracy, the right to work and a more equitable distribution of resources and charged that it was anti-property, anti-family and anti-religion. Democ-soc spokesmen, however, could turn this argument around, saying it was the working-class family that was most threatened by economic misery and rather than threatening property they were defending the only property possessed by the working-class, its labor. As for religion, Edward Berenson has shown how montagnard propaganda, rather than attacking religion, often appropriated religious language and images for republican ends. It eschewed much of traditional dogma, focusing instead on temporal application of Christian ideals of brotherhood and charity.

In the Gard the democ-soc spokesman, Pierre-Germain Encontre contrasted the simple and practical faith of republicans with that of the so-called defenders of religion. By religion, he charged, "you mean that religion which you disdain for yourselves, but which you feel is good enough for the people to keep them humble and submissive and for preserving their ignorance and prejudices." Elites dared to call society "civilized and Christian" while two-thirds of the population "languishes in misery and is dying of hunger while rubbing shoulders with opulence without pity." These are not Christians, he declared. "[They are] men without faith, shameless hypocrites" who defend their privileges "in the name of a religion they themselves degrade." Instead of attacking

Christianity, Encontre, a former student at the Protestant seminary at Montauban, cast democ-socs as reformers seeking to "purify religion so it will enlarge our souls, sanctify our thoughts, and through reason, conscience and love, bring humanity closer to the Divine." Thus radical republicans, not unlike Protestant evangelicals, claimed a purer gospel than that preached and practiced in the churches. But where followers of the Réveil focused on personal spiritual renewal in this life with rewards delayed until the next, democ-socs were concerned with the present and put forward a project for the reformation of society.[22]

This message found a hearing among many in the popular classes of the Reformed community. Police reports from the Second Republic document the spread of republican clubs, often cast as charitable associations or mutual aid societies, through the Protestant communes of the south, punctuated by an occasional public demonstration or confrontation with Catholic Legitimists. The Montagnard Committee for the Gard even acknowledged a certain affinity between republicanism and the "Protestant principle" of liberty of conscience, though it insisted it was "not necessary to be born Protestant in order to be republican. Republicanism is not a right of birth. It is a principle, the fruit of a holy conviction." When the call went out in early December 1851, for republicans to resist Louis-Napoleon Bonaparte's coup, in regions where Protestants lived in strength they were the ones who responded. Thus, half of the Gardois communes that joined the rebellion were more than three-fourths Protestant. The same pattern held in the Drome and Ardèche, where Protestant towns like Privas, Dieulefit, Salavas and Vallon were centers of unrest.[23]

This sympathy for political and social radicalism was deeply disturbing to Protestant elites, and seems related to their further generosity in behalf of their impoverished coreligionists. Funding for all Protestant charities grew throughout the 1850s. Revenues for the Maison de Santé more than doubled from 3,900 francs in 1850, to 9,800 francs in 1859. Increases for the Consistory of Nîmes were larger in volume. The annual collection climbed from nearly 14,400 francs in 1851, to 19,500 francs in 1859. Offerings increased from 4,300 francs to 7,500 francs, and special gifts, which averaged 3,035 francs during the Second Republic, averaged 7,600 francs between 1854-1859.

Even though the Reformed Church, despite competition from evangelicals and socialists, remained the single largest provider of social assistance to the Reformed community, it was losing a degree of control over the use of these funds. There was an increasing tendency for donors to the church to designate their gifts towards specific projects. One of the first of these came from an unlikely source, Baron de Feuchères, commanding general for the district of the Gard and a Roman Catholic. In 1842, he donated 25,000 francs to the Consistory of the Nîmes as part of 514,000 francs he handed out that year to a variety of military, civil and religious organizations. His gift to the Protestant community came, however, with instructions that it be put into government bonds bearing 5 percent interest with the income used to create grants of 150 francs to 200 francs each, and given out every six months for "the relief of unfortunate families in Nîmes."[24]

Grateful for such generosity from a Roman Catholic, the Consistory of Nîmes immediately named the trust after its benefactor and determined that the grants be used to aid "unfortunate families well known for their morality, for whom illness, serious accident, lack of work, or the lack of the tools necessary for their profession, has deprived them their livelihood." But reflecting their distaste for dependence, church leaders sought to apply the Feuchères grants in ways that would enable recipients to become self-supporting, or at least to tide them over until they could resume their regular occupations. Thus eleven of the first fifteen grants were used to purchase capital goods for small-scale production, such as looms, shoe leather and forms, tinker's tools, and to pay off a wagon driver's loan for his horse and wagon. By enabling workers to labor for themselves without the encumbrance of debt or on machinery owned by someone else, Reformed leaders hoped to give working-class families a better chance at economic viability and moral autonomy. As a further inducement to self-reliance the consistory prohibited for one year those receiving Feuchères grants from getting other forms of consistorial aid.[25]

This sort of modest attempt at using charitable gifts for social engineering continued in the 1850s. A few months after Louis-Napoleon's coup d'état, a rich Protestant gave the Reformed Church of Nîmes 32,500 francs from the sale of a piece of property to endow apprenticeships for graduates from the consistory's schools, thereby both encouraging primary education and opening a path for poor youths without resources into the skilled trades.[26] In October 1851, an elder gave 1,000 francs in memory of his recently deceased wife to create twenty savings accounts for an equal number of deserving heads-of-households. A year later another elder followed this lead, but lowered the target age-group when he marked his retirement from the consistory with a gift of 500 francs for ten savings accounts, five for Protestant girls and five for boys. These savings accounts were explicitly intended to provide assistance in a time of need, but more importantly to teach members of the working class the value of foresight and thrift.[27]

These projects demonstrated Protestant leaders' belief in the moral and civic virtues of the self-disciplined and independent worker. They were confident that with proper education and training a sober, hard-working and thrifty person not only could meet the demands of life, but would develop the personal integrity and social responsibility on which a harmonious modern society could be built. This did not necessarily preclude more conventional forms of charity. They generally recognized that in times of particular need help and guidance might be necessary from one's coreligionists, but the ideal was independence in community. In 1863, the Consistory of Nîmes did consider transforming its system of poor relief into a mutual aid society along lines similar to the Société de prévoyance, but the proposal was rejected and direct aid remained the single largest element of its charitable spending.

This type of assistance was also supported by the population. Beyond the increase in discretionary funds for direct aid, the Consistory of Nîmes was also receiving large individual gifts for the same purpose. Mme. Mazoyer, a prosperous widow who died in 1842, named the consistory the primary beneficiary of her estate with explicit instructions that it be used to endow the purchase of bread for the Protestant poor. Later, Antoine Granier, a retired baker, did the same, but with conditions that essentially reduced the Consistory of Nîmes to the invisible administrator of a private foundation. Granier's will forbade the consistory from selling the two houses comprising the estate or using them in any way other than to finance the purchase of bread for the poor. Those benefitting from the trust would be given a card reading "Foundation of Antoine Granier, Former Baker," which they would then redeem for a loaf of bread. The bread itself was to be made at Granier's former establishment, with the baker paid the going rate without discount or rebate.

In another case, Pauline Vincent, mother of the late pastor Samuel Vincent, left the Consistory of Nîmes 6,000 francs, half of which was for the women's association of the Société de prévoyance. The other half she directed towards a form of assistance that had fallen out of favor with church leaders. At one time the church had provided poor catechumens with money for clothes for their first communion. The practice was suspended in 1847, because it was felt the money was being used to buy clothes fancier than were appropriate to the child's station in society. Now Madam Vincent dedicated 3,000 francs to clothe impoverished girls for their first communion. The consistory had little choice but to comply.

In another case, the Consistory of Nîmes was left the estate of a wealthy bachelor in order to establish an orphanage for boys. This was a project church leaders had wanted to pursue for some time, especially since the nearest such institution was the evangelicals' orphanage at Saverdun. But it never felt it had the necessary funds. By the time the bequest was received, however, church leaders favored a form of foster care. The conditions of the bequest made such a use impractical, forcing them to create a centralized institution despite the fact they believed it would take a child out of his natural geographic and familial environment.[28]

This type of designated giving marked a change in attitudes towards church, charity and patronage. Private benefactors of course had always been part of the network of relations in the Reformed community. In some cases the very building in which Protestants worshiped was the gift of a member of the community. In general, however, most donors had been content to let the church allocate their funds as it saw fit. As the nineteenth century progressed they wanted more of a say in how their money was used. By specifying the conditions under which the money given the church was to be used contributors were able to direct their charitable giving to a particular need and form, and thereby feel more personally involved as patron.

Iindividualization was also part of the attraction of independent religious associations. They provided a greater degree of personal choice and identification. Rather than the submissive anonymity of the established church, one engaged directly and actively in a particular cause even if it was only once a year at the annual meeting, or as a name in the list of contributors published in the yearly report. For example, the Société des Dames in Nîmes and its counterparts in towns throughout the region, actively raised funds for poor relief. It usually cooperated with the local consistory, especially since in smaller areas they were frequently chaired by the pastor's wife. In being independent, however, they could also allocate funds as they desired. Thus, in the same year the Maison de Santé was announced several women's organizations in Nîmes raised 4,490 francs in four separate charity auctions, but only 790 francs went to the consistory. Of the rest, 300 francs was given to the Maison des Orphelines protestantes du Gard, and 1,400 francs went to the Société des missions évangéliques and the Société évangélique de France, neither of which had the blessing of the Church of Nîmes. They also kept 2,000 francs to distribute to the poor themselves, thereby allowing them to determine the criteria for who should receive it and to identify themselves personally as benefactors to the poor.[29]

As seen, however, many independent associations reflected the theological divisions in the Reformed Church. The Maison de Santé was one of the more significant and perhaps controversial of these. It was followed in 1847, by a Société des Amis de Pauvres which gave assistance in goods and counsel to those for whom consistorial assistance was either unavailable or insufficient. At Lyon, a group of evangelicals, most of whom belonged to the local free church, opened the Infirmerie protestante évangélique in 1844. The Maison de Vieilles, for elderly and infirm women at Montauban, was founded the same year by Madam Sarrazin, an evangelical. Though it later expanded to become a full hospital, it remained entirely independent of the established church. Considerably later a Protestant hospital was established at Alès as well. As at Nîmes the municipal hospital was staffed by Catholic orders whose commitment to confessional neutrality was "illusory." After a Protestant patient abjured the faith *in extremis*, the Protestant chaplain had enough and with a few like-minded laity opened a hospital. Though many Reformed leaders opposed the project as "reckless and imprudent" it opened in August 1866, with a nurse and three beds, but grew to serve much of the Protestant Cévennes.[30]

Facing competition from evangelicals and voluntary associations, and worried by the threat of social instability, Reformed consistories expanded their own commitment to poor relief. For Ferdinand Fontanès, writing in his newsletter for liberal clergy, the issue was not whether the church should expand social assistance, but the need to control its growth so as not to overextend itself and thereby subject it to ridicule. By 1859, at least twenty-three Protestant charitable societies were operating in the Gard alone, not including those at Nîmes. Five were mutual aid societies similar to that of the Consistory of Nîmes. Six others, such as the Association national évangéliste at Vergèze and the Société religieuse et protestante at Uzès, were simply described as charitable. Elsewhere, the Consistory of Montpellier founded an Asile protestante in 1845, for the sick and infirm, and also took in a few elderly pensioners without family to care for them. In a similar vein the Consistory of Mazamet, in the department of the Tarn, began a Refuge de Vieillards in 1850, for the "honest and abandoned" elderly of both sexes.[31]

Other institutions mingled personal and ecclesiastical patronage. The Maison des Orphelines Protestantes du Gard, was founded in Nîmes in 1822, by several prominent women led by the mother of François Guizot. Located in the former home of Paul Rabaut, the celebrated pastor of the Eglise du désert, the orphanage was independent of the Reformed Church, but operated in close association with its leaders, many of whom were the husbands, sons or fathers of members of the orphanage's directing committee. At Anduze, Martin-Rollin, upon retiring after several decades service as pastor at Caen, founded the Asile de Bon-Secours in his home town. Though he built and directed this home as a personal project for elderly men and women in the consistorial of Anduze, religious services were provided by the two pastors of the Reformed Church of Anduze. The Recouvance de Champagne-les-Lyon was begun in 1846, by a prominent woman from Lyon, but was directed by local church leaders through a committee of women to give indigent girls of the Reformed Church of Lyon a brief respite in the countryside. In the same city, a home for destitute women over the age of seventy and without family owed its existence to Mme Déthel. Her inspiration came from Pastor Basin, President of the Consistory of Lyon, and though she ran the institution herself, on her death it passed to the consistory which entrusted it to a Comity des Dames.[32]

Over time the distinction between consistorial and non-consistorial associations declined in relevance. In 1852, the Consistory of Nîmes voluntarily gave the independent Société de patronage responsibility for a large endowment it had received to support apprenticeships for Protestant youths. Similarly, a decade later the Church of Nîmes came to the rescue of the Protestant Asyle [sic] Maternal when it got into financial trouble by expanding too quickly. In doing so Gustave de Clausonne, who first proposed the action, pointed out that though the refuge was independent of the consistory it alleviated some of the burden on the church's own resources. "Besides," he observed, "the consistory cannot do everything," and when a benevolent work was as "effectively exercised with as praiseworthy zeal" as was that of the women of the Comité de l'Asyle, the consistory would not depart from its prerogatives by assisting it, especially if the consistory was not in a position to do the work itself. His colleagues agreed and offered the Asyle Maternal 6,000 francs provided that it develop formal guidelines and accept Pastor Viguié as the consistory's official representative to the agency's board of directors. Cooperation with more evangelically oriented institutions was longer in coming, but where the founders of the Maison de Santé had complained about the Consistory of Nîmes acting as if it had a monopoly on charity, by the early 1860s Frossard claimed the hospital's utility was acknowledged by all. Whether or not this was true, a level of comfort had developed with private initiatives in social assistance that earlier was unthinkable.

Initially leaders of the established church were deeply disturbed by the appearance of voluntary organizations in the field of charity. Perceiving in these institutions a threat to their own influence that sometimes was explicit, and later fearing the consequences of social instability, they assimilated some of the activism characteristic of the Réveil and intensified their own activity in behalf of the poor. Their efforts were echoed by the willingness of parishioners to support these projects. The consistories of the established church remained the primary patron to the Reformed community, but they now acted amidst a multiplicity of charitable institutions and organizations operating within the Reformed community from a variety of cooperative and competitive positions. Even in their own activities church leaders often found their freedom of action limited by restrictions donors placed on the use of funds they channeled to the poor through the Reformed Church. In the charged atmosphere of the Réveil religious diversity ended up being mirrored in a fragmentation of charitable action, but with a significant expansion in the number and variety of Protestant social institutions as well.

Equally significant was the spread of evangelical forms of worship and devotion within the established churches of southern France. Perhaps the most dramatic example of tradition yielding to emerging sensibilities is in the changing role of the Reformed Church in rituals surrounding death. Calvinism, more than other branches of the Protestant Reformation, self-consciously broke with Catholic liturgical practices. In France, where Catholic/Protestant tensions remained strong for several centuries, the discipline of the French Reformed Church prohibited prayers and discourses at funerals "for fear of approaching too closely the ceremonies of the Catholic Church and imperceptibly supporting belief in purgatory and the intercession of the saints."[33]

The rigid separation of the church from rituals surrounding death persisted into the nineteenth century. In part this was because repression made pastoral participation impractical. Baptisms, communion and marriages all had to wait until a pastor was in the area to perform them. The same could not be done with the dead, and burials were often small, private affairs taking place in a quiet corner of the family's land.[34] As toleration increased attitudes began to change. A conference of Pastor-Presidents of Reformed consistories held at Paris in 1804, allowed "ceremonies such as exhortations or prayers, either in the temple, at the grave, or in the house of the deceased" so long as they avoided "all that could lead to superstitious practices." The Consistory of Nîmes and many other southern churches did not attend the conference, and refused to adopt its directives. Here the churches' involvement in death remained largely limited to providing a carriage, black coverings for the casket, and the necessary attendants for the funeral procession, as well as the grave in which the dead were buried. In less prosperous districts, not even these accouterments were available.[35]

As the church strengthened institutionally, and as the clergy professionalized and assumed a larger presence in communal life, pressure mounted for a larger ecclesiastical presence at the time of death. For the most part the initiative seems to have come from the laity. Perhaps reflecting an increased sentimentalization in personal relations that both fed into and was fed by the romantic mood of society, people desired greater spiritual consolation for themselves and more sacralized burial rituals for their dead.[36] Church leaders, for both theological and logistical reasons (for clerics who already felt over-worked the thought of adding funerals to their many other duties was daunting) were, however, reluctant to become more intimately involved with the dead.

Independent revivalists, by contrast, were quite willing to step in where the established clergy hesitated. In part this was a logical outgrowth of their emphasis on the need for Christianity to permeate all aspects of life. They also, at least initially, saw funerals as an opportunity to proselytize. Rather than consoling the bereaved, they tended to use the proximity of death as an object lesson to the living of the need to repent before it was too late.[37] As disturbing as this practice might seem, many of the bereaved apparently found warnings of eternal damnation preferable to no religious component to the funeral service at all.

Gradually a softer approach took hold. Among all evangelicals, and the Methodists in particular, funerals honoring their own emphasized the heroic element of the deceased's faith and the peace and tranquility with which they were thereby able to face death. This type of sentimentalized ritual was deeply attractive and though the Reformed Church of Nîmes may have been slower than many to adjust, even here the demand for a religious presence at funerals grew to the point that the President of the Consistory of Nîmes decided the matter could no longer be ignored. A commission was appointed in 1838, to determine whether "there is reason to interdict this usage which could lead to some abuses, or to regularize it by organizing funeral services for which a liturgy would be established."[38]

This committee never reported back, but two years later Pastor Tachard raised the topic again. He observed that religious funerals:

are today nearly generally established in the Protestant churches of large cities such as Lyon, Marseille and Montpellier, and above all in the countryside. The need is even being felt in our city, and if the consistory does not charge itself with regularizing these services, it will see other persons from outside the consistory preach in the cemeteries under the consistory's administration, acting outside of the consistory's inspiration and influence.[39]

The consistory was again urged to adjust to changing priorities in the population in order to keep control of its own institutions. Church leaders, however, were divided on the issue. Some argued that if unauthorized persons were conducting funerals in the church's cemetery the answer was more discipline not a new type of worship service. On the other side, were those who thought it would be enough to say a liturgical prayer in the home of the deceased. Others opposed this limited involvement, and instead urged that it be left to the pastor's discretion "to speak words appropriate to the circumstances, the age, sex and life of the deceased." This would allow them to "respond more particularly to the people and elevate their interest in religious services."

At this point the question also became involved with other issues as well. The committee entrusted with the matter recommended a pastoral presence at burials, but feared orthodox pastors would use the occasion to evangelize. To prevent this from happening they recommended an entirely liturgical funeral service, neither "preceded nor followed by any discourse or funeral oration." The formula for the service would be standardized with modifications allowed only for the deceased's name, sex, age and station in life. Still the consistory could not agree. The issue was taken up in each of the next three sessions, sometimes quite heatedly, but without resolution. Finally it was tabled indefinitely, leaving pastors to follow their own conscience when a family asked them to officiate at the burial of a loved one. These requests became common enough that most pastors eventually agreed to take part. Six months after the consistory set the question aside, a pastor who had refused to take part in funerals as a matter of conscience complained that he felt compelled in the future "to respect the wishes of the families." By 1846, the question for Ferdinand Fontanès was no longer whether the Reformed Church should condone prayers and orations at funerals, but if Reformed pastors should cooperate with dissident pastors in such services.[40]

The gradual adoption of an ecclesiastical role in funerals was indicative of the way religious practices characteristic of the Réveil altered the ritual life of the Reformed Church. Evangelicals may have led the way, but as shown by demand, the sacralization of burial rites was not limited by doctrinal considerations. Liberals, orthodox and the indifferent alike desired a church presence as they put their loved ones to rest. Casting-off traditional prejudices against the practice was not easy, particularly when the simplicity of Reformed funerals was taken by many as a point of pride against the elaborate rituals, emotionalism, and superstition they saw in Catholic services.[41] But the popularity of religious funerals had leaders of the Reformed Church reluctant to refuse their participation for fear of providing an opening to revivalists. Consequently, in the rituals of death the presence of the church in the life of the community was affirmed and increased, even if by default.

In other rituals marking life stages the Réveil had less direct impact. The evangelical concern for a believers' church might be expected to de-emphasize infant baptism, but there is little evidence to suggest this was the case. The vast majority of Protestants continued to adhere to the customs of their faith by having their children baptized with little delay after birth. Methodists, who were the largest dissident group, did not object to the practice, and the orthodox faction of the Reformed Church was accurate on this point in its claim to Calvinist orthodoxy. Marriage was another matter. The law's requirement for a civil marriage marginalized church ceremonies. Reformed leaders had to remind Protestants of their duty to have their unions blessed by the church as well.[42] Most did, but some did not bother. Perhaps the awakening was less effective in addressing this problem than was Louis-Napoleon's reform in 1852, of the process for selecting church elders, opening it to direct democratic election. In setting criteria for participation in these elections many consistories required proof of baptism and marital status based on church records. Men whose marriages had not been celebrated in a church wedding frequently were not eligible to vote.

The Réveil did have an effect on the ritual of confirmation, but not in terms of the number of participants. The practice was widely observed throughout the Reformed communities of southern France. Rather its influence could be seen in the increased attention the Reformed Church gave to instructing the young in the faith prior to their first communion. In Nîmes this was first apparent in the consistory's decision to make catechetical training free for all who desired it. By custom the consistory exempted poor children from paying for this education, but all others paid 1 franc 50 per month. It was pointed out, however, that if primary schooling was offered free in the church's schools than the same should be the case for religious instruction. In 1837, this change was made. The consistory also regularized catechetical training by establishing a framework for consistorial oversight of religious education and developed a set of regulations to guide the tutors in their duties.[43] Then the church changed the day on which first communion was celebrated. The event had coincided with the Feast of God. This was usually a workday, and many working-class families were reluctant to lose a day's wages and so were not present when their children took their first communion. To make it easier to join their children for the occasion, and thereby accentuate the importance of the event and further associate the family with the church, first communion was moved to Pentecost Sunday.[44]

Reformed Churches in the region also began to pay more attention to the quality of religious education in general. They came to share the evangelicals' concern about what had often become a perfunctory examination of catechumens prior to confirmation. The orthodox faction insisted this denigrated the spiritual significance of communion and perverted the church's nature. Acting on this belief could lead to unpleasant situations, as when Clement Ribard, pastor at Roquedur [Consistory of St-Hippolyte-du-Fort], refused to allow several catechumens to take communion, claiming their behavior did not indicate they had taken the catechism to heart. His consistory thought this was overly severe and successfully petitioned the government to remove the minister. In another case, an evangelically minded pastor was known as so vigorous a catechist that several of his parishioners sent their children to a neighboring minister for confirmation.[45] The Consistory of Nîmes took a gentler approach, but one of the concerns about moving first communion to Pentecost was that the examination of catechumens would come only a few weeks before they were to participate in communion, making it impossible to give additional instruction if necessary. Consequently, there was considerable pressure on pastors to pass children they did not feel were properly prepared, rather than subject them to the embarrassment of holding them back. To alleviate the problem, a preliminary examination was instituted in February, in addition to the regular examinations held shortly after Easter, thereby allowing time for extra work when it was needed.[46]

Catechetical training, however, remained a source of concern. In the mid-1840s it was observed that boys, because of their "indifference, frivolity, ill will and ignorance," were not learning their lessons as well as the girls. To improve their performance, two pastors instead of one were given responsibility for catechism. This apparently still did not take care of the problem, as only a few days after news arrived of the February

Revolution in Paris, the Church of Nîmes doubled the hours of religious instruction to four hours a week.[47]

Other aspects of the Réveil impacted upon the worship practices of the Reformed Church. Ferdinand Fontanès, though a leading liberal in southern France, found much that was favorable in evangelical styles of worship, particularly when compared to the tradition laden practices in the established church. Unwilling to risk going to revival services in the Gard where he might be recognized, he admitted to his colleagues that he took advantage of a visit to Switzerland to attend a night service of Swiss dissidents. He was immediately struck by the contrast between "the rigid, arcane, and inflexible language and liturgy used in the official Reformed Church," and the warmth and familiarity of the evangelical service. In French Reformed Churches, for example, seating arrangements in the sanctuary still reflected the hierarchies of society. Church officials and civil dignitaries commonly sat in a prominent place before the pulpit, separated from the rest of the congregation. In addition many of the remaining seats were rented. At one point so many seats were rented in the Petit Temple at Nîmes that there was no longer room even at the back of the church for those who could not afford the 5 to 7 francs each year to reserve a seat.[48]

By contrast, Fontanès said one of the first things he noticed about the evangelical gathering was the ease with which the worshipers interacted with each other.

> I was in a large room with about two hundred-fifty people present. There, one saw people from all orders, of which about a third were men and none were children. Those arriving seated themselves wherever they liked, and prayed seated or standing before taking part in the session. They seemed generally to acknowledge one another and squeezed together voluntarily to make room for newcomers. Each appeared little concerned for the lack of comfort, seeing that the hall was full.
>
> It still was not full, however, when a group of men entered, one of whom, without ecclesiastical dress, placed himself in a small, slightly elevated pulpit. He opened the session with a short prayer simply for the purpose of requesting blessings from on high upon the meeting. He announced a hymn, read it and began to sing, joined by the assembly. . . A stranger to the words and music I remained silent, but my neighbor seeing this quickly offered me his hymnal.[49]

This was quite different than the French Reformed Churches where the pastors almost always wore dark clerical robes, preached from an elevated pulpit, and participants were much more protective of their seats, hymnals and social station.

The evangelical service itself was simple and familiar, and "the assembled audience seemed to follow it with a lively interest." There was much about it that impressed the pastor from Nîmes, from the welcome with which the worshipers received him and each another, the informality of the liturgy, and the warmth of the hymns, to the focus of the service on how the faith actually related to the daily life of the believer. "The emotion of the assembly won me over," Fontanès concluded.

This did not mean he had a conversion and joined the ranks of the orthodox, but he did find much in revivalist practices from which the Reformed Church could benefit. Fontanès asked of the established churches:

> Is there no means to prod into action an assembly of men that duty or habit has led to meet together in a temple; to persuade them that they are there to enter into communion with God, and not simply to listen to a man; to express their gratitude and repent; to request the fullness of grace, aid, consolation, and ask for it themselves; in a word, to pray themselves and not rely upon a single man to pray for all? Is there no means to convert an audience, that is to say a meeting of men who limit themselves to the passive role of listeners, into an assembly of worshipers?[50]

Few evangelicals could have stated the challenge as succinctly. Fontanès essentially accepted the orthodox critique that the practices of the Reformed Church were incapable of waking those in its congregations who attended more out of custom than conviction out of their spiritual malaise. He urged the national church to modify its form of worship to involve the congregations more fully in the life of the church. Too many attended out of custom and were content to let the clergy perform the acts of religion much as any other public official charged with a civic function. And too many pastors were content to operate within this circumscribed role. This complacency, Fontanès argued, would not equip the church to withstand the challenges of modern society. Neither would it satisfy those who wanted more from religion than a civil or cultural exercise.

Fontanès still felt the orthodox insistence on doctrine was too exclusive in that they limited participation in the church to those who adhered to a confession of faith and devotional behavior. The customary practices of the Reformed Church, however, tended to exclude the individual, were repetitive and tedious, and therefore ultimately without much intrinsic meaning. Through their use of hymns, congregational prayer and practical preaching, Fontanès believed evangelicals were able to draw those who attended into the rituals of worship and connect the Christian faith to personal life. He saw no reason why these methods could not be used to similar ends in the Reformed Churches of France. "Among the causes of fervor just enumerated," Fontanès concluded, "there are perhaps none the national church could not use to its profit."[51]

On a personal level Gustave de Clausonne, a frequent collaborator with Fontanès in liberal causes, testified to the influence of the Réveil on his own faith. In the midst of a caustic letter to Pastor Frossard regarding the Maison de Santé, he told Frossard the Réveil had led him "to feel a need to give greater account to my beliefs, in my affections and my ideas, than I had until then judged necessary - to take steps towards a more concrete and better coordinated Christianity."[52]

As a consequence of the Réveil, even liberals like Fontanès, Clausonne and others were altering their understanding of the relation between the church and the Reformed community. While rejecting the orthodox wing's "spirit of separation . . . and of an exclusive salvation," even opponents of the Réveil gradually adopted an evangelical emphasis on individual commitment to the faith. They were coming to the conviction that if their own churches were to be more than hollow institutions the faithful had become more than passive listeners, attending church out of habit or a sense of duty. Instead of being satisfied with an identification with the Reformed faith based on culture and custom, they believed it was necessary to make the individual an active participant in the life of the church. Liberals continued to define the church in broad and inclusive terms, but there was a growing awareness that it was necessary to attract or persuade Protestants to accept a deeper spiritual identity. Thus they too were coming increasingly to treat the Reformed Church as a sort of voluntary institution.

This semi-revivalistic perspective derived out of a defense to the growing influence evangelicals, but also out of a genuine regard for the spiritual nature of the church. A significant number in the Reformed community desired a deeper religious experience but did not find the practices of the Church spiritually fulfilling. It was among these individuals that the dogmatic principals of the orthodox faction and the outright dissidence of the sects were gaining acceptance. If the Reformed Church was to remain united and retain religious vitality it had to meet the expectations of these people. Fontanès, in the *Correspondance pastorale*, which he edited for the liberal clergy in France, declared it was time to find ways "to bring ourselves closer to our parishioners Methodism or indifference has seized while we remained distant." He exhorted his colleagues to become more active pastors in their communities, to "visit the sick. Reunite your catechumens after their first communion. Collect subscriptions for religious societies. Circulate good books and brochures. Profit from occasions that present themselves to turn the conversation to religious topics. Search for means to enlighten public opinion upon events relative to the church and to piety." In short to assume many habits of the evangelical clergy. To drive the point home he quoted his mentor, Samuel Vincent, who had advised, "the means to resist Methodism was to do much of what it does, but do it in a larger and more enlightened spirit." Fontanès added his own warning to his colleagues. "If souls do not find with you the nourishment for which they feel the need, they will go search for it elsewhere, and then they will slip away from you. You will remain a good pastor, but a pastor without a congregation or a pastor of the indifferent."[53]

By the mid 1840s, many pastors were following this advice. The *Correspondance pastorale* noted that among "pastors who are friends of liberty" there were many "devoted to the service of God and full of activity for the reign of the Gospel. Through their care, liberal churches are moving towards health and devotion." In other words, a liberal version of the Réveil was taking place, but as Fontanès said, it was "without foreign assistance and without the resources that the confessional party receives from England and America. But, it still is necessary to continue and propagate this good movement."[54]

Much of the evidence of how leaders of the established church in southern France were in fact trying to improve the state of worship in their congregations comes from the Consistory of Nîmes which met more frequently and left better records than most other consistories. The Consistory of Nîmes also set the agenda which many churches in the region often later followed. The establishment at Nîmes of the *culte de l'Oratoire* was one example of an evangelical innovation to which the Church of Nîmes, by adopting it, gave a degree of legitimacy which other pastors and consistories could then be less apprehensive about adopting themselves. A few years after instituting this form of informal worship, Nîmes set out on a program to make all worship services more accessible. To those who could not afford to rent a pew would have a place in worship one service was set aside for which no pews were rented, and restrictions were placed on the number of pews available for rent in others. In addition, noting the relative absence of men in church, side chapels in the Petite Temple were reserved for men only, hoping more men would attend if there was someplace for them to sit without women or children. Apparently this worked at least enough so that a few years later the same was done in the Grand Temple as well.[55]

Attention was also given to congregational singing which Fontanès said was in a "deplorable state," claiming it lacked "harmony, spirit and dignity, all at the same time." In late 1839, the consistory hired a music teacher to conduct lessons for the congregation. More than three hundred people attended the three-week long course. The results were favorable enough that the course was added to the curriculum of the consistorial schools. To facilitate these lessons the consistory bought several copies of a new hymnal containing sixty-eight of the old Psalms and twenty-four hymns. Introduction of these hymns was a more dramatic step than it might seem at first. The Psalter used in the French Reformed Church dated back to the seventeenth century. Attempts during the Empire to update it had not been well received, but by the 1830s, some pastors were openly complaining that the traditional Psalms were antiquated. A participant at a Pastoral Conference in 1833 declared, "The introduction of some new hymns would be seen with pleasure."[56] In Nîmes at least, nothing was done until the service of the *Oratoire* in 1836. Even then only a few hymns were adopted, and their use was expressly limited to this service. Yet, two years after sponsoring the music lessons for the congregation, adding music to the consistory's schools, and buying a Psalter that included hymns, these became a regular part of Sunday morning services. By 1846, the consistory was prepared to buy for the *Oratoire* a hundred copies of a song book containing nothing but hymns.[57]

The growing emphasis within the Reformed Church on catechetical training and communal worship was also more than simply a response to the challenge posed by the orthodox wing of the church. Liturgical innovations often are introduced only when the current practices of worship no longer satisfy the emotional and spiritual needs of the worshiper. The new practices introduced by the Réveil were attractive because they seemed better matched to the changing spirit of the times as manifested in the church's congregations. Social and political forces were taking an increasing toll upon Protestant solidarity. Economically the individual was increasingly isolated and subject to the whims of the market. At the same time social divisions seemed to harden while ties between classes diminished. In these circumstances many in the Reformed community were attracted by the less formal and more affective beliefs and forms of worship propagated by the religious renewal. The revival offered spiritual certainty in the midst of temporal uncertainty. It provided a new sense of fellowship, based upon shared beliefs and piety, that did not take into account social or economic position, and its forms of worship strengthened this sense of community.

Where the established church segregated the community through pew rentals and seating in the parquet for notables, evangelicals emphasized familiarity, mutual acceptance, and equality of the faithful. By custom the pulpit in Reformed Churches was elevated high above the congregation and the pastor who preached from it was further distinguished from his audience by his ministerial robes. In the meetings of the dissidents the pastor was barely distinguishable from anyone else. In the same way the evangelicals' use of congregational singing helped reinforce individual participation within cooperative harmony. The hymns that were sung were contemporary, written in a language familiar to the people, set to attractive tunes, and designed to emotionally involve the singer. By contrast, the Reformed Churches continued to sing the Psalms translated and put to music centuries before.

In a similar way the evangelicals' use of congregational prayer involved the laity as active participants in corporate worship. In the worship services of the national church prayers were usually liturgical and led by the pastor. By contrast, the Réveil propagated the belief that simple, extemporaneous prayer was more sincere and therefore more effective. It was certainly more flexible in form and often times more comprehensible. They might well be led by a lay person, were easily adjusted to the context and nature of the congregation, usually were relevant to immediate events and concerns, and often times more understandable by the audience. Fontanès noted that they were not as poetic and well-formed as the liturgical prayers, but "though they were generally diffuse, full of repetition, and too uniform in color and tone, they had feeling and the audience heard them with a visible interest and emotion."[58] Each member of the congregation, through the communion of prayer, could "associate himself with the works, the success, the weariness, and the persecutions of the evangelists, the missionaries, and the small churches hindered in their development."[59]

This identification with other believers was something the traditional practices of the Reformed Church were unable to provide. As the evangelicals gained strength and effectively challenged the established churches, the forms of worship characteristic of the Réveil were gradually incorporated into the liturgy of the Reformed Church. As a result the church was better able to meet the spiritual needs of a broader section of the Protestant population, thereby helping to maintain ecclesiastical unity while strengthening the sense of commonality and fellowship among its faithful.

In making these adjustments, however, the Reformed Church also implicitly adapted some of the orthodox party's' exclusionist view of the church. The sociologist of religion David Martin noted in his book, *The Breaking of the Image*, the way changes in liturgy can impact a church having a broad identification with the its society. Their impact can be particularly disorienting for those who are infrequent attenders. When they do attend, during a time of personal distress or for a special occasion, they find the familiar patterns are no longer present. The order of worship, the music, the words are different from what they were accustomed to. The result is a sense of confusion and foreignness that can end-up distancing the casual participant from the church altogether.

Martin wrote in the context of liturgical reforms in the Church of England, but his conclusions can just as well apply to the Reformed Churches of southern France. The established church rejected the revivalists' restrictions on the basis of doctrine and piety for participation in the church, and fought to maintain a communal church, but the changes they little by little incorporated implicitly separated the less assiduous. The church did not set up confessional tests for participation, but for the youth who was set apart for additional instruction with the pastor before first communion, or the occasional worshiper who no longer knew the hymns or when to sit and stand, the message was clear. Membership in the Reformed Church was contingent upon more than just the fact one's parents and grandparents belonged to that confession. A distinction was being drawn between the Reformed community and the Reformed Church. The Reformed Church did not formally change its inclusive ecclesiology, but it did try to work out a compromise between community and spiritual identification.[60]

The French Churches of Bas-Languedoc did not intend to disestablish itself from the community. It was simply a byproduct of the perceived need to require a greater degree of commitment. Particularly after the political and social disruptions of the Second Republic liturgical and disciplinary reforms were paired with programs designed to reach out to the Protestant population to increase participation in the regular life of the church. For example, the Consistory of Nîmes, again showing its concern about declining attendance by men, began holding an annual conference for men during the six weeks before Easter. These conferences dealt with religious topics thought to be of a broad interest, and were led by a visiting pastor of some stature and known for his ability as a public speaker.[61]

A more dramatic example of how leaders of the Reformed Church had changed their view of the relation of church and community, was the Pastoral Conference of the Gard's organization of the Mission intérieur operating within the Protestant heartland. Unlike the earlier Société d'évangélisation des protestantes désséminées, which was designed to provide pastoral services for Protestants who didn't live near a Reformed Church, the Comité des missions intérieur had the explicit mandate to plan, organize and carry-out activities that would resurrect interest in the Reformed faith, even in areas fully served by a consistory and a resident minister.[62]

By far the most popular activities sponsored by the Mission intérieur were the outdoor services it organized. Inspiration for these events came from the often noted interest the ordination services for new pastors attracted in the Reformed community. The services usually were attended by several pastors and the speaker, often a senior minister of some note, delivered a sermon written specifically for the occasion. Trying to capitalize on the broad interest raised by these services as popular spectacle the Mission intérieur organized special events in the various consistories that duplicated the structure of the ordination services without the focus of initiating new ministers into their vocation. At first these events were held in area churches, but almost immediately had to be moved outside because the size of the crowd exceeded the capacity of the temples. It was not long before organizers realized that the very fact of an outdoor service was itself part of the attraction. It had the additional advantage of linking these events with memories of the assemblies of the *Eglise du désert*. In this way, the events both served to reinforce Protestant identity by involving those in attendance in a vicarious participation in the heroic sacrifices made by their ancestors for the Reformed religion, and of affirming the link between the Reformed Churches of France in the nineteenth century with the church of the Huguenots. The events themselves were explicitly religious, but did not require a great deal of personal commitment. One could attend, reaffirm his or her place in the Reformed community without even having to pass through the doors of the church, or subject himself or herself to the scrutiny of the pastor and elders, let alone give an accounting of his or her beliefs or actions.[63]

These efforts to build and maintain a balance of religious persuasion and discipline while supporting a common identity within the Reformed population were also reflected in attempts by the consistories of Bas-Languedoc to resurrect the ecclesiastical structure of the French Reformed

Church. The strongest move towards this end came as an indirect result of plans to establish a school at Nîmes to prepare Protestant youths for seminary and eventual service in the Reformed Church as pastors. Bas-Languedoc supplied by far the largest percentage of pastors in the Reformed Church. Of the 220 pastors ordained between 1815-1830, 24 percent came from the Gard. When those pastors from the seven departments bordering the Gard are included, the proportion rises to nearly 46 percent. By 1848, the percentage of those for whom an origin is known that came from the Gard had declined to 21 percent, but grew for the region as a whole to 68 percent. The number of students entering the seminaries, however, did not match the demand for new pastors, especially as those ministers who had served before and during the Revolution retired or died. Consequently, Reformed Churches were having difficulty finding replacement pastors. Even when candidates were available there were only one or two from which to choose.[64]

One reason seen for the shortage of new pastors was the lack of quality secondary schooling, particularly in rural communes. As a result, youths who might have gone into the ministry did not do so due to their lack of education, and several who did go were so unprepared academically they could not keep pace. To combat the problem, the President of the Consistory of Nîmes asked his consistory, in July 1846, to consider founding a preparatory school for theological studies. The "constant fact of many vacant churches," he argued, indicated the need to increase the number of pastoral candidates. A preparatory school would help do this, while also encouraging "the students to assume early-on the spirit of their vocation. From this one will have both quality and quantity." The other members of the consistory readily seconded the idea. Some remarked that, "Nîmes, through its position and its large congregation, is a providentially appropriate" location for such an institution. "Small churches could not put themselves at the head of such establishments. The Consistory of Nîmes, therefore, has a great duty to fulfill in this regard."[65] The proposal was approved unanimously.

Once the consistory agreed to explore founding such an institution, however, the session took an unusual direction. Gustave de Clausonne, as secretary for the consistory, turned the discussion to the continuing absence of church synods. He claimed, "a lack of organization is generally felt in our churches. The synods only exist on paper and the churches remain isolated one from the other." Independent religious societies and pastoral conferences had helped alleviate this problem, but they "also have the inconvenience of annihilating more and more the consistories which are, however, the legal representatives of the church."

Clausonne proposed that the consistories act immediately to organize synods on a departmental basis, even if the government would not authorize them. His proposal was well received by the his colleagues. As for the problem of government approval, it was believed that though the civil authorities might not condone the assemblies they would not forbid them as they already were tolerating pastoral conferences. Since these synods would not, however, have official sanction their authority necessarily would be more moral than real. Still, it was believed that the advantages of having the legal representatives of the church in regular contact made even these limited synods desirable. With support secured in principle, Clausonne proposed that the Consistory of Nîmes lead the way by arranging a meeting of the consistories of the Gard. "The establishment of a preparatory school would be a naturally indicated subject for the first conference." This also was approved and sent to the Extraordinary Commission for amplification. A month later this commission reported back with its recommendations. Its members concluded that "the utility of the preparatory school is superabundantly demonstrated," but the ways and means of establishing it was a more difficult matter. They estimated that the annual expenses for the school would run approximately 12,000 francs including 4,000 francs for scholarships. Half of this sum would have to come from other consistories in the Gard and other sources outside of the department.[66]

Once the details were laid before the consistory there was more hesitation about the project. Some feared that after the enthusiasm of the initial years wore off the Consistory of Nîmes would be left responsible for funding the entire institution. While this was seen as a serious though solvable problem, the greatest criticism was leveled against offering scholarships to some students at the school. Several members of the consistory believed this financial aid would encourage "incompetent young people, or those belonging to the inferior classes of society to enter into the ministry." That this possibility was undesirable was never disputed. Instead, it was simply argued that scholarships were "a necessary evil in order to have pastors."[67] Despite the risks, the consistory determined to pursue the project pending the approval of a Conference of Consistories which would convene for the first time to consider the new institution. Letters went out to the various consistories inviting them to send a pastor and a layman to Nîmes to discuss creating a theological preparatory school to serve the Protestant population of the Gard and the Midi. On September 9, 1847, representatives of sixteen of the eighteen consistories in the Gard unanimously endorsed the project.

While all consistories present promised financial support for the school, the amount actually allocated was less than hoped for. As of December 7, 1846, fifteen consistories had promised a total 2,842 francs in addition to the 2,000 francs set aside by the Consistory of Nîmes. Still, the pastors and elders of the Church of Nîmes were satisfied with this initial show of support and expanded the appeal for funds to all of France and in particular to the other Reformed consistories in the Midi. This brought in an additional 695 francs; still 4,000 francs short of the estimated cost. Despite the shortage of funds it was decided to continue with the project and open the school in October 1847. For this purpose a second Conference of Consistories convened April 21. Again the response was satisfying and the Ecole préparatoire pour le Ministère évangélique went ahead as planned.[68]

In this way the Consistory of Nîmes, at least for the time being, reasserted its customary position at the lead of the Reformed Churches of Bas-Languedoc in their effort to ease the need for more and better qualified pastors, while at the same time they tried to reconstruct the traditional structure of the French Reformed Church. The precedent involved in the Conference of Consistories was acknowledged by their instigator, Gustave de Clausonne, in his 1847 annual address as President of the Société Biblique de Nîmes. "Two times in the space of one year," he told his audience:

> the churches of the department of the Gard have sent to Nîmes a pastor and an elder from their consistory to meet in an official conference. In this they followed the [path?] traced by our ancient discipline and the law Germinal. This was a promising start which raised prospects that such assemblies might become a regular occurrence.

But Clausonne also noted the absence of a few consistories which broke, "as lightly as it was, the unanimity for which we would have been pleased." This was regrettable, he said, but it also left hope for the future. "For the Protestant family of the Gard must not be divided. These words I leave to your hearts, for they need no commentary."[69]

This attitude was quite different from that expressed by the Consistory of Nîmes in 1835, in its response to a project sponsored by the Commission of Pastoral Correspondence at Paris which sought to lobby the government for the establishment in the Reformed Church of an authority superior to that of the consistories.[70] The leaders of the Church of Nîmes again opposed the idea in 1839, when the government asked the consistories to comment upon its plan to modify the administration of the Reformed Church.[71] But in 1847, after several years of dissension and conflict with the orthodox wing of the church, the old concern for the unity of the Reformed community led the Consistory of Nîmes to seek a means to reestablish regular ties between consistories. The fact that Nîmes would be in the lead of the effort only added to its attraction.

The convening of a Conference of Consistories in the Gard was then put forward as a model for a national project to establish "General Assemblies of the French Protestant Churches."[72] Though this project was never accepted by the other consistories in France it fed into the broader movement that followed the February Revolution of 1848 to take advantage of events to convene a general assembly of French Reformed Churches. A number of proposals, including one from the Church of Nîmes similar to its plan of the previous year, were put forward to govern the distribution, selection and powers of delegates to this conference. In a preliminary conference held at Paris, May 10, 1848, it was decided that delegates would be chosen through indirect election by all adult male Protestants.[73] These representatives would then officially meet as the Assemblée générale du protestantisme français in Paris September 9, 1848.

This assembly had to confront two major questions. These were the relations between the Reformed Church and the French state, and the writing of a confession of faith. Both issues were highly charged due to the Réveil. The more adamant members of the orthodox faction demanded the complete separation of church and state and favored writing a conservative statement of faith that would be authoritative for the church. Liberals opposed both measures. Therefore the division of the assembly between liberal and evangelical delegates would determine the general results of the meeting.

Though the extremist rhetoric made it appear that this assembly would be the forum for a showdown between liberals and orthodox, most of the church was more moderate in temperament. In much of southern France, church leaders seemed genuinely concerned with preventing a schism. This sentiment was explicitly expressed by the Consistories of Lasalle and Vauvert. Though these two consistories, one dominated by liberals the other by evangelicals, expressed their desire to improve the Organic Articles, they charged their representatives to do everything possible "to maintain in one body the Church of France," and to do nothing against "the union of church and state."[74]

The other consistories in the department demonstrated a similar concern in choosing those who would represent them at the General Assembly. The eighteen consistories of the Gard were allotted eighteen delegates to this meeting. When each church sent its democratically elected representatives to Nîmes, August 17-18, 1848, to choose the delegates to Paris, it was decided to select five evangelicals and thirteen liberals, a figure both sides thought was fair representation for the two doctrinal tendencies. The actual vote, however, only provided four evangelicals. A lengthy debate followed which was settled by the nomination of an additional orthodox delegate, meaning the Gard sent to Paris nineteen, rather than its allotted eighteen, lay representatives. This accommodation to the evangelicals was vigorously criticized by liberals from other regions of France. The presence of an extra delegate also raised problems for accrediting the representatives in the first session of the General Assembly. Eventually, all nineteen delegates from the Gard were admitted as voting members of the Assembly.[75]

Once the Assembly was officially seated the representatives began the formal deliberations. First, a report was made on the general content of the *cahiers* sent by the consistories to guide their delegates. These revealed that thirty-seven of the ninety participating consistories opposed any separation of the church from the state. The cahiers from thirty-eight consistories, including those in the Gard, did not treat this question directly, but they had already expressed their desire to remain part of the civil structure. Sixty-three consistories directed their representatives to abstain from all dogmatic discussions, and the consistories of the Gard further limited this aspect by telling its representatives, "questions of organization must not be treated upon dogmatic terrain." In other words, the churches of the Gard did not want the structure of the church altered according to evangelical doctrinal or devotional principles.[76]

Despite the fact that the majority of the churches asked that the dogmatic debates be avoided, three days after it had chosen its officers the Assembly opened discussion on a confession of faith. Over the next five sessions the various parties aired their thoughts, criticisms and protests regarding a formula of doctrines that would serve as a guide for the Reformed Church. But when the matter came to a vote it was a proposal sponsored by Clausonne and Louis Delmas, a moderate evangelical pastor at La Rochelle, that was accepted by the deputies by a vote of sixty-seven for, six against, and seven abstentions. This measure left the doctrinal position of the church as it was, citing the fact that most of the cahiers opposed deliberations on dogmatic questions, and the discussions that had been held on the issue demonstrated that, "the moment has not come to touch the status quo in this regard." It further called for the establishment of a commission to write an address to the churches that would serve as a preamble for the Assembly's deliberations on church organization. To guarantee bipartisan support for this letter this commission was composed of four members from each of the two wings of the church.[77]

A week later this commission reported back with its compromise statement. As such it represented the minimum of what the evangelicals required and the maximum of what the liberals would allow. It was a vague and sentimental statement of doctrines about which few Protestants could object. It did not go into detailed specifics on doctrines such as the nature of Christ's divinity or the atoning nature of his sacrifice. Instead it simply stated, "Jesus Christ and Jesus Christ crucified," was "the only foundation" upon which Christianity was established. This "divine liberator" was "the same yesterday, today, eternally. In him exists corporally the full plenitude of divinity, and he is always able to save those who come before God through him."[78]

The refusal of the delegates to draft a more definitive statement of faith did lead a few of the most zealous evangelicals, such as Frédéric Monod, to withdraw from the Assembly. Eventually he and others of a similar perspective withdrew from the French Reformed Church entirely and established the Union of Evangelical Churches, a loose confederation of several independent Protestant congregations. The vast majority of evangelical Reformed pastors and laity did not follow this example. Only a few pastors from the south withdrew from the national church. The most notable of these were Emile Arnal, pastor at Bréau in the Consistory of Le Vigan, and Louis Bassaget, pastor at St-Laurent-d'Aigouze, Consistory of Vauvert. There were only four independent congregations in the Gard at this time, and these were quite small.[79]

Though the liberals in the Reformed Church were strong enough to keep the General Assembly from adopting a confession of faith as a standard for participation in the church, they did not use this strength to attack their orthodox rivals. Neither did the evangelicals flee the church when their agenda was not accepted. Instead, a compromise was developed that allowed continued coexistence between the two factions. In this result the consistories of the Gard, and the Consistory of Nîmes in particular, played a significant part. Though church leaders in the region were largely liberal in disposition, they at least made a nominal effort to maintain the integrity of their congregations, and at the General Assembly at Paris, Gardois liberals such as Gustave de Clausonne were prominent in the compromises that held the conference together.

These accommodations to evangelicalism were reflected in the internal life of the Reformed Churches of Bas-Languedoc. Though the Réveil raised tensions within the Reformed community and challenged the ecclesiastical and spiritual status quo, it also helped revive the religious life of this community. Both through its moral influence upon the faithful and the spirit of competition it raised among the leaders of the established church, revivalism prodded the Reformed Church into making changes. These were evident in its renewed efforts in behalf of the Protestant poor, as well as its deeper concern for the religious education of the young, the acceptance of responsibility in the burial of Protestant dead, and the inclusion of new forms in its worship services.

In this way the Reformed Church could better respond to the needs of men and women caught up in what were often bewildering social changes. As an institution closely tied to a community formed by centuries of persecution and custom, the Reformed Church had difficulty innovating in religious practice. The traditional bonds, however, that had united individuals in this community were weakening. The Réveil furthered this sense of deterioration by challenging the religious cohesion of the Protestant population. But at the same time revivalism, through its implicit egalitarianism, participatory practices, and emphasis upon sentimental attachment to the faith, could provide a renewed if altered sense of community. Through the creativity and energy of the spiritual awakening French Protestantism was able to adapt to the changing needs of its faithful in an increasingly commercialized and politicized society, while preserving the outward face of Protestant solidarity.

EPILOGUE

MAY 1859: PROTESTANTISM IN MODERN FRANCE

On the morning of May 26, 1859, a crowd of 15,000 to 20,000 people gathered outside Nîmes in a walled field next to the Protestant cemetery. They were there to celebrate the three-hundredth anniversary of the Synod of 1559 that marked the founding of the Reformed Church of France. People began arriving soon after daybreak at the site where a century before the Church of the Desert had worshiped clandestinely. By seven o'clock so many had gathered that the gates were opened an hour ahead of time so that traffic could pass by on the road. At 9:30 in the morning 110 pastors from across the region formally processed in black clerical robes to seats reserved for them on the platform and in front of the podium. Once seated, David Tachard, senior pastor of the Reformed Church of Nîmes and President of its consistory, opened the service with a prayer that included the requisite request for God's blessings on the Emperor and Empress, the Imperial Prince, the success of French armies fighting Austria in northern Italy and for the personnel of the departmental and municipal administrations. After this Eugène Buisson, Pastor and President of the Consistory of Lyon, took the podium and spoke for an hour and twenty minutes on the character of the Reformed faith and the circumstances of the founding of the French Reformed Church. Those in attendance then returned to their homes for the noon meal or to a special banquet prepared for the many dignitaries.

This event was one of many held over the next few days throughout the region and across France, wherever Reformed Protestants resided in any number. As with most of these the gathering at Nîmes was deemed a rousing success. Fears on the part of civil and clerical authorities alike that so large a gathering of Protestants for what could be a highly charged event would provoke another round of confessional violence went happily unmet. Many from the Catholic community did crowd into an adjacent field to see what the Protestants were up to, but this was only out of curiosity, and the Prefect for the Gard reported to his superiors in Paris with some relief, "All passed calmly and in good order." The only negative was a violent thunderstorm that struck in mid-afternoon, ripping away tents and canopies, and drenching those who had returned early for the afternoon meeting, which had to be canceled.[1]

A month later, however, Monsignor Plantier, Bishop of Nîmes, published a pamphlet challenging the Protestant commemoration of the Synod of 1559. Plantier had been appointed to the diocese of Nîmes a few years before. He brought to his position a more aggressive style in Protestant/Catholic relations than had his predecessors. A leading ultramontane, he seldom hesitated to jump into a fray. The Procureur-Général for the region observed that in taking Protestants to task for the self-congratulatory tone of their celebrations Bishop Plantier showed himself a man of "vast learning and a talent of the first order as a writer." In fact his publication caused quite a stir and set off a minor pamphlet war between him and the Reformed clergy that was widely followed through much of the summer.[2] In this exchange the Catholic bishop forced Protestant church leaders to openly confront in a public forum the relation between the French Reformed Church in the modern era with its predecessor of the sixteenth century. In doing so they provided a window onto the ambiguities in which the Reformed community found itself in mid-nineteenth century France.

After an aside to the "indiscreet storm" that dampened the day's festivities, Bishop Plantier began his assault on French Protestantism by asserting his astonishment they should want to celebrate the Synod of 1559 at all. "Rather than speak of this synod and exalt it," he declared, "if you truly understood your own interests you would bury it in eternal silence." Priding himself on citing only Protestant sources such as Théodore Bèze's *Histoire ecclésiastique* and a number of contemporary Reformed writers, he laid out two main critiques. The first, which consumed the bulk of the brochure, was that the founding synod of the French Reformed Church violated Reformed principles. Much of this was a reworking of well-tilled soil in the polemic between Protestants and Catholics. He did point out, however, that the twelve churches that participated in the first synod of the French Reformed Church were not a majority of the more than forty Calvinist churches then active in France.

In addition they had no official status according to Reformed polity to speak for their own congregations let alone the thirty or so not present. Yet they wrote and approved a document that became the standard for all Reformed Churches in France. In addition, and perhaps here Plantier was more original, he argued backwards from the contemporary propensity of French Protestants to identify freedom of conscience as the essential principle of their faith to assert that the Synod of 1559 violated this core ideal. Even if delegates to the synod had the authority to do what they did, the Confession of La Rochelle they adopted and to which ministers were required to ascribe their assent, denied the liberty Protestantism claimed to resurrect from Catholic tyranny.[3]

This point led the Bishop of Nîmes into his second critique. He observed that by their own admission Reformed Protestants no longer respected the work of their Church's founders.

> The Synod of 1559 is no longer anything more to you than a historical memory. Its acts have passed into the state of dead letters. For a long time you have seen them as neither necessary foundation nor obligatory rule. Completely swept along by the current of free inquiry and the private interpretation of the Scriptures this beacon raised by your fathers to illuminate and guide the march into the future has been entirely lost from view.

Was it logical, Plantier asked in conclusion, "to celebrate a council whose traditions and ordinances you have abandoned?"[4]

This struck a sensitive nerve among Protestants. Already bruised by internal divisions, the celebrations of May 1859, were a rare demonstration of religious unity and enthusiasm in the Reformed community. On other occasions Reformed leaders had been somewhat reluctant to draw too much attention to their Reformation traditions, concerned that it might exacerbate confessional relations much like Roman Catholic processions often did. At the same time, theological liberals worried that it might further inflame doctrinal debates within the Reformed Church itself.[5] Some of these same reservations were voiced about the nation-wide commemoration of the Synod of 1559. The proposal for the celebration that came from the fledgling Société de l'histoire du protestantisme français had been careful to emphasize that the events would be in honor of a historical fact, the founding of the French Reformed Church, not the theological project it adopted. Ultimately, the attractions of an opportunity to celebrate their common heritage proved too appealing to pass up. The churches of French

Protestantism's heartland threw themselves into the preparations. In the weeks and months leading up to the event they produced numerous publications, speeches and sermons preparing the way by recalling to the Reformed community its valorous past, its integrity and suffering for the faith, and its distinctiveness and superiority to Roman Catholicism. These themes remained a prominent aspect of the festivities themselves. In fact Plantier claimed it was the persistence of the anti-Catholic rhetoric that led him to write his tract in the first place. His critique, which hit upon many of the points French Protestants were debating amongst themselves, was as sobering as the downpour that washed-out the afternoon festivities at Nîmes.[6]

Consequently responses were quick and widely followed. The first was not a response at all. *Les Pasteurs de Nîmes aux Fidèles de leur Eglise*, took the form of a pastoral letter from the ministers of the Reformed Church of Nîmes to their parishioners. Its stated concern was to prevent "the salutary impulsion with which you received the glorious memories of the Reformation" from being lessened by the "intemperate attacks against the purity of our faith and the heroism of our martyrs." The pastor's letter did, however, chastise Plantier for violating "the mission of peace and love he is called to fulfill among us." More conventional was *Réponse à la lettre aux Protestants du Gard, de Mgr. L'Evèque de Nîmes*, by the future Senator and masonic leader, Frédéric Desmons, and the rejoinder to the bishop from one of the pastors of the Reformed Church of Nîmes, Charles Dardier's *Réponse à la lettre aux Protestants du Gard, de Mgr. l'Evèque de Nîmes*. Both pamphlets did address Mgr. Plantier and matched the bishop point by point, but they also shared the pastoral letter's concern for Protestant sensibilities.[7]

Thus both responses were quick to praise their coreligionists for their calm in the face of this attack, but did not shy away from taking up the challenge set before them. The *Letter* from the pastors of Nîmes may have ignored the Bishop of Nîmes but it did not ignore his charges. They explained to the Reformed community, after the fact, that the celebration was not to glorify the Reformers or to recognize the Synod of 1559 as a definitive authority. Protestants, they pointed out, did not regard any human teaching as infallible. Therefore the fact they believed differently in the nineteenth century than in the sixteenth century did not mean they were any less faithful to the Reformation. "Each age and each church," the pastors said, "has the right and the duty to formulate its faith according to the inspiration of its Christian conscience."[8]

Dardier pursued the same line of argument in his more detailed

Response. He quoted from the letter of the Société de l'histoire du protestantisme français to show that they had celebrated a "grand historical fact," the founding of the French Reformed Church. The three hundredth anniversary of the Synod of 1559 was chosen because, as a French and Reformed community of faith, they could not very well celebrate an event, like Martin Luther's posting of the Ninety-five Theses to the doors of the church in Wittenberg, which belonged to another church or people. The question of whether the conference in 1559 had the authority to found the French Reformed Church was spurious. It was a constitutive assembly and as such established the system by which future deliberations would be governed, but it could not be held to these regulations themselves. In addition, though the Synod of 1559 was only attended by a minority of the Calvinist churches in France none of the other congregations were forced to submit to the deliberations of this assembly. They entered into association freely and thereby agreed to be governed by its articles. Three hundred years later, when the Reformed Church of France chose to commemorate the Synod of 1559, it honored what had grown out of that assembly, not the Confession of La Rochelle that it produced. This confession, Dardier said, was not an infallible formulation of the faith. It was a human construction and as such was open to modification. The Synod of 1559 recognized this principle and provided for later conferences to add or change the articles of La Rochelle. Dardier did concede that the Confession of La Rochelle was historically contingent and misguided in its contradiction of Protestant liberty. But at the time, he declared, the Protestant faith was still not fully developed. Since that time it had progressed enough to recognize the limitations of its beginnings and to go back to the original principles of the Reformation. What mattered was the purity of faith, not the definitions by which it was understood. "If we do not have . . . the same definition of the faith, we have the same faith, and that is the essential thing. The formula is that which is human. It can be modified without harm. The faith, this is what is divine, this is what is immutable, this is what is eternal like God, like the conscience." [9]

This was an able defense and consistent with notions that the Protestant faith was based on free inquiry. The problem was that saying the French Reformed Church no longer recognized the authority of the Confession of La Rochelle may have been technically accurate, but for many in the Reformed community it was unsettling. The battles between liberals and evangelicals in the Reformed Church were cast in exactly these terms. It was true that evangelicals departed from strict Calvinism on several points, but they claimed, and were called "orthodox." It is not surprising therefore, that in the exchange provoked by the Bishop of Nîmes' pamphlet evangelicals were for the most part content to stay on the sidelines. Liberals for their part used the orthodox faction's dogmatism and willingness to break the tie between church and community by excluding those who did not meet their doctrinal and devotional standards to question their legitimacy. The majority of the Reformed people likely did not follow the doctrinal particulars of this debate, but most thought of themselves as inheriting the faith of their ancestors. The catechisms with which they were trained in the faith were generally consistent with the Confession of La Rochelle, and points where they may have differed were largely passed over in silence. The liturgical formulas and the creedal statements they used in worship were written with the theology of the Confession of La Rochelle in mind. And few ministers declared from the pulpit their dissent from the dogmatic formulas of the past. Those who did were often as roundly criticized by their congregations in the same way that orthodox pastors were who refused to serve communion to those they deemed unworthy. For a large number of Protestants continuity with the past was important. Discovering from the pen of a Catholic bishop that this continuity was largely illusory, despite the enthusiasm with which they had just celebrated the founding event of the French Reformed Church, was quite disconcerting.

At its heart the question Bishop Plantier raised for the Reformed community was what it meant to be Protestant in modern France. As such the ambiguity Plantier showed in the theological relation of Protestantism at mid-nineteenth century to its sixteenth-century origins mirrored ambiguities in Reformed identity. The French Reformed community of Bas-Languedoc entered the nineteenth century as a religious minority whose identity was forged out of loyalty to the Reformed faith amidst the experience of persecution and isolation. They took great pride in their distinctiveness from the Catholic majority, and tended to enshrine the faith of their ancestors and the suffering they had endured for its sake as cultural icons and confirmation of their special mission to French society.

Yet Protestants in Bas-Languedoc were also aware their history kept them on the margins of French society. They lived with an underlying insecurity, an awareness of their vulnerability and the possibility that persecution might resume. They were sensitive to the charges of rebellion and subversiveness leveled against them by their opponents on the basis of their ancestors' actions and were at pains to justify their loyalty. While they had little doubt about the legitimacy of their presence in France they also recognized they could not belong in a France structured according to the Ancien Regime's absolutisms of throne and altar. Instead, they were confident rather that as a people that had suffered because of the tyranny and superstition that marred France's past, and armed with the religious principles of their ancestors, they would lead the nation out of this darkness into the bright future of a society founded on tolerance and freedom.

In venerating their history the Reformed community was also to a degree enslaved by it. Both for the sake of security and fidelity to the traditions that formed them, there was little room for change and adaptation. In this sense the work of the Synod of 1559 had become, and in fact was elevated in the celebrations of 1859, as an icon of the founding myth of the Reformed community. Yet the widening inclusion of Protestants into the larger society exposed the community to commercial and social forces that weakened many of the bonds that had united it. In addition, the application of the very principles of individual liberty and free inquiry that they so often championed increased the diversity of opinion and conflicting priorities within their midst. Finally, as Protestant confidence in a tolerant society increased the imperative for solidarity lessened, though the continuing hostility of many in France, and particularly the Catholic community of southern France, meant it did not disappear entirely.

One of the few bonds that remained common to all was the shared religion in which much of their identity was involved. As internal tensions and anxieties increased many looked to the Protestant religion and the Reformed Church to reinforce the community and solidify its identity. Benefitting as an established church from state financial support the church expanded institutionally to assume a much larger presence in the daily life of the community. But there were needs an increase in the number of pastors and places of worship could not necessarily address. Establishment under the state helped solidify church organization but at the cost of some of the church's freedom of action and modifications to its polity. These made church governing bodies more remote from the average individual, cost the consistories some of their legitimacy and denied the church the system of provincial and national synods on which it had depended to maintain ecclesiastical discipline and cooperation. In addition Reformed Protestantism emerged from the French Revolution spiritually exhausted and encumbered by the legacy of rationalism from its alliance with the philosophes in the struggle for toleration, while its ritual life remained embedded in practices reaching back to the sixteenth century and could seem remote and perfunctory in the romantic mood of the early nineteenth century. Consequently the Reformed Church had come to depend as much on anti-Catholic rivalry and cultural custom for its vitality as it did on spiritual devotion.

By the 1820s and especially after the July Revolution of 1830, a growing number in the Reformed community were no longer satisfied with this causal religious identification and began to seek spiritual renewal for themselves and their community. In this context the Réveil emerged and continued on through the 1850s. Though it revitalized and strengthened individual spiritual commitments, it also proved to be a very divisive force in Reformed community. In terms of religion the awakening seemed a conservative movement to preserve the Reformed faith from dilution and corruption by modern culture and philosophy. Certainly its evangelical partisans cast themselves this way by championing the *essential* doctrine of the faith, claiming they were the true inheritors of the Reformation faith, and attacking liberals as innovators corrupted by their worldly attachments. But as their opponents observed, though evangelicals claimed the title of "orthodox" they would be little more comfortable than liberals with a strict application of the ancient discipline of the French Reformed Church. Meanwhile, Protestant sectarians like the Methodists and Darbyites, rejected the Calvinist tradition outright. Conversely, as Bishop Plantier noted with such effect, Protestant liberals explicitly broke with Reformation dogma, were proud of their openness to modern philosophy and the new biblical criticism, and extolled the Protestant values of the priesthood of all believers and the right of free inquiry. In practice, however, they had grave hesitations about an open society, were jealous of consistorial privilege, were reluctant to tamper with traditional forms of worship to make them more open and familiar, and were very protective of the corporate relation of the Reformed Church and community.

It was in this latter respect that evangelicals and the Réveil were the most radical. The orthodox faction may have been concerned to preserve what they saw as the truths of the Reformed faith, but they were not interested in conserving an organic relation between the Reformed Church and the Protestant community. It was true that they were not entirely comfortable with the Confession of La Rochelle, but they felt it or a new statement of faith was necessary in order to separate true believers from the false. Their objective was to create a church of believers that more closely approximated spiritual reality. It was not enough to have been baptized and confirmed in the Reformed Church. These rituals had become so closely identified with familial life and the temporal community that they could not be regarded as reliable indicators of belief. Protestantism was not subject to birth and culture, but was the product of personal commitment and affection to the Christian faith. For this reason the orthodox faction favored restricting the sacraments to those who gave evidence of the confession of faith as the effective rule for their salvation and daily lives. In doing so they sought to raise a barrier to participation in the Reformed Church where none had previously existed. Given the organic connection that existed between the Reformed community of Bas-Languedoc and the Reformed Church, such a change involved more than just religious policy. Redefining the church implied a redefinition of Protestant identity. The Réveil, therefore, not only tried to exclude many French Protestants from heaven, it threatened to remove them from what was a unifying institution of their temporal community.

Consequently, the debate between evangelicals and liberals encompassed much more than elevated points of doctrine. It spilled over into the pews where the progress of the Réveil could often be followed by the divisions it raised within congregations. Individual belief may have been becoming a private matter, but the Reformed Church was not. Through tradition, charity, education and leadership in civil life it was deeply embedded in the fabric of the community. Therefore religious divisions were deeply disturbing both for reasons of security and communal integrity. The presence of independent congregations were particularly disturbing in this regard. Though they were few in number, in a region where loyalties still formed according to a Catholic/Protestant divide they were a visible symbol of fragmentation.

From this perspective religious awakening could be seen as another of the forces dissolving traditional social bonds in the nineteenth century. Religion, however, was both a reflection of social changes and a response to them. On one hand, as new commercial, civil and political relations altered how individuals and groups interacted, the Réveil changed how they worshiped by transforming Protestantism into a voluntary association which rejected those who did not meet the necessary standards for acceptance. Ultimately this would result in a smaller church, but that was not the Réveil's objective. With missionary enthusiasm and charitable works its followers reached out to include those its doctrines excluded. Those who joined, meanwhile, were united into a new community based on the common acceptance of a doctrinal core. In this community devotion to God was the defining principle, and the hierarchies of wealth, status and politics that divided the secular world were at least theoretically irrelevant.

In many ways evangelicals, despite their willingness to restrict the freedom of conscience by doctrinal standards, were more attuned to the demands of an open society than were their counterparts. Organizationally they depended upon the structures of a voluntary society. In their recruitment of new members they relied on the ability of the individual to decide for herself or himself. Once within the fold they integrated the new member into a new community reinforced by forms of piety and worship that were affective, participatory, and egalitarian. Instead of the Psalms chanted in the French Reformed Church since the Reformation, evangelicals sang together stirring hymns by César Malan, Charles Wesley and other modern hymnists. Where Reformed worship tended to be remote and formal, and sermons were often technical and abstract, those who shared in the awakening met for common extemporaneous prayer, and heard sermons that were more exhortative and reverential than the dry expositions on morality or Biblical scholarship that were frequently characteristic of more traditional ministers. There were also visual and positional reinforcements of equality. In the established church the custom was for pastors to wear robes, members of the consistory and other dignitaries sat in the parquet before the pulpit, and much of the remaining seating was rented. By contrast, seating in evangelical meetings was open. Participants greeted each other warmly and made room for new arrivals regardless of social status, while pastors officiated without distinguishing garb and often were as much participant as leader.

The influence of such practices extended considerably beyond the ability of evangelicals to gain converts and establish new churches. Even critics of the Réveil gave testimony to how the awakening influenced them towards a deeper, more experiential spirituality. On a broader scale this subsidiary influence encouraged the adoption of revivalist forms of devotion, liturgy and charity by even the most liberal of consistories. The Réveil exposed many of the weaknesses in traditional Reformed practices, and the need to compete with evangelicals for influence in church and community often forced the implementation of reforms that previously had been resisted. As pastors and consistories saw a number of the more energetic and committed members in their congregations accept evangelical ideas or even participate in separatist services and institutions, they came to realize that in a society in which individuals were free to choose their associations it was necessary to compete for their affections and persuade them to participate. To remain secure in the strength of traditional institutions and patterns of identification was to risk abandonment and irrelevancy. Consistories increased efforts to reach out to the community through charitable and devotional societies. The number of religious services grew. Worship was made less formal. Special celebrations like those of the Mission intérieur and that of May 1859, were interspersed with regular services to break-up monotony. Hymns were introduced, and sermons that spoke to the heart replaced those dealing with intricacies of theology and philosophy. Sunday schools became commonplace, catechetical training was expanded, and the examination of catechumens prior to first communion was more tightly regulated.

In this way even liberals subtly altered their interpretation of the nature of the church. By adopting practices characteristic of the Réveil they implicitly transformed the Reformed Church into a voluntary association. On one hand they sought to persuade Protestants to become more involved in their church and faith, while on the other they tightened discipline to restrict participation to those willing to make a commitment to the church. They did not set up confessional tests, but for the infrequent worshiper who no longer recognized the hymns or knew when to stand and sit during the service, or for the youth set apart for additional instruction before first communion, the message was clear. Participation in the Reformed Church required more than just the fact one's parents and grandparents had adhered to the Reformed confession. In a sense the Reformed Church was becoming disestablished as the distinction grew between the Reformed community and participation in the Reformed Church.

In this respect the Réveil acted as a secularizing agent in the Protestant community. Though the awakening revived the spiritual life of the Reformed Church it also advanced the development of a secular perspective in the community. The Réveil rejected any inherent connection between religious faith and the historical community by defining as Christians only those who confessed and internalized certain beliefs. Over time the Reformed Church became identified with a particular population. The renewal emphasized personal responsibility in matters of faith over the communal aspects of religion. For evangelicals' inclusion in the church resulted from an individual decision and not a circumstance of birth or culture. Where before one thought in terms of a Reformed community, evangelicals thought in terms of the faithful. Through their enthusiasm, their inclusive and egalitarian forms of worship, and, on the part of the established churches, a fear of marginalization in a society increasingly characterized by voluntary forms of association, the distinction between the Reformed Church and community was generalized throughout the Protestant population. In the process the line between temporal and spiritual realities became more distinct. The moral imperative for confessional solidarity declined, and the traditional sense of a Reformed community diminished.

Protestant identity remained a powerful force. The near universal enthusiasm with which Protestants celebrated the three hundredth anniversary of the Synod of 1559 demonstrated its continuing force, but it was an identity that was now much more open to diversity. Following the White Terror the Reformed community in Bas-Languedoc was in many ways a closed society in which the need for confessional solidarity limited its capacity for change and adaptation. The Réveil challenged that solidarity at its religious core. As a result, in 1859 it was difficult to identify a theological basis for Reformed identity beyond a belief in individual liberty that was shared by an increasing number outside the Protestant faith. But the Réveil also left the community with a greatly expanded network of voluntary associations and social institutions that bound Protestants together without specific reference to a single church or ideology. These interactions, interpreted according to a common heritage, provided a basis for greater flexibility to deal with and accommodate internal diversity and external influences. Protestant identity remained, but not in a way that necessarily excluded or was threatened by other, less particular forms of identity and allegiance.

NOTES

Introduction

1. There are exceptions of course. James Osen's biography of the noted preacher Adolphe Monod, Robert Zaretsky's study of Protestant resistance to German occupation in WW II, and Burdette Poland's examination of Protestantism during the French Revolution are the only historical monographs in English on modern French Protestants of which I am aware. Robert Zaretsky, *Nîmes at War: Religion, Politics, and Public Opinion in the Gard, 1938-1944* (State College, PA: Pennsylvania State University, 1995); James L. Osen, *Prophet and Peacemaker: The Life of Adolphe Monod* (Lanham, Maryland: University Press of America, 1984); Burdette Poland, *French Protestantism and the French Revolution: A Study in Church and State, Thought and Religion (1685-1815)* (Princeton: Princeton University Press, 1957). French Protestants do figure less directly in a variety of other studies. Some examples are Philip Nord, *The Republican Moment: Struggles for Democracy in Nineteenth-Century France* (Cambridge, MA: Harvard University Press, 1995); John Woodbridge, *Revolt in Prerevolutionary France: The Prince de Conti's Conspiracy against Louis XV, 1755-1757* (Baltimore: Johns Hopkins University Press, 1995); Gwynne Lewis, *The Second Vendée: The Continuity of Counterrevolution in the Department of the Gard, 1789-1815* (Oxford: Clarendon Press, 1978); Brian Fitzpatrick, *Catholic royalism in the department of the Gard, 1814-1852* (Cambridge: Cambridge University Press, 1983).

More exists in French, including the recent book by William Edgar, *La Carte protestante. Le protestantisme francophone et la modernité (1815-1848),* (Geneva: Labor et Fides, 1997). This work covers the same period as the present one, but Edgar's purpose "is not strictly historical, even though historical givens are useful for situating thought in its context. In other words, our attention will bear less on events and circumstances than on apologetical production." He focuses on how attitudes towards modernity are revealed in Protestant apologetics. Ibid., 146. Though using a different approach his conclusions largely confirm our own. See also Daniel Robert, *Les Eglises réformées en France, 1800-1830* (Paris: Presses Universitaires de France, 1961); André Encrevé, *Protestants français au milieu du XIXe siècle: Les réformés de 1848 à*

1870 (Geneva: Editions Labor et Fides, 1986); Idem., *Les protestants en France de 1800 à nos jours: histoire d'une réintégration* (Paris: Stock, 1985); Jean Baubérot, *Le Retour des Huguenots: La vitalité protestante, XIXe-XXe siècles* (Paris: Les Editions du Cerf; Geneva: Les Editions Labor et Fides, 1985), 301-307; Alice Wemyss, *Histoire du Réveil, 1790-1849* (Paris: Les Bergers et les Mages, 1977).

    2. Philippe Joutard, "The Museum of the Desert: The Protestant Minority," in *Realms of Memory,* vol. 1, *Conflicts and Divisions,* ed. Pierre Nora, trans. Arthur Goldhammer (New York: Columbia University Press, 1996), 366. Some contemporary Protestant commentators are concerned by the invisibility of their confession in French society. Jean-Paul Willaime worries that Protestantism is so closely connected to modernity in its doctrinal and ecclesiastical diversity and individualism that it is being subsumed by society. Similarly, Jannine Garrisson, who claimed the "Homme protestant" is one who takes pride in difference, asks whether Protestants should resume the struggle in order to remain Protestant. In a public speech, the jurist Jean Carbonnier warned that Protestantism is "in danger of crumbling away," and that "wasting away is perhaps a mortal danger worse than perishing." In the same vein, the sociologist of religion, Jean Baubérot, published a book asking the question "Must Protestantism Die?" Jean Baubérot, *Le Protestantisme, Doit-il mourir?* (Geneva: Labor et Fides, 1988). Jean-Paul Willaime, *La précarité protestante: Sociologie du protestantism contemporain* (Geneva: Labor et Fides, 1995), 9-10. Jannine Garrisson, *L'Homme protestant* (Paris: Hachette, 1980).

    Reason for this anxiety is hinted at by a Gallup-L'Express poll conducted in France in October 1985. Of those asked their feelings about Protestantism 31 percent said they viewed it favorably, while only 4 percent had a negative attitude towards the confession. Nearly two-thirds, however, were entirely indifferent. Moreover, when asked which term best fit Protestantism, a majority (54 percent) answered "Anglo-Saxon." Only 13 percent replied "socialist" even though at the time seven Protestants were serving as ministers in the Socialist government and since then two of the last three Socialist Prime Ministers were Protestants (Michel Rocard and Lionel Jospin). For a recapitulation of the Gallup-L'Express poll see, Baubérot, *Protestantisme, Doit-il mourir?,* 11.

    3. Georges Thiébaud, *Le parti protestant* (Paris, 1895), 18; Charles Maurras, *Le Soleil,* April 23, 1898; Edouard Tavanier, *L'Univers* February 15, 1901; cited in Jean Baubérot, "L'Anti-protestantisme politique à la fin du XIXe siècle," *Révue d'histoire et de philosophie religieuses* 53 (1973): 175-221, 183, 188. Marvin L. Brown, *Louis Veuillot: French Ultramontane Catholic, Journalist and Layman, 1813-1883* (Durham, NC: Moore Publishing Company, 1977), 139. Louis Veuillot, *L'Univers,* August 26, 1851. Félicité de Lamennais, *Essay on Indifference in Matters of Religion,* Lord Stanley of Alderly, trans., (London: John MacQueen, 1895), 87-132; Idem, *Défense de l'Essai sur l'indifference en maitère de religion,* 2eme édition (Paris: Méquignon fils ainé, 1821), 212-220. Robert Gildea, *The Past in French History* (New Haven: Yale University Press, 1994), 230-243. See also the introduction Prévost-Paradol wrote to the second edition of

Samuel Vincent, *Le Protestantisme en France*, 2 ed. (Paris: Michel Lévy frères, 1860).

4. Samuel Vincent, *Le Protestantism en France* (Nîmes: Bianquis-Gignoux, 1829), 480.

5. On Protestantism and politics see André Siegfried, *Géographie électorale de l'Ardèche sous la Troisième République* (Paris: Colin, 1949); Stuart Schram, *Protestantism and Politics in France* (Alençon, 1954); Jean-Daniel Rocque, "Positions et Tendances politiques des protestants nîmois au XIXe siècle," in *Droite et Gauche de 1789 à nos jours* (Montpellier, 1975), 199-232; Alain Sabatier, *Religion et Politique au XIXe siècle. Le canton de Vernouz-en-Vivarais* (Vernoux, 1975); Pierre Poujol, "Socialistes et chrétiens (1848-1948)," *Questions de notre temps*, January 1956, 1-60; Ibid., December 1956, 1-79. André Encrevé agrees that Reformed Protestants voted with the Left in the nineteenth century, but sees it as more a measure of their anti-Catholicism than of an inherent affinity for the leftist agendas. Encrevé, *Protestants français*, 367-506, 909-976.

6. A similar argument is made more recently by the sociologist Steven Bruce, who argues that despite periodic renewals the internal logic of Protestantism's approach to modern culture leads it into a "spiral of decline." Steven Bruce, *A House Divided: Protestantism, Schism and Secularization* (New York: Routledge, 1990), 11.

7. Two recent books have again drawn attention to the charged religious language and symbols with which the shape of French society was debated in the nineteenth century. Philip Nord, *The Republican Moment,* and Robert Gildea, *Past in French History*. See also Adrian Dansette, *Religious History of France in the Nineteenth Century* (New York: Herder and Herder, 1961); Gérard Cholvy and Yves-Marie Hilaire, *Histoire religieuse de la France* Contemporaine,vol. 1 *1800/1880* (Toulouse: Privas, 1985); Jean Baubérot, *Le protestantisme doit-il mourir?*, 53-70.

8. For example the popular movie of René Allio, *Les Camisards* (1972), the novels of André Chamson, *La Superbe* (Paris: Plon, 1967), Max Olivier-Lacamp, *Les Feux de la Colère* and Jean-Pierre Chabrol, *Les fous de Dieu* (Paris: Gallimard, 1967); or memoirs like André Chamson's, *Le chiffre de nos jours* (Paris: Gallimard, 1954) and Jean-Pierre Chabrol, *Le bonheur du manchot* (Paris: Editions Robert Laffont, 1993). On the power of memory and geography in French Protestantism see Joutard, "The Museum of the Desert," 353-377.

9. Gwynne Lewis, *Second Vendée*; Brian Fitzpatrick, *Catholic royalism*.

10. On this broader awakening see W. R. Ward, *The Protestant Evangelical Awakening* (Cambridge: Cambridge University Press, 1992); Clarke Garrett, *Spirit Possession and Popular Religion: From the Camisards to the Shakers* (Baltimore, MD: Johns Hopkins University Press, 1987); Nathan O. Hatch, *The Democratization of American Christianity* (New Haven: Yale University Press, 1989); Richard Carwardine, *Transatlantic Evangelicalism: Popular Evangelicalism in Britain and America, 1790-1865* (Westport, CT: Greenwood Press, 1978); Jay P. Dolan, *Catholic Revivalism: The American Experience, 1830-1900* (Notre Dame, IN: University of Notre Dame Press, 1978).

11. Eugen Weber, *Peasants into Frenchmen: The Modernization of Rural France, 1870-1914* (Palo Alto, CA: Stanford University Press, 1976); André Siegfried, *Géographie électorale,* 66-73; idem, *Tableau politique de la France de l'Ouest sous la Troisème République* (Paris: Colin, 1913), 3-7. On the origins of this thesis see Roger Chartier, *Cultural History: Between Practices and Representations,* Lydia G. Cochrane, trans. (Ithaca, NY: Cornell University Press, 1988), 172-200.

12. Peter Sahlins, *Forest Rites: The War of the Demoiselles in Nineteenth-Century France* (Cambridge, MA: Harvard University Press, 1994); James R. Lehning, *Peasant and French: Cultural contact in rural France during the nineteenth century* (Cambridge: Cambridge University Press, 1995); Tessie P. Liu, *The Weaver's Knot: The Contradictions of Class Struggle and Family Solidarity in Western France, 1750-1914* (Ithaca, NY: Cornell University Press, 1994); Maurice Agulhon, *La République au Village: les populations du Var de la Révolution à la II*ᵉ *République* (Paris: Seuil, 1979); Edward Berenson, *Populist Religion and Left-Wing Politics in France* (Princeton: Princeton University Press, 1984).

13. David Blackbourn, *Marpingen: Apparitions of the Virgin Mary in Nineteenth-Century Germany* (New York: Alfred A. Knopf, 1994); Thomas Kselman, *Miracles and Prophecy in Nineteenth-Century France* (New Brunswick, NJ: Rutgers University Press, 1984); Michael Graetz, *The Jews in Nineteenth-Century France: From the French Revolution to the Alliance Israélite Universelle,* Jane Marie Todd, trans. (Stanford: Stanford University Press, 1996); Judith Devlin, *The Superstitious Mind: French Peasants and the Supernatural in the Nineteenth Century* (New Haven: Yale University Press, 1987); Alex Owen, *Women, Power and Spiritualism in Late Victorian England* (Philadelphia: University of Pennsylvania Press, 1987); Jonathon Sperber, *Popular Catholicism in Nineteenth-Century Germany* (Princeton: Princeton University Press, 1984); Hugh McLeod, *European Religion in the Age of Great Cities, 1830-1930* (New York: Routledge, 1995); idem, *Religion and the People of Western Europe, 1789-1970* (London, New York: Oxford University Press, 1981); David Hempton, *Religion and the People: Methodism and Popular Religion c. 1750-1900* (New York: Routledge, 1996). Also the review essays of David Blackbourn, "The Catholic Church in Europe since the French Revolution: A Review Article," *Comparative Studies in Society and History* 33 (1991): 778-90; Caroline Ford, "Religion and Popular Culture in Modern Europe," *Journal of Modern History* 65 (1993): 152-175.

14. Suzanne Desan, *Reclaiming the Sacred: Lay Religion and Popular Politics in Revolutionary France* (Ithaca, NY: Cornell University Press, 1990); Caroline Ford, *Creating the Nation in Provincial France: Religion and Political Identity in Brittany* (Princeton: Princeton University Press, 1993); David Blackbourn, *Class, Religion and Local Politics in Wilhelmine Germany: The Centre Party in Wurttemberg before 1914* (New Haven: Yale University Press, 1980); David Hempton, *Religion and Political Culture in Britain and Ireland: from the Glorious Revolution to the Decline of Empire* (Cambridge: Cambridge

University Press, 1996). A valuable overview of scholarship on religion and politics in Germany is Lavinia Anderson, "Piety and Politics: Recent Work on German Catholicism," *Journal of Modern History* 63 (1991): 681-716.

15. Peter Berger, *The Sacred Canopy: Elements of a Sociological Theory of Religion* (Garden City, NY: Doubleday, 1967); Thomas Luckmann, *The Invisible Religion: The Problem of Religion in Modern Society* (New York: Macmillan, 1967).

16. Karel Dobbelaere, "Secularization Theory and Sociological Paradigms: A Reformation of the Private-Public Dichotomy and the Problem of Societal Integration," *Sociological Analysis* 46 (1985): 378-387.

17. Brian Wilson, *Religion in Sociological Perspective* (Oxford: Oxford University Press, 1982), 50-55.

Chapter 1

1. Thus the Methodist evangelist Charles Cook found in 1819, that he could only get to the village of Boissières, in the agriculturally rich Vaunage, after a two-mile walk as the road was impassable by coach despite favorable weather. Methodist Missionary Society [hereafter MMS] FBN European Correspondence 4 #110-111, Charles Cook to Committee of Methodist Missionary Society in London, June 22 - November 5, 1819.

2. Emilien Frossard, *Tableau pittoresque, scientifique et moral de Nîmes et de ses environs à vingt lieues à la ronde* (Paris: Delay, 1846), 95. "An olive or a fig tree, a grape vine, sometimes a mulberry tree, the small masets [sic], reduced to their simplest expression, offer stone mounds in oriental forms. All that lacks is a protective date tree to transport the viewer to the soil of Syria." Mazets were the small parcels of land popular with residents of Nîmes as retreats from the city and a means to supplement their diet and income with fruit and vegetables. See Leslie Page Moch, *Paths to the City: Regional Migration in Nineteenth-Century France* (Beverly Hills, California: Sage Publications, 1983), 86-90.

3. Archives du département du Gard (hereafter ADG) 6M 111, Recensement de 1851.

4. Ibid.; ADG 6M 108, Recensement de la population - 1846. J.D. Roque, "Positions et tendances politiques," 200-202.

5. Frossard, *Tableau de pittoresque*, 354-355.

6. According to statistics published in 1842, more than 19,000 hectares in the arrondissement of Le Vigan were in chestnuts. Hector Rivoire, *Statistiques du département du Gard*, 2 vols. (Nîmes: n.p., 1842), 2:796-797. ADG uncatalogued, *Annuaire du Gard, 1849* (Nîmes: n.p., 1849). Roger Price, *An Economic History of Modern France, 1730-1914*, revised edition (London: The MacMillan Press, Ltd.,1981), 58. Also, Emmanuel Le Roy Ladurie, *The Peasants of Languedoc*, trans. John Day (Chicago: University of Illinois Press, 1980), 66-73. Jean Vidalenc, *La société française de 1815 à 1848: Le peuple des campagnes* (Paris: Editions Marcel Rivière, 1970), 237; Fitzpatrick, *Catholic royalism*, 4-5.

7. Vidalenc, *Le peuple des campagnes*, 236-237; Suzanne Savey, "Essai de reconstitution de la structure agraire des villages de Sardan et d'Aspères (Gard) sous l'ancien régime à l'aide des compoix," *Annales du Midi*, 81 (1969): 41-54. Hector Rivoire, *Statistiques du département du Gard*,2:73. According to Rivoire, an employee of the Prefecture at Nîmes and a follower of Saint-Simon, 116,098 hectoliters of eau-de-vie were produced in the Gard, 1,154 hectoliters of which was consumed locally and the rest shipped to external destinations. *Annuaire du Gard - 1849*, n. p.

8. Rivoire, *Statistiques du Gard*, 2: 776-797; *Annuaire du Gard - 1849*, n. p.; Leo A. Loubère, *Radicalism in Mediterranean France: Its Rise and Decline, 1848-1914* (Albany, NY: State University of New York Press, 1974), 84, 98.

9. Hugh D. Clout, *Agriculture in France on the Eve of the Railway Age* (London: Croom Helm, 1980), 144.

10. Frossard, *Tableau pittoresque*, 355; Rivoire, *Statistiques du Gard*, 2:67.

11. Raymond Huard, *La préhistoire des partis: Le mouvement républicain en Bas-Languedoc, 1848-1881* (Paris: Presses de la fondation national des sciences politiques, 1982), 34-35; G. Lautier, "La sériculture et les industries de la soie dans le pays cévenol," *Bulletin de la Société Languedocienne de Géographie*, série 2, 4(1930):79-86. According to the census of 1851, women made up more than half of the work force in textiles. ADG 6M 111, Recensement du 1851.

12. Rivoire listed the towns of Uzès, Alès, Genolhac, St-Côme, Calvisson, Quissac, Sauve, St-Hippolyte, Sumène, St-Laurent, Anduze, St-Jean-du-Gard, Le Vigan, and most of the Vaunage. In addition, Sommières was an important producer of woolens, where seventeen establishments employed 1,310 workers, and produced 1,485,700 kg of cloth worth 2,870,900 francs. Rivoire, *Statistiques du Gard*, 2:44-45, 69; Fitzpatrick, *Catholic royalism*, 11, 14.

13. ADG 6M 111. Many workers in the textile industry were children and many of those working within the family were likely not included in the census figures. For a more detailed look at the relations of family and production in the textile industry see Tessie P. Liu, *The Weaver's Knot*.

14. Gwynne Lewis, "A Cevenol Community in Crisis: The Mystery of L'Homme à Moustache," *Past & Present*, 109 (November 1985):144-175, 167.

15. Moch, *Paths to the City*, 201-205; Raymond Dugrand, *Villes et campagnes en Bas-Languedoc* (Paris: Presses Universitaires Françaises, 1963), 401-415.

16. Already in 1842, large quantities of raw and spun silk were being shipped from Anduze and St-Jean-du-Gard to Marseille, Lyon, St-Etienne and Paris. Rivoire, *Statistiques du Gard*, 1:160-161.

17. Ibid., 1:53. See also the description of filatures in Frossard, *Tableau pittoresque*, 311-312.

18. Ibid., 2: 160-161; Fitzpatrick, *Catholic royalism*, 11-13.

19. Ibid., 12; Price, *Economic History of Modern France*, 122, 124; Huard, *Mouvement républicain*, 29-30.

20. Ibid. On his visit to the foundries around Alès, Frossard reported "the ear

is singularly struck by the sounds which arrive to it. It is German, Belgian and English above all, then various French dialects, from the drawling sound of the St-Stephenois to the less accentuated sound of the inhabitants of Valenciennes." Frossard, *Tableau pittoresque*, 359.

21. ADG 6M 111.

22. Le Roy Ladurie, *Les Paysans de Languedoc* (Paris: S.E.V.P.E.N., 1966), 98-102; Moch, *Paths to the City*, 34-37, 41-78.

23. Jean Pitié, *L'Homme et son espace: L'Exode rural en France du XVI* *siècle à nos jours* (Paris: Editions du CNRS, 1987), 523-525, 541-545, 575-579.

24. Pitié provides a valuable bibliography of *l'exode* rural, in *L'Homme et son espace*. Most studies examine the question from a national perspective and tend to overlook regional variations and characteristics. Leslie Moch provides a corrective by examining the migration patterns from the three towns of Le Vigan, Villefort and Langogne. Moch, *Paths to the City*, 39-78.

25. Le Vigan gained only eighty-four residents (1.71 percent) during the period 1831-1851. ADG 6M, 105, 111. For 1851-1856, taking into account birth and death rates, Moch estimates a net migration loss for Le Vigan of 5.77 percent, Langogne and Villefort showed similar results, 5.17 percent and 6.38 percent respectively. Moch, *Paths to the City*, 47, 57.

26. There does not appear to be any correlation between confession and demographic change. Trèves, a canton with one of the smallest Protestant populations, was one of only two cantons to experience a net population loss. See also Paul V. Adams, "The Determinants of Local Variations in Fertility in Bas-Languedoc and Roussillon during the Mid-Nineteenth Century," *Annales de démographie historique* 1990: 155-172.

27. The canton of Lasalle for example, had a net growth of less than one percent. The population of the town of Lasalle itself, however, increased by nearly 10 percent, while four of its dependant communes showed a net loss or no change at all. The same process was at work in St-Jean-du-Gard. Mialet, a commune of 1,381 in 1831, had only seven more residents in 1851, while the cantonal seat grew nearly 9 percent. ADG 6M 111, Recensement de 1851.

28. Fitzpatrick, *Catholic royalism*, 140-141; ADG 5M 118-122, Epidémie de choléra 1835, 1837; ADG 42 J 170, 115-122, Conf. pastorale, 2 mars 1836.

29. In 1847 the Municipal Government gave the Consistory of Nîmes an extra 6,000 francs for distribution to destitute Protestants in the city. ADG J 196, Budget de l'Eglise. On the Second Republic in the Gard see, Raymond Huard, "Souvenir et tradition révolutionnaires: Le Gard: 1848-1851," *Annales historiques de la Révoltion française*, N° 258 (1984): 207-245.

30. This is evident in the electoral success of the Protestants under the censitairy regime of Louis-Philippe. They were not able to repeat this success with the universal suffrage of the Second Republic, and they had been nearly totally excluded from office by the much higher tax qualification under the Bourbons. Fitzpatrick, *Catholic royalism*.

31. One artisan remarked, "It is necessary to always keep in mind that at Nîmes a Catholic artisan has a mostly Catholic clientele and a Protestant artisan

a clientele mostly Protestant." Quoted in J.D. Roque, "Protestants nîmois au XIXe siècle," 205. Brian Fitzpatrick has found evidence that mine owners in the region of Alès tried to exclude Protestants from their work force, going to the extent of importing Piedmontese rather than hiring local Protestants. He also tells of a scheme of Catholic entrepreneurs to maintain the loyalty of the Catholic unemployed by building a desalination plant in the Camargue which would employ 2,000. Fitzpatrick, *Catholic royalism*,141-142, 147.

32. On the Second Republic and early-Empire in the Gard see Huard, *Mouvement républicain*, 27-141; Huard, "Montagne rouge et Montagne blanche en Languedoc-Roussillon sous la Seconde République," in *Droite et Gauche en Languedoc-Roussillon*, 139-160; André Encrevé, "Protestantisme et politique. Les protestants du Midi en décembre 1851," *Droite et Gauche en Languedoc-Roussillon*, 161-187.

33. Vidalenc, *Peuple des campagnes*, 238.

34. Félix de Lafarelle, *Du Progrès social au profit des classes populaires non indignes, ou Etudes philosophiques et économiques sur l'amélioration matérielle et morale du plus grand nombre*, 2 vols. (Paris, 1839). De Lafarelle received a prize from the Académie française for this work.

35. ADG V 348, Affaire de Gallargues, 1832-1833, particularly, Préfet to Ministre de la Justice et des Cultes, Nîmes, Oct. 20, 1832; Préfet to Ministre de la Justice et des Cultes, Nîmes, Oct. 27, 1832; ibid., Commissar du Police to Préfet, Sommières, Feb. 3, 1840. The police report noted that Reboul was not favored by the *gens aisés*, and for this and his appeals to the people he not only recommended against Reboul's appointment, but also that Reboul be forced to leave the area. Reboul did not receive the position but was later appointed as a pastor in the Consistory of Calvisson. In 1854, however, he was dismissed under charges of homosexuality. ADG V 491, Affaire du Pasteur Reboul.

36. ADG 42 J 25, B-73, Affaire de Valleraugue, 1844-1845.

37. Maurice Agulhon, *The Republic in the Village: The People of the Var from the French Revolution to the Second Republic* (Cambridge: Cambridge University Press, 1982); Philippe Vigier, *La Seconde République dans la région alpine*, 2 vols. (Paris: Presses Universitaires de France, 1963). On the Midi in the Second Republic see Ted W. Margadant, *French Peasants in Revolt: The Insurrection of 1851* (Princeton: Princeton University Press, 1979), 3-103.

38. An exception was the brief career of Louis Roque, a rural bandit of the type described by E. J. Hobsbawm in *Primitive Rebels: Studies in Archaic Forms of Social Movement in the 19th and 20th Centuries* (New York: W.W. Norton & Co., 1965); especially Chapter II, 13-29. Roque roamed the Protestant regions of the Gard and Lozère with a band of followers between 1823 and 1826, frustrating attempts to apprehend him with the tacit complicity of the general population. Lewis, "A Cevenol Community in Crisis," 144-175.

Chapter 2

1. ADG 4 U 5 26, Rapport du Procureur général (Thourel), undated [1849]. Forcade la Roquette, Ministre de l'Intérieur, Discours prononcé au corps législatif, 27 janvier 1869; quoted in Raymond Huard, *Mouvement républicain*, 17. Archives nationales (hereafter AN) F^{19} 10433, Plainte contre M. de Sabatier-Plantier, pasteur à St.-Frezal-de-Ventalon, Mende, 17 aout 1875.

2. James N. Hood, "Protestant-Catholic Relations," *Journal of Modern History* 43 (1971): 247. Jansenists also suffered under the religious absolutism of the French monarchy, as a division within Catholicism it was much more difficult for the state to marginalize them in society than was the case with the Huguenots. On Jansenism and the French state see Dale K. Van Kley, *The Damiens Affair and the Unraveling of the Ancien Régime, 1750-1770* (Princeton: Princeton University Press, 1984). It is important to note that though repressed, French Protestants did influence, if indirectly, state policy. See John D. Woodbridge, *Revolt in Prerevolutionary France*, 4-23, 144-183.

3. Garrison, *L'Homme Protestant*, 7. Brian Fitzpatrick, identifies a similar tendency for the Catholic population to define itself, and especially its politics, in counter-distinction to Gardois Protestants. Fitzpatrick, *Catholic royalism*.

4. It was as a result of the Albigensian Crusade, preached against the heretics of southern France, that the area became part of the Capetian patrimony. Le Roy Ladurie, *Peasants of Languedoc*, 165.

5. Archives municipale de Nîmes, LL 5, fol. 244, Registre des délibérations du conseil de ville, published in *Textes et documents sur L'Histoire du protestantisme dans le Gard*, ed., Pierre Fanguin (Nîmes: Archives départementales du Gard, 1983), 15, 17.

6. Quoted in Le Roy Ladurie, *Peasants of Languedoc*, 165.

7. Ibid., 171.

8. However, only four Huguenots were executed. The rest escaped into the Cévennes. Léonard, *Histoire générale du protestantisme*, 114-115; Louis Ménard, *Histoire de Nismes*, 5 vols. (Paris, 1850), 5:10-60; Le Roy Ladurie, *Peasants of Languedoc*, 176-178.

9. Fanguin, *Textes et documents*, 35-40; Ménard, *Histoire de Nismes*, 5:585-589; Léonard, *Histoire général du protestantisme*, 2:332-333.

10. Fanguin, *Textes et documents*, 35; Léonard, *Histoire général du protestantisme*, 2:357.

11. Quoted in ibid., 363. Another pastor, Elie Merlat, after suffering persecution and fleeing his ministry to seek refuge at Lausanne, still wrote: "The sovereigns, whom God has permitted to arrive at absolute power, have no law which rules them in respect towards their subjects. Their only law is their will, and that which pleases them is allowable to them in this relation." Merlat further argued that resisting a monarch was equivalent to placing the temporal over the eternal, and persecution only made one long more for heaven. "He who only looks at the present life can only weakly interest the children of God, and for that why refuse the obedience which is their due? . . . The greater the miseries the

greater the Christian's dislike of the world, the greater his desire for heaven where he contemplates his repose. Thus, death, which seems the greatest of evils, becomes the greatest good." Quoted in Joutard, *Les Camisards* (Paris: Editions Gallimard/Julliard, 1976), 26.

12. Ibid., 358-359. Jon Butler, *The Huguenots in America: A Refugee People in New World Society* (Cambridge: Harvard University Press, 1983), 15.

13. Quoted in Joutard, *Les Camisards*, 31-32.

14. Quoted in Charles Bost, *Les Prédicants protestants des Cévennes et du Bas-Languedoc, 1684-1700*, 2 vols. (Paris, 1912), 1:13.

15. Léonard, *Histoire général du protestantisme*, 2:367-372.

16. Samuel Mours, "Essai d'évaluation de la population protestante réformée au xvii° et xviii° siècle," *Bulletin de la société de l'histoire du protestantisme français*, (hereafter *BSHPF*) 103 (1958): 17.

17. Léonard, *Histoire generale du protestantisme* 2:374.

18. Cited in Bost, *Prédicants protestants*, 1:40.

19. Ibid., 1:39.

20. Léonard, *Histoire générale du protestantisme*, 2:381-389; Joutard, *Les Camisards*, 28-30.

21. For example the call of Paul Coulagnac, a.k.a. Dauphiné, to serve as minister at one of these assemblies. *BSHPF*, 1901: 339. Charles Bost counted sixty such preachers in Bas-Languedoc between 1686 and 1700.

22. Joutard, *Les Camisards*, 38-52.

23. Ibid., 63-69.

24. Ibid., 61. For a fuller discussion of this prophetism and its possible links with other prophetic movements of the eighteenth and early nineteenth centuries see Clarke Garrett, *Spirit Possession and Popular Religion*, 13-59.

25. Philippe Joutard, *La Légende des Camisards: Une sensibilité au passé* (Paris: Editions Gallimard, 1977), 25-28.

26. Joutard, *Légende des Camisards*, 28-39; Fanguin, *Textes et documents*, 107-109.

27. Joutard, *Légende des Camisards*, 294-300.

28. Charles Coquerel, *Histoire des églises du désert depuis la fin de règne de Louis XIV jusqu'à nos jours*, 2 vols. (Montpellier, 1861), 1:25.

29. Hood, "Protestant-Catholic Relations," 251.

30. Garrett, *Spirit Possession and Popular Religion*, 13-34; Denis Ligou et Philippe Joutard, "Les Déserts," in *Histoire des protestants en France* (Toulouse: Privat, 1977), 189-262; Poland, *French Protestantism and the French Revolution*, Chapters 2-3.

31. On Protestant relations with the monarchy and involvement in the rebellion of the Prince de Conti see Woodbridge, *Revolt in Prerevolutionary France*, 48-71, 115-160; Hood, "Protestant-Catholic Relations," 252.

32. For references to local schisms see Articles XXXII and XXXVI of "Actes du Synode national des églises réformées, depuis le prémier du mois de juin 1763, jusqu'au dixième inclusivement," in M. M. Haag, *La France Protestante, ou vies des Protestants Français qui sont fait un nom dans l'histoire depuis les prémiers*

temps de la Réformation jusqu'à la reconnaissance du principe de la liberté des cultes par l'Assemblée Nationale, 10 vols. (Geneva: Slatkine Reprints, 1966), 10:452-458. Alice Wemyss, "Les Protestants du Midi pendant la Révolution," *Journal du Midi* 69 (1957): 310, 318.

33. Haag, *La France Protestante,* 10:458.

34. Burdette Poland, *French Protestantism and the French Revolution: A Study in Church and State, Thought and Religion (1685-1815)* (Princeton: Princeton University Press, 1957), 230-236; Robert, *Eglises Réformées,* 9-16; Denis Ligou, "L'Eglise Réformée du Désert, fait économique et social," *Révue d'histoire économique et sociologique* 32 (1954): 162-163.

35. This hermeneutic was evident even in the moderate pastor, Paul Rabaut, who died in 1793, and once calculated from Biblical evidence that the end times were near, and a "prince-restorer" of the church would appear in 1802, the year Napoleon Bonaparte promulgated the Concordat which established the Reformed Church as a state church. Paul Rabaut, *Lettres à divers,* 2 vols. (Paris: Charles Dardier, 1892), ed., Charles Dardier, 2:88-89.

36. Georges Dieny, "Essai sur la prédication de Rabaut de Saint-Etienne" (thèse de théologie: Faculté de théologie de l'Eglise Réformée à Paris, 1907), 19. John D. Woodbridge, "L'Influence des philosophes français sur les pasteurs réformés du Languedoc pendant la deuxième moitié du XVIIIᵉ siècle" (Thèse de la 3ᵉ cycle: Faculté des Lettres de L'Université de Toulouse, 1969), 291-371.

37. Rabaut de Saint-Etienne, son of Paul Rabaut, is said to have drafted the cahier. "Cahier de doléance, plaintes, et réprésentations du tiers-état de la sénéchausée de Nîmes, pour être porté aux Etats généraux de 1789," *Archives parlementaires,* 4: 242, chap. 4, art. 2. Charles H. Pouthas, *Une famille de bourgeoisie française de Louis XIV à Napoléon* (Paris, 1934), 83, n. 2.

38. "Procès-verbal 26 juin 1790 - Récitation des événements à Nîmes du 13, 14, 16, et 17 juin 1790, envoyé par l'administration du département du Gard," *Archives parlementaires,* 16:482-483, 509, 685. See also Ibid., 20:47, 67, 143; 22:406, 503, 540-544, 587, 663.

39. Jacques Godechot, *La Contre-Révolution (1789-1804)* (Paris: Presses Universitaires de France, 1961), 248-253; Tackett, "Women and Men in Counterrevolution," 691-701.

40. Joséphine Siméoni, "Club et Société populaire à Nîmes," (Mémoire de maîtrise, Université de Montpellier, 1972); Anne-Marie Duport, "La Société populaire de Nîmes 1791-1795," *Annales Historiques de la Révolution* Française 1984: 519-520.

41. Among those guillotined was André Guizot, father of François Guizot. Ibid., 523-526; Hood, "Patterns of Popular Protest," 291-293; Jean Sentou, "Révolution et contre-révolution," in, ed., Philippe Wolff, *Histoire du Languedoc* (Toulouse: Privat, 1967), 467-468.

42. "Rapport de Feydall à Peré, septembre 1793," in *Rapports des Agents du Ministre de L'Interieur dans les Départements (1793-an II),* 3 vols., ed., Pierre Caron (Paris, 1933) I: 354.

43. G. Lautier, "La sériculture," 79-86.

44. Lewis, *The Second Vendée*, 41-79.

45. It should be noted that one reason the process proceeded so peacefully among Catholics was that much of this population was loyal to the refractory clergy. See Michel Vovelle, "Essai de Cartographie de la déchristianization sous la Révolution française," *Annales du Midi* 76 (1964): 531; Michel Vovelle, *Religion et Révolution: La déchristianization de l'an II* (Paris: Librairie Hachette, 1976), 32-64; Robert, *Eglises Réformées*, 8; John D. Woodbridge, "The Reformed Pastors of Languedoc Face the Movement of Dechristianization, (1793-1794)," *Problèmes d'Histoire du Christiamsme* 13 (1984): 77-89. Of the 106 Reformed pastors in Languedoc studied by Woodbridge only three are known to have persisted in their duties.

46. Robert, *Eglise Réformées*, 32-40. According to Robert, in 1788-1789 there were thirty-eight pastors active in the province of Bas-Languedoc. In 1799, there were only twenty-seven. See also Emile Léonard, *Histoire ecclésiastique des Réformés français au XVIII* siècle* (Paris, 1940), 204-210.

47. Lewis stated, "[f]or the only time in the Revolution political, patriotic, and socio-economic forces triumphed over the historic struggle between the Catholic and the Protestant elites." Lewis, *Second Vendée*, 223; Hood, "Patterns of Popular Protest," 290-291.

48. Lewis, *Second Vendee*, 81-115, 153-218. See also Gwynne Lewis, "The White Terror of 1815 in the Department of the Gard: Counter-Revolution, Continuity and the Individual," *Past & Present* 58 (February 1973): 108-135.

49. See for example the letter of the Prefect of the Gard praising the Protestants for their support of the Empire. Daniel Robert, *Textes et documents relatifs à l'histoire des Eglises réformées de France (periode 1800-1830)* (Geneva: Labor et Fides, 1962), 169; Lewis, *Second Vendée*, 154-156.

50. ADG 42 J 56, Correspondance du consistoire de Nismes, B 53²⁴, Olivier-Desmonts au Garde des Sceaux; Robert, Eglises Réformées, 267-301; Fitzpatrick, *Catholic royalism*, 28-59; Lewis, *Second Vendée*, 153-218.

Chapter 3

1. Robert, *Eglises réformées*, 67, n. 2, 262-265.

2. Based on Robert, *Eglises réformées*, 608-611. Only eight new temples were built during the first seven years of the July Monarchy compared to eleven that were constructed in the final two years of the Restoration. By 1848, there was a total of 131 Reformed temples maintained by the state in the Gard. ADG V 347, Tableaux des circonscriptions dressés en 1839 pour l'ensemble de département; ADG V 356-362, Dossiers des pasteurs Réformés. During the July Monarchy eighteen new positions were created in the Gard, making a total of seventy-three.

3. Corinne Negre, *Le Protestantisme nîmois à l'oeuvre*; Samuel Ingrand, *La Maison de santé protestante 1842-1945* (Nîmes: Lacour, 1992), 53.

4. Cited in Robert, *Eglises réformées*, 321-322.

5. Archives nationales [henceforth AN] BB¹⁸ 984 4302, Arrondissement de

Florac, juin-juillet 1818; BB¹⁸ 1129 6221, St-Hippolyte-du-Fort, juin-juillet 1825. On the abduction of Protestant youths see AN BB¹⁸ 1001 5852, Plainte du Sʳ Bonifas, protestant, à Lenoux (Tarn) aout 1820-mai 1821; BB¹⁸ 1168 1617, Plainte du Président du Consistoire de La Carme (Tarn) jan-mars 1825.

6. Samuel Vincent's funeral oration for Pastor Olivier-Desmonts, July 20, 1825, quoted in Pierre Petit, *Une Métropole protestante en Languedoc: Nîmes 1802-1848, Chronique et Textes* (Nîmes: Lacour/Eruditae Indagationes, 1989), 51. Robert, *Eglises réformées*, 320-324, 327-329. ADG 42 J 70, E-23; MMS FBN European Correspondence 4, Extracts from the journal of Charles Cook, June 22, 1819 - September 30, 1819. Jacques Olivier-Desmonts to Reverend C. Smith, Nîmes, 10 janvier 1815, in Frank Puaux, ed., "Lettres du Révérand Perrot et du Pasteur Olivier-Desmonts," *BSHPF* 67(1918): 221.

7. Fitzpatrick, *Catholic royalism*, 125.

8. Ibid., 125-126.

9. AN BB¹⁸ 1315 3998, Troubles politiques dans le Gard et occasionment dans l'Aude et le Tarn 1830-31. Also Emilien Frossard, *Evénements de Nîmes depuis le 27 juillet jusqu'au 2 septembre 1830* (Nîmes, 1830); Armand Cosson, "La Révolution de 1830 à Nîmes," *Annales historiques de la Révolution Française* 258 (Oct.-Dec. 1984): 528-540.

10. From Fitzpatrick, *Catholic royalism*, 101.

11. Frank Puaux, *Les Oeuvres du protestantisme français au XIXᵉ siècle* (Paris: Comité Protestant Français, 1893), xxii. ADG V 356-362, Dossiers des pasteurs réformées; Robert, *Eglises réformées*, 604-615.

12. Vincent, *Protestantisme en France*, 15, 255, 271. Olivier-Desmonts to C. Smith, Nîmes, 10 janvier 1815, *BSHPF*, 1918, 221; ADG 42 J 170, Conf. pastorale, 10 novembre 1830. For more on Protestant education in France see Garrisson, *L'Homme protestant*, 165-184; François Furet and Jean Ozouf, *Reading and Writing: Literacy in France from Calvin to Jules Ferry* (Cambridge: Cambridge University Press, 1982), 58-63; on largely Catholic education in the Gard see Richard Gildea, *Education in the Provinces: A Study of Three Departments* (Cambridge: University of Cambridge Press, 1986), 66-83, 138-156.

13. ADG 42 J 47, Consist. of Nîmes, 10 avril 1829; 1ᵉʳ mars 1833. ADG 42 J 170, Conf. pastorale, 19 février 1832.

14. Quoted in Furet and Ozouf, *Reading and Writing*, 120, 121. For Guizot on Christianity and revolution see François Guizot, *L'Eglise et la société chrétienne en 1861* (Paris: Michel Lévy frères, 1861), 264-265.

15. Gildea, *Education in Provincial France*, 66-83. Many in Reformed circles were skeptical of Guizot's willingness to make common cause with the Catholic Church. In April 1860, he was roundly criticized for his address to the Société pour l'encouragement de l'instruction primaire parmi les protestants de France, in which he called on all Christians to support the Roman Catholic Church in its trials during Italian unification. Guizot, *Eglise et la société*, 1-3.

16. Vincent, *Protestantisme en France*, 14, 271, 480. ADG 42 J 170, Conf. pastorale, novembre 1831.

17. Quoted in Gildea, *Education in the Provinces*, 79. Ibid., 233; Vincent,

Protestantisme en France, 276.

　18.　Gildea, *Education in the Provinces*, 233; Furet and Ozouf, *Reading and Writing*.

　19.　Vincent, *Protestantisme en France*, 272; ADG 42 J 170, Conf. pastorale, 10 novembre 1830; Petit, *Metropole protestante*, 42; Gildea, *Education in Provincial France*, 71-72.

　20.　Vincent, *Protestantisme en France*, 272; Furet and Ozouf, *Reading and Writing*, 308, also, 134-135; Jean-Marie-Robert de Lamennais, *De L'Enseignement mutuel* (St-Brieuc, 1819).

　21.　One pastor advised, "Sunday Schools are a complement to weekly schools. They reunite the children long after they leave the school bench and keep them from forgetting what they learned. Moreover, these schools have a religious aspect that is very useful." ADG 42 J 170, Conf. pastoral, 10 novembre 1830. Also, ibid., 2 mars 1831; 19 février 1832.

　22.　Vincent, *Protestantisme en France*, 268, 282. ADG 42 J 170, Conf. pastorale, 10 novembre 1830.

　23.　Rivoire, *Statistiques du Gard*, 2:390; MMS FBN European Correspondence, Extracts of the Journal of Charles Cook, Sept. 15, 1819.

　24.　ADG 42 J 47, Consist. of Nîmes, 11 mars 1831; 20 mai 1831; 3 février 1832. Rivoire, *Statistiques du Gard*, 2:390. The area had a better than average literacy rate for a department south of the Saint-Malo-Geneva line. Furet and Ozouf, *Reading and Writing*, 5-47. Gildea, *Education in Provincial France*, 73-75.

　25.　ADG 42 J 48, Consist. of Nîmes, 19 juin 1840. Ibid., 12 sept 1846; ADG 42 J 51, Consist. of Nîmes, 2 février 1866.

　26.　Between 1835 and 1840, this was about 6,000 francs a year in assistance. ADG 42 J 96, Consist. of Nîmes, Administration et comptabilité, 1828-1859; see also *Correspondance pastorale*, septembre 1845, n° 148: 1. This publication was edited by Ferdinand Fontanès, a pastor at Nîmes, to allow clergy of liberal theological dispositions to discuss issues of common interest.

　27.　Les Articles Organiques des Cultes Protestants, Art. 18, Art. 19, Art. 23, and Art. 24, reprinted in Robert, *Eglises réformées*, 78-83. In December 1852, the government of Louis-Napoleon Bonaparte, perhaps trying to co-opt the Protestant public, democratized the election of elders. Though in practice this had limited impact on the personnel of the consistories, the Consistory of Nîmes fiercely opposed the reform, and Jean-Paul Hugues, pastor at Anduze, declared the principle of Calvin's polity was not democracy "but rather *oligarchy* or if you prefer *aristocracy*." Of the 1852 reforms he complained, "oligarchy was replaced by mob rule." J.-P. Hugues, *Rapport lu à la Conférence pastorale du Gard, le 8 juin 1854, sur cette question: A l'aide des articles du Concordat concernant tous les cultes, de la loi de germinal, des décrets de mars 1852, des usages généralement accepté dans nos Eglises, déterminer la discipline aujourd'hui en viguer, et la comparer dans ses principales dispositions avec notre discipline historique* (Alais: Mme Veirun, 1854), 41, 42.

　28.　ADG V 491-492, Elections for the Tri-annual Renewal of Consistories,

1812-1853; ADG 3M 45, Listes électoraux. The only electoral lists for the Gard surviving from the July Monarchy are for the arrondissement of Vauvert (1841, 1843, 1846), and Uzès (1839, 1842, 1847), which includes the consistories of Vauvert, Calvisson, Sommières, St-Chaptes and Uzès. In addition to those paying at least 200 francs in yearly taxes, a few individuals chosen by the Prefect were also allowed to vote. Thus, the elder at Uzès, Pierre-Abraham Lafont, a retired lieutenant-colonel and Justice of the Peace, could vote though he only paid 111 francs in taxes. See also Bernard Serre, "Le protestantisme dans l'Eglise consistoriale de Lasalle (Gard), 1802-1848" (mémoire de Maîtrise, Montpellier, Université Paul Valéry, 1979), 58; Encrevé, *Protestants français*, 82-84; Robert, *Eglises réformées*, 112-116, 469-470.

29. See for example the dispute between the congregation of Mialet and the Consistory of St-Jean-du-Gard, or that in Valleraugue. AN F[19] 10389, Pastor Paul Laune; ADG 42 J 25, Correspondence of the Consist. of Nîmes, B-73, Affaire de Valleraugue. ADG 42 J 60, Correspondence of the Consist. of Nîmes, février 1845. AN F[19] 10440, Pétition de Mialet, 10 octobre 1834; ADG 42 J 47, Consist. of Nîmes, 23 mars 1834. Serre, "L'Eglise consistoriale de Lasalle," 58.

30. Hugues, *Rapport lu à la Conférence pastorale du Gard*, 37, 39.

31. AN F[19] 10389, Paul Laune, 1er septembre 1835 - 14 mars 1836.

32. Vincent, *Protestantisme en France*, 233-255; ADG 42 J 170, Conf. pastorale, 26 juin 1833; 25 mars 1835. Ibid., 25 mai 1831; 8 juin 1854; Hugues, *Rapport lu à la Conférence pastorale*, 38-41, 70. See also Robert, *Eglises réformées*, 91-97, 265-267, 314-316; Encrevé, *Protestants français*, 77-82. Jurisdictional conflicts and questions of legitimacy persisted even when synods returned in the Third Republic. Claude-France Hollard, "Conflits de pouvoir en Vaucluse dans l'Eglise réformée concordataire" *BSHPF* 144 (1998): 617-646.

33. ADG 42 J 170, Conf. pastorale, 19 septembre-20 septembre 1821.

34. Ibid., 19 février 1832; 5 mars 1834; 2 mars 1836.

35. Encrevé, *Protestants français*, 80. The extent of Nîmes' influence is difficult to gauge as it divided on many issues. For example, Pastor Ferdinand Fontanès was prominent nationally among liberals, while Pastor Emilien Frossard was a leader of the evangelical movement. Liberals, however, dominated the Consistory of Nîmes, and as a rule the Conference followed a liberal line.

36. ADG 6M 770, Sociétés religieuses et de bienfaisance.

37. AN F[19] 10170; Douen Orentin, *Histoire de la Société biblique protestante de Paris, 1818-1868* (Paris, 1868), 165; ADG Chartier de Clausonne, 89, *Onzième séance anniversaire de la Société biblique de Nismes* (Nismes: n. p., 1833), 25.

38. Ibid., 3.

39. ADG 42 J 94, G 19[0], *Société d'Evangélisation pour les Protestants desséminés - établie à Nismes - prémière annèe, 1839* (Nismes: Triquet, 1839); ibid., G 19[42], Lezan, 1838. ADG 42 J 170, Conf. pastorale, 30 mai 1838. Bibliothèque de la Société de l'histoire du Protestantisme français [henceforth Bib..SHPF], Archive Jaucourt, liasse 9, #36.

40. ADG 42 J 170, Conf. pastorale,12 novembre 1834; 25 mars 1835. "Assemblées générales des sociétés religieuses à Paris," *Archives Evangéliques,*

1842 (23-24):1-9. Robert, *Eglises réformées*, 439-442.
    41. *Archives Evangéliques*, 1842 (33-34): 1. The pastors were the evangelicals, Emilien Frossard, Abraham Borrel and Jean-Jacques Gardes. Two négociants, Léon Noguier and Boissier-Heimpel, later became elders.
    42. Ibid.; ADG Chart. Clausonne, 89, Gustave de Clausonne to the Comités des Sociétés bibliques Branches et Sectionelle de Nîmes, 18 décembre 1833; ADG 42 J 47, Consist. of Nîmes, 3 janvier 1834.
    43. ADG 42 J 170, Conf. pastorale, 25 mai 1831; 26 juin 1833. ADG V 491, Jean-Paul Hugues, *Quelques mots à l'occasion d'un réglement dressé par le vénérable Consistoire d'Aiguesvives pour la nomination des diacres de son resort*, (unpublished manuscript, 1ᵉʳ juin 1844).
    44. ADG 42 J 170, Conf. pastorale, 26 juin 1833.
    45. Ibid.

Chapter 4

    1. Abraham Borrel, *Histoire de l'Eglise Chrétienne Réformées de Nismes* (Nismes: Bianquis-Gignoux, 1844), 236. Puaux, "Lettre du Pasteur Olivier-Desmonts," 219-221.
    2. Vincent, *Protestantisme en France*, 357. ADG 42 J 47, Consist. de Nîmes, 23 mars 1832. MMS "Extracts from the Journal of Charles Cook"; Puaux, "Lettre du Révérand C. Perrot," 217-218. Edmond Jaulmes, *Les Quakers Français: Etude historique* (published thèse, Université de Paris, Faculté de théologie protestante, 1898), 39-51. On the Catholic renewal see Gérard Cholvy and Yves-Marie Hilaire, *Histoire religieuse*, 9-148.
    3. Vincent, *Protestantisme en France*, 517, also, 376-424. ADG 42 J 47, Consistoire de Nîmes, 18 juin 1830,16 mars 1832, 30 mars 1832. ADG 42 J 170, Conf. pastorales, 27 mai 1829; ibid., 25 mai 1831. ADG 42 J 47, Consist. de Nîmes; ADG Chart. Clausonne, 89, *Onzième séance de la Société biblique de Nismes*, 9.
    4. Rev. William Berrian, *Travels in France and Italy in 1817 and 1818*, (New York: T. and J. Swords, 1821), 49-50. MMS FBN European Correspondence 4, 110-111, Extracts from the journal of Charles Cook.
    5. Woodbridge, "Reformed Pastors of Languedoc," 85-86; Jacques Perrier, "Les Difficultés des pasteurs du Gard pendant la Révolution," BSHPF 1993: 375-389; Robert, *Eglises réformées*, 1-46, 108-132.
    6. Cook, *Vie de Charles Cook*, I, 55-56; Frossard, *Tableau pittoresque*, 89.
    7. Borrel, *Notice historique sur l'Eglise chrétienne réformée de Nismes* (Nismes, 1837), quoted in Petit, *Une Metropole protestante*, 74-75; Timoléon Béziés (pastor-suffragant à St-Jean-du-Gard), *Sermon sur ces paroles: Et Jésus leurs dit: Je suis le Pain de Vie* (Nîmes: Triquet père et fils, n.d), 5; Jean-Paul Cook, *La Vie de Charles Cook, pasteur méthodiste et docteur en théologie, par son fils*, 2 vols. (Paris: Librairie Evangélique, 1862) 1:55-56; Frossard, *Tableau pittoresque*, 89.

8. ADG 42 J 47, Consist. de Nîmes, 23 mars 1832; ADG Chart. Clausonne, 89, *Onzième séance de la Société biblique de Nismes*, 9.

9. Jean-Pierre Aguet, *Les Grèves sous la monarchie de juillet (1830-1847): Contribution à l'étude du mouvement ouvrier français* (Geneva: , 1954); Charles Tilley and Edward Shorter, *Strikes in France, 1830-1968* (Cambridge: Cambridge University Press), 360; William H. Sewell, Jr., *Work and Revolution in France: The Language of labor from the Old Regime to 1848* (Cambridge: Cambridge University Press, 1980), 194-218.

10. Armand Cosson, "L'Industrie textile à Nîmes: la fin d'une hégémonie (1790-1850)," *Le Mouvement social*, 133 (1985): 5-24, p. 11, 23; idem, "La Révolution de 1830 à Nîmes," *Annales historiques de la Révolution française* 556 (1984): 528-540; Fitzpatrick, *Catholic royalism*, 97-121.

11. ADG Chart. Clausonne, 89, *Onzième séance de la Société biblique de Nismes*, 9. ADG 42 J 47, Consist. de Nîmes, 16 mars 1832, 30 mars 1832.

12. Ibid., 16 mars 1832.

13. Alfred Vincent, *Histoire de la prédication protestante de la langue française au XIXᵉ siècle, 1800-1866* (Geneva, 1870), 4. ADG 42 J 170, Conf. pastorale, 27 mai 1829, 13 mars 1833.

14. Pasteur Samuel Bruguier, letter of abdication, Mont Mamert, 24 floréal an II, reprinted in Jacques Perrier, "Les Difficultés des pasteurs du Gard pendant la Révolution," *BSHPF* 139 (1993): appendix 2, 384-385. See also the abdication of Daniel Encontre of Anduze, ibid., 386-387.

15. "La voix d'un ami, addressé à un jeune pasteur le jour de sa consecration - 'Prends garde à toi et à la doctrine, et persiste en ces choses. I Timothée IV, 16,'" *Archives Evangéliques*, 1842 (31-32): 7. ADG 42 J 170, Conf. pastorales, 27 mai 1829.

16. Vincent, *Protestantisme en France*, 290, 313.

17. Robert, *Eglises réformées*, 119, 377-379; ADG Chart. Clausonne, 89, *Discours prononcé à la séance publique de la Société biblique de Nîmes, le 13 août 1837 par M. de Clausonne, Président, extrait du journal L'Evangeliste, 1 septembre 1837* (Valence: Imprimerie de Marc Aurel Frères, n.d.).

18. Samuel Vincent was a member of the Académie de Nîmes, the local Société d'agriculture, the Conseil académique, and the council of the Ecole normale. He was elected to the Conseil général du Gard, and was chosen by Guizot as president of the Commission protestante de l'enseignement primaire. He was also awarded the status of Chevalier de la Légion d'honneur.

19. ADG 42 J 47, Consist. de Nîmes, 4 août 1837. Samuel Vincent, *Catechisme à la usage de l'Eglise réformée de Nismes, suivi d'un abrégé de l'histoire sainte, d'un petit recueil de passages et de quelques prières* (Nismes: Gaude fils, 1817). Vincent translated from English works of the common-sense theologian William Paley and the Scottish evangelical Thomas Chalmers. From German he translated works by the rationalist Bretschneider. Bernard Reymond, "Redécouvrir Samuel Vincent," *Etudes théologiques et religieuses*, 54 (1979): 411-423. Vincent's response to Lamennais are, *Observations sur l'unité religieuse* (Nîmes, 1820); and *Observations sur la voie d'autorité appliqué à la Religion*

(n.p.). On this exchange see Bernard Reymond, "La controverse entre l'abbé Félicité de Lamennais et le pasteur Samuel Vincent," in M. Peronnet, ed., *La Controverse religieuse (XVIe-XIXe siècles)* (Montpellier: Université Paul Valéry, 1980), vol. 2, 135-141.

20. Samuel Vincent represented this merger of traditions in a genetic sense as well. Adrien Vincent, his father, was a rationalist pastor at Nîmes from 1785 to 1794, who voluntarily resigned during the dechristianization campaign. Because of this, the faithful of Nîmes refused to accept him back as their pastor, and he closed out his days as pastor in the small village of Gajan (Gard). Spiritually and in prestige, however, Vincent was the heir of Paul Rabaut, the eminent pastor of the Eglise du Désert in Nîmes during the last-half of the eighteenth century. Edgar, *Carte protestante*, 217-222, 224-227; Robert, *Eglises réformées*, 151, n. 4, 378-379, 574; Léonard, *Histoire Générale*, 3:232-236; ADG Chart. Clausonne, 89, Clausonne, "Discours prononcé à la séance publique de la Société biblique de Nîmes le 13 août 1837," 8-10.

21. ADG 42 J 170, Conf. pastorale, 13 mars 1833.

22. Borrel, *Histoire de l'Eglise de Nîmes*, 368. Citing the integrative benefits of teaching the catechism this way the pastors tried in 1855, to eliminate private catecheses. The move was rejected by the elders. ADG 42 J 50.

23. ADG 42 J 47, Consist. de Nîmes, 16 mars 1832, 23 mars 1832, 30 mars 1832.

24. ADG V 491, dossier, Anduze; MMS FBN European Correspondence 4, card 110-111. Extracts from the journal of Charles Cook, Sept. 22, 1819; Sept. 24, 1819. Robert, *Eglises réformées*, 392-393.

25. ADG 42 J 47, Consist. de Nîmes, juin 1830; 18 juin 1830.

26. "Review of 'Bishop Milner's Charge,' &c," *Methodist Magazine,* March 1814: 189-198. "Religious Intelligence," ibid., 235.

27. MMS FBN 4, Journal of Charles Cook., Sept. 4 - Nov. 5, 1819.

28. In Wemyss, *Histoire du réveil*, 132; Cook, *Vie de Charles Cook*, 1:77.

29. MMS FBN European Correspondence 4, card 111, Cook to M. G. Marsden, Nismes, October 4, 1819. J.-P. Cook, *Vie de Charles Cook*. In addition to Cook, Henri de Jersey served the Reformed Church at Caveirac (Gard) and Armand de Krepezdron served at Mer (Loire-et-Cher). Robert, *Eglises réformées*, 376, n. 1. Also Théodore Roux, *Le Méthodisme en France: Pour servir à l'histoire religieuse d'hier et d'avant-hier* (Paris: Librairie Protestante, 1940), 31-54, 66.

30. In his first visit to the region Cook noted the hesitancy of the Reformed Churches to risk provoking the Catholic Church. MMS Journal of Charles Cook, Sept. 4 - Nov. 5, 1819. On suspicions of Methodist practices and the composition of their meetings see MMS FBN European Correspondence 4, card 149, A Reformed pastor at Nîmes to Cook, March 12, 1832; MMS FBN European Correspondence 5, card 169, Philip Le Bas to Methodist Missionary Society, London, 1 March 1836; AN BB¹⁸ 1414, n° 7056, Procureur Général au Garde des Sceaux, Nîmes, 28 août 1843; AN F¹⁹ 10927, Procureur Général au Garde des Sceaux, Nîmes, 11 octobre 1843,.

31. ADG 42 J 170, Conf. pastoral, 13 novembre 1833; 5 mars 1834.

32. Roux, *Méthodisme en France*, 74-77; also James C. Deming and Michael S. Hamilton, "Methodist Revivalism in France, Canada and the United States," in George A. Rawlyk and Mark A. Noll, eds., *Amazing Grace: Evangelicalism in Australia, Britain, Canada, and the United States* (Grand Rapids, MI: Baker Books, 1993), 137-153.

33. Quoted in Roux, *Méthodisme en France*, 72-73. J.P. Cook, *Vie de Charles Cook*, 51-57.

34. ADG 42 J 170, Conf. pastoral, 5 mars 1834; ADG 42 J 47, Consist. de Nîmes, 10 avril 1835.

35. ADG 1M 609, Pasteur Gardes au Préfet du Gard, Nîmes, 30 mai 1853. The Consistories of Valleraugue and St-Chaptes protested to the government the Methodist presence in their towns. ADG 1M 607, Pasteur Sarrut au Sous-Préfet du Vigan, Le Vigan, 20 juin 1855, 2 juillet 1856; AN F[19] 10931, Louis Braces au Minister des Cultes, St-Chaptes, 6 novembre 1859.

36. AN F[19] 10436, dossier Bosc, Consist. de Privat, Plainte contre Pasteur Bosc, Privat, 14 aout 1837. AN BB [18] 1414, n° 7056, Procureur Général au Minister des Cultes, Nîmes, 27 octobre 1843.

37. ADG 42 J 170, Conf. pastorales, 28 juin 1837.

38. ADG 42 J 170, Conf. pastoral,13 mars 1833, 1 mars 1837, 28 juin 1837.

39. ADG 42 J 47, Consist. de Nîmes, 9 sept. 1836, Règlement pour les exercises d'édification de l'Oratoire, Art. 5. This service departed from regular services where the pastor rarely spoke from anywhere but the pulpit, most seats were rented, and the parquet, in front of the pulpit, was reserved for the Consistory and other notables. Article 4 of the regulation stated that each person present be seated, which was often impossible in the regular services for those who could not afford the pew rental. In addition, the seating arrangement for the culte de l'Oratoire required men and women to sit in separate areas. This related to a belief that one of the reasons few men attended church was because there was no seating set aside expressly for them. Ibid., 10 avril 1835.

40. ADG 42 J 71, E 35[1], Deux pétitions, 9 novembre 1836. ADG 42 J 47, Consist. de Nîmes, 11 novembre 1836. This door-to-door solicitation was similar to one made yearly for Protestant poor relief. In 1836, the collection for the poor raised over 12,000 francs. ADG 42 J 163, H-82, Comptabilité, relevés des comptes de l'Eglise réformée de Nîmes, 1821-1852.

41. ADG 42 J 47, Consist. de Nîmes, 16 décembre 1836.

42. ADG 42 J 170 Conf. pastoral, 5 mars 1834.

43. The revival in St-Hippolyte first emerged in a group led by Soulier fils, a Moravian convert to Calvinist predestination. He appealed to Pastor Lissingol at Montpellier, who arranged with the Société évangélique de Geneva to send an evangelist who stayed six weeks with Soulier, and preached up to six times a day with success especially among the rural population. Wemyss, *Histoire du réveil*, 195-196. AN F[19] 10436, dossier Bosc, Consist. de Privat, Plainte contre Pasteur Bosc, Privat, 14 août 1837.

44. ADG 42 J 170, Conf. Pastorale, 26 mai 1830, 13 novembre 1833, 5 mars 1834; *Archives du Christianisme*, 15 (1832): 177-180.

45. W. R. Ward, *The Protestant evangelical awakening* (Cambridge: University of Cambridge Press, 1992), 355. Ward's book is one of the few examining the trans-national aspect of the evangelical awakening. Its trans-Atlantic character has begun to receive attention in works like Richard Carwardine's, *Transatlantic Revivalism*; David Bebbington, Mark Noll, eds., *Evangelicalism in Britain, America and Beyond* (New York: Oxford University Press, 1992). These, however, still treat the awakening as essentially an Anglo-American phenomenon.

46. Samuel Vincent, *Catechism*. Ferdinand Fontanès, *De l'unité religieuse dans l'église réformée de France* (Nîmes, 1844), 25. The generational difference in liberal Protestantism is clearly evident in the confrontation pitting Gustave de Clausonne and several other long-time elders with newer liberals for control of the Consistory of Nîmes, during which Clausonne was charged with being an evangelical. ADG 42 J 51, Consist. de Nîmes, 10 janvier 1866. On theological development in the French Reformed Church see Encrevé, *Protestants français*, 87-131, 239-312, 601-678.

47. Fontanès, *Unité religieuse*, 13, 18.

48. "La voix d'un ami," *Archives Evangéliques* 1842 (31-32):3, 4-5. Marc Forissier, *Emilien Frossard, l'apôtre des Pyrénées* (Tarbes, France: n.p., 1946); *Dictionnaire de biographie française* (Paris: Librairie Letouzey et Ane, 1979), 1392.

49. Emilien Frossard, for example, was an amateur geologist and co-founded the *Société d'encouragement pour l'agriculture et l'industrie*. His son Charles-Louis bypassed a career as a mineralogist to serve as a pastor with his father. André Encrevé, ed., *Dictionnaire du monde religieux dans la France contemporaine. Tome 5: Les Protestants* (Paris: Beauchesne, 1993),

50. Béziés, *Sermon sur ces paroles*, 4-5, 30. "Meditations - Le Réveil de L'Ame," *Archives Evangélique*, 1842 (5-6): 1-2.

51. Jean Calvin, *Institutes of the Christian Religion*, vol. 2, ed., John T. McNeil, Ford Lewis Battles, trans. (Philadelphia: Westminster Press, 1960), 920-979.

52. "Le Dévouement Chrétien," *Archives Evangéliques*, 1842 (9-10): 2.

53. Béziés, *Sermon sur ces paroles*, 5. Ferdinand Fontanès, *De la Lutte engagé dans les Eglises protestantes de France* (Valence: Marc Aurel frères, 1842), 4-5.

54. Fontanès, *Unité religieuse*, 22, 23.

55. Frossard charged that the church suffered "under the three greatest plagues of Satan. . . . Here it suffers under the shadow of profound ignorance, there it stoops under the yoke of Caesar, elsewhere it has become the prey of a prideful priesthood." "Meditation - Celui qui-est sur le trône dit . . .," *Archives Evangéliques*, 1842 (1-2): 2-4.

56. According to Frossard, to be saved one must "recognize the rigor and the sanctity of divine law, the real and inveterate misery of the natural man, his absolute incapacity for salvation without the intervention and the immense mercy of God and the effusion of the blood of Christ the just, the action of the Holy

Spirit which directs the moral world and leads the repentant man, as if by the hand, in the new route of regeneration." Frossard, "La voix d'un ami," *Archives Evangéliques*, 1842 (31-32): 3. See also Emile Arnal, *Ma démission* (Le Vigan: n.p., 1849).

57. Evangelicals argued that such a practice was consistent with the early Reformed practice of reviewing members of the congregation for worthiness prior to communion. James L. Osen, *Prophet and Peacemaker: The Life of Adolphe Monod* (Lanham, MD: University Press of America, 1984), 129-148.

58. Fontanès, *De la Lutte engagé*, 2. In the pages of the journal he edited for liberal pastors Fontanès wrote, "One does not understand the language of the Bible because one is ignorant of the historical givens necessary for its comprehension, and therefore does not read it." *L'Evangéliste*, 1 (15 juillet 1837): 1, "Introduction." In *De la Lutte engagé*, which he wrote for a more popular audience, he argued that the Bible had to be read in its textual and cultural context, taking into account "the time, the place, the people, the customs of oriental language, and all the circumstances which might aid in recovering the particular idea the writer." Fontanès, *De la Lutte engagé*, 2-4, 5. "L'Evangile," *L'Evangéliste*, 1 janvier 1837: 2-3. It was only after 1848, when the positivist spirit grew stronger, that theological liberals began openly questioning doctrines such as the divinity of Christ. Edgar, *Carte protestante, 147-148*. In addition to continuing the theological legacy of Samuel Vincent, Fontanès was also Vincent's nephew by marriage and contributed to some of his uncle's publications.

59. *L'Evangéliste,* I (15 janvier 1837), 10.

60. Reformed consistories showed little tolerance for incorrect politics, particularly in its pastors. After the July Revolution of 1830, the Consistory of Nîmes purged itself of its Pastor-President, Olivier de Sardan, a Bourbon sympathizer. Jean Buchet, was dismissed from the ministry in 1834, by the Consistory of St-Jean-du-Gard for his alleged republican opinions. After Louis-Napoleon Bonaparte's coup d'état in December 1851, the Consistory of Lasalle did the same with one of its pastors, Jean Aubanel, for democ-soc sympathies. ADG 42 J 48, Consist. de Nîmes, 20 septembre 1830; AN F¹⁹ 10440, dossier Jean Buchet; AN F¹⁹ 10389, dossier, Pasteur Paul Laune; AN F¹⁹ 10440, dossier, Pasteur Jean Aubanel.

61. Fontanès, *De la Lutte engagé*, 4-5, 15-16. Vincent, *Protestantisme en France*, 305.

Chapter 5

1. ADG 42 J 170, Conf. pastorales, 9 novembre 1836.

2. David Bebbington, *Evangelicalism in Modern Britain: A History from the 1730s to the 1980s* (Grand Rapids, MI: Baker Book House, 1992), 10-12.

3. ADG Chart. Clausonne, 89, "Discour à la Société biblique de Nîmes, 13 août 1837," 11, 13.

4. Ibid., 14, 15.

5. Doctrine did not seem to be central to this division. There was no dissent to promoting Emilien Frossard, an evangelical, from pastor/catechist to full pastor, or to the election of David Tachard, a liberal, President of the Consistory. ADG 42 J 47, Consist. De Nîmes, 31 juillet 1837. It was a different matter when they tried to select a new pastor/catechist. One election was annulled due to the narrow margin of victory. Three months later, in an equally close decision, the consistory settled on the moderately liberal Aristide Fermaud, suffragan for the section of Milhaud. Ibid., 11 août 1837; 14 août 1837.

6. ADG V 356, Garde des Sceaux au Préfet du Gard, Paris, 30 mai 1837. ADG V 349, Petition des habitants de la ville de Nages et de Boissières, n.d. Ibid., Pasteur/Président du Consistoire de Calvisson au Préfet du Gard, Calvisson, 20 mai 1839. The gendarmerie occupied Valleraugue for several days after simmering animosity between two factions in the area erupted into a riot set off by the removal of Pastor Sarradan for his alleged illicit relations with a prominent woman. AN BB[18] 1425, n° 9173, Affaire de Valleraugue.

7. The government authorized the election of Frédéric-Claude Dussant over Eugène Moutier. ADG V 356, Ordinance Royale, 26 septembre 1837. ADG V 355, Sous-Préfet du Vigan au Préfet, Le Vigan, 19 avril 1837. ADG V 356, Procès-verbaux du séance du 28 février 1837; ibid., Garde des Sceaux au Préfet du Gard, Paris, 30 mai 1837; ibid., Petition des maires et membres du consistoire du commun de Soudorgues, Ste-Croix et Vabre, 15 mai 1837.

8. Liberals often complained of the Faculty of Montauban's evangelical bias, and nearly every appointment was bitterly contested. With its influence at Paris the orthodox party usually won the nomination. More liberal students tended to go to Geneva for seminary, but the Organic Articles required that French pastors receive their degree from a French faculty. To meet this requirement students at Geneva would transfer to the Lutheran Faculty at Strasbourg which then awarded the degree. Robert, *Eglises réformées*, 204-223, 387-390, 394-397, 465-469; Encrevé, *Protestants français*, 299-302; Wemyss, *Histoire du réveil*, 170-172. ADG V 491, Procès-verbaux du séance du 4 avril 1837. Soulier was part of an earlier clash between local evangelicals and several notables in Anduze.

9. ADG V 491, Ministre des cultes au Préfet, Paris, 3 août 1837.

10. Ibid., Soulier au Sous-préfet d'Alès, Anduze, 17 août 1837.

11. Ibid., Ordinance du Roi, 26 octobre 1838.

12. ADG V 360, Garde des Sceaux au Préfet du Gard, Paris, 23 septembre 1837. Laune caused a later controversy at Mialet when he refused to distribute communion to prevent giving it to someone unworthy of its reception. AN F[19] 10440, Paul Laune, *Ma Tentative de réforme et ma défense anticipée devant le Consistoire de Saint-Jean-du-Gard* (Alais: Vve Veirun, 1851).

13. The Swiss evangelist, Reymond, made a tour of the region in 1832, leaving a small group of followers in Avèze and Le Vigan. At about the same time, Moureton, an independent revivalist who later became a disciple of John Nelson Darby, was gaining an audience in Avèze. Encrevé, *Protestants français*, 141, n. 301; Wemyss, *Histoire du réveil*, 196, 209.

14. ADG V 360, Louis Boussez au Préfet du Gard, Le Vigan, 9 décembre

1837. Ibid., Pour le Sous-Préfet en congé, Le conseiller d'arrondissement délégué au Préfet, n.d.; Wemyss, *Histoire du réveil*, 196.

15. The Prefect said, "The population of Avèze and Molières, will soon tire of its sulking. It was said of M. Dussant's nomination at Soudorgues, that tempers would flare if this pastor was confirmed, and to the contrary, soon after he arrived he was received with acclamation." ADG V 360, Préfet au Ministre des Cultes, Nîmes, 9 février 1838.

16. ADG V 359, Préfet aux pasteurs de St-Martin-de-Corconac et de St-André-de-Valborgne, Nîmes, 14 juin 1842. *Archives du Christianisme*, 23 juillet 1842: 127. AN BB[18] 1425 n° 9173, affaire de Valleraugue.

17. ADG V 491, affaire de Sauve, 1842.

18. ADG 42 J 48, Consist. de Nîmes, 6 mai 1842.

19. Bianquis, *Société des Missions Evangéliques*, I, 90-93.

20. Louis-Philippe's eldest daughter married the Lutheran King of Belgium, Léopold de Saxe-Cobourg-Saxfeld. His second daughter married Duke Alexander of Wurtembourg, also a Lutheran. In 1837, the heir to the throne, Ferdinand-Philippe duc d'Orléans, married the duchess Helen of Mecklembourg-Schwerin in a ceremony officiated by the president of the Lutheran Consistory of Paris. According to Emile Léonard, "the Protestants of the Cévennes were so proud of their *dauphine* that, when the princely couple passed through Sommières they unhitched the carriage to pull it triumphantly along the promenade." Léonard, *Histoire générale*, t. 3. *Archives Evangéliques*, 1842 (21-22): 15-16. On Protestant evangelism see, James Lynn Osen, "French Calvinists and the State, 1830-1852" *French Historical Studies* V (Fall 1967): 220-232.

21. Jean Pédézert, *Cinquante ans de souvenirs religieux et ecclésiastiques, 1830-1880* (Paris: Librairie Fischbacher, 1896), 87-90; Ingrand, *Histoire de la Maison de Santé Protestante Evangélique de Nîmes* (Nîmes: Maison de Santé Protestante, 1986), 10-11.

22. Pédézert, *Cinquante ans de souvenirs religieux*, 90.

23. ADG 42 J 48, Consist. de Nîmes, 6 mai 1842.

24. *Archives du Christianisme*, 10 (1842), published a list of pastors and consistories supporting the new agency. In five consistories in the Gard more than one pastor supported the society. All of the pastors in the Consistory of Vauvert supported this association though as a body the consistory did not.

25. ADG 42 J 48, Consist. de Nîmes, 6 mai 1842.

26. Pédézert, *Cinquante ans de souvenirs religieux*, 94.

27. ADG 42 J 48, Consist. de Nîmes, 6 mai 1842. This portrayal seems to overlook the Camisards whom liberals were inclined to regards as lamentably fanatical. See Joutard, *La légende des Camisards*, 185-276.

28. Ibid.

29. Henri Dubled, *Les Eglises protestantes de Gardonneque de 1802 à 1906* (Nîmes: C. Lacour, 1990), 27, 56. The names of supporters of the Société généraux were published in *Archives du Christianisme*, 28 mai 1842: 83; 11 juin 1842: 97; 25 juin 1842: 107; 23 juillet 1842: 125; 13 août 1842: 135. See also the dossier on the society in AN F*19* 10170, Sociétés religieuses.

30. Ingrand, *Histoire de La Maison de Santé*, 11.

31. Ibid., 11-12. Frossard used essentially the same argument to justify the Maison de Santé. ADG 42 J 48, Consist. de Nîmes, 10 juin 1842.

32. Ingrand, *Histoire de La Maison de Santé*, 14.

33. Ibid. Only two of the laymen then served the Church of Nîmes in an official capacity, and both of those as deacons. Years afterwards Frossard said of his idea for the hospital, "I believed then that the thought came from him whose constant and sovereign intervention we recognize, and I believe it more now than ever." Ibid., 13.

34. "Le Riche et le pauvre," *Archives Evangéliques*, 1843: 59-63.

35. In 1830, the consistory persuaded the administration of the Hôpital général to create a separate ward for Protestants. But two years later the Comité des Dames told the consistory that Protestant women in the hospital had no nurses assigned to them, were often isolated from one another, and pressured to convert. One woman was denied entry altogether. The consistory brought sufficient pressure to bear to have such abuses corrected, but in 1840, the reputation of the hospitals were still such that the consistory had to demand that the seriously ill enter the public institutions or forfeit all consistorial charity. ADG 42 J 47, Consist. de Nîmes, 19 novembre 1830, 9 novembre 1832; ADG 42 J 93 G 14[4], L'Administration de l'hospice Général au Consistoire de Nîmes, Nîmes, 4 juin 1831; ibid., G 14[5], Comité des Dames de l'hospice au Consistoire de Nîmes, Nîmes, 4 janvier 1832. ADG 42 J 61, Règlement pour la distribution des aumônes.

36. "Maison de Santé pour les Malades Protestantes à Nismes," *Archives du Christianisme*, 13 (9 juillet 1842): 121-122.

37. Negre, *Protestantisme nîmois à l'oeuvre*, 52.

38. ADG 42 J 47, Consist. de Nîmes, 12 janvier 1838, 10 janvier 1840. ADG 42 J 93, G 16[15], Clauzel, médecin, au Président du Consistoire, Nîmes 10 Septembre 1840. Figures for the Budget of Charities from ADG 42 J 96, Administration et comptabilité.

39. Ingrand, *Maison de Santé*, 14.

40. ADG 42 J 48, Consist. de Nîmes, 3 juin 1842.

41. Ibid.

42. Ibid.

43. ADG Chart. Clausonne, 90, G[ve] Clausonne au Emilien Frossard, pasteur, Nîmes, 7 juin 1842.

44. The only petition found from a Reformed Church in the Gard was that of St-Laurent-d'Aigouze in the Consistory of Vauvert. AN F[19] 10094, Extrait de la séance du 20 mars 1843, Consistoire [sectionelle] de St-Laurent-d'Aigouze. James L. Osen, "Revival of the French Reformed Church, 1830-1852," (Ph.D. diss., University of Wisconsin, 1966), 55. On the conversions at Senneville see Jean Baubérot, "L'évangélisation protestante non concordataire en France et les problèmes de la liberté religieuse au XIXe siècle: la Société évangélique de 1833 à 1883" (thèse du 3e cycle, Ecole Polytechnique des Hautes-Etudes, 1966), 68-72.

45. ADG 42 J 48, Consist. de Nîmes, 1er décembre 1843. *Correspondance*

pastorale, 23 (mars 1843): 3.
46. ADG 42 J 48, Consist. de Nîmes, 1ᵉʳ décembre 1843.
47. Ibid.
48. ADG 42 J 94 G 19[116], Ministre de la Justice et des Cultes aux Préfets, Paris, 28 février 1844. ADG 42 J 48, Consist. de Nîmes, 8 mars 1844. See also Osen, "French Calvinists and the State," 230-232. Though local officials could block independent chapels and evangelists, dissidents in southern France did not encounter systematic obstruction until the first years of the Second Empire.
49. AN F[19] 10094, petition, Nîmes, 2 février 1844. Other petitions came from Boissières, 1ᵉʳ février 1844; Beauvoisin , 18 février 1844; Aymargues, 25 janvier 1844; St-Gilles, n.d.; Bréau, 24 décembre 1843; Bernis, 18 décembre 1843; Codognan et Vergèze, n.d.; and Le Vigan, 15 décembre 1843. "Consistoire de Nîmes - Circulaire," *Archives du Christianisme*, 12 (13 janvier 1844): 4. The Consistory of Montpellier also separated itself from Nîmes' opposition to freedom of worship. ADG 42 J 94 G 19[114], Consist. de Montpellier au Garde des Sceaux et Ministre de la Justice et des Cultes, Montpellier, 8 janvier 1844. ADG V 491, Jean-Paul Hugues, "Quelques mots à l'occasion d'un règlement dressé par le vénérable Consistoire d'Aiguesvives pour la nomination des diacres de son resort" (unpublished manuscript, Gallargues, 1ᵉʳ Juin 1844), 29-30.
50. Ibid. The sections dominated by evangelicals were Bernis, Codognan and Vergèze. Their petitions for absolute freedom of religion, signed by the deacons, pastors and several residents, were sent to the Paris in 1843. AN F[19] 10094, petition, Bernis, 18 décembre 1843; Ibid., petition, Codognan et Vergèze, (n.d.).
51. ADG V 491, Hugues, "Quelques mots," 31-32; "Consistoire d'Aiguesvives," *Archives du Christianisme*, 12 (14 septembre 1844): 155.
52. ADG V 491, Hugues, "Quelques mots," 27. The view of the Réveil as a foreign import has been adopted more recently by Alice Wemyss, *Histoire du réveil*. It ignores, however, the many evangelical leaders who were French and domestic organizations such as the Société biblique française et étrangère and the Société évangélique de France.
53. Ibid., 28-29.
54. ADG 42 J 48, Consist. de Nîmes, 18 mars 1842, 8 avril 1842, 22 avril 1842; 20 mai 1842; 19 mai 1843. Though as Coquerel's biographer said, Gardes felt his assistant was "born into heresy, raised in heresy, and was baptized and received into the church by a heretical pastor," the two actually got along quite well. Ernest Stroelin, *Athanase Coquerel Fils: Etude biographique* (Paris: Librairie Fischbacher, 1886), 113. Jean-Marie Mayeur et Yves-Marie Hilaire, eds., *Dictionnaire du monde religieux dans la France contemporaine*, volume 2, *Les Protestants*, André Encrevé, ed. (Paris: Beauchesne, 1993), 161-162.
55. Ibid., Consist. de Nîmes, 5 décembre 1842; ADG 42 J 61, Extrait de la séance du 23 décembre 1842, Nouveau règlement sur les Prédicateurs étrangers.
56. AN F[19] 10436, dossier Bosc (1836-1838).
57. Hugues, "Quelques mots," 12-20. In opposing the Consistory of Sauve's request for a second pastor, Justin Fraissinet, pastor at Sauve, mentioned that several of his supporters had recently been forced out of the sectional consistory.

ADG V 491, Fraissinet à M. le Préfet, Sauve, 17 octobre 1845.

58. As would be expected, when the change was implemented several complaints were made to the Prefect. These included the opposing elders, the deacons and several notables from Vergèze, Codognan and Bernis, as well as the deacons for the communes of Uchaud, Vistric and Aubord, who do not seem to have been directly involved. At first the Prefect seemed sympathetic with the plaintiffs. But after investigating further he acknowledged that the Organic Articles did not allow him to interfere in behalf of a body that did not have a legal status. He only warned Laget and Hugues to keep the controversy from getting out of hand, and thereby become a "legitimate concern of the civil authorities." ADG V 491, H. Laget, P^{tr}, à Monsieur le Préfet, Bernis, juillet 1844. Ibid., Cabinet du Préfet au Président du Consistoire d'Aiguesvives, Nîmes, 23 avril 1844. Ibid., Préfet du Gard au Pasteur Hugues, Nîmes, 23 juin 1844; ibid., Préfet du Gard au Monsieur Laget, pasteur-président, Nîmes, 11 juillet 1844.

59. Henri Dubief, "Réflexions sur quelques aspects du premier Réveil et sur le milieu ou il se forma," *BSHPF* CXIV (1968):373-402, 378. Dubief's conclusions agree basically with those of Emile Léonard, *Histoire générale*, 3: 222-229. ADG V 348, dossier, Affaire de Gallargues, 21 septembre 1832-29 novembre 1833; ADG 42 G 47, B 73, Affaire de Valleraugue.

60. ADG V 491, dossier, Consist. d'Anduze. Ibid., dossier, Consist. de Sauve.

61. ADG V 492, Composition des Nouveau Consistoires et Conseils presbytéraux. ADG 6M 770, Sociétés Religieuses et de Bienfaisance, 1860.

62. See *Union des Eglises Evangéliques de France: Constitution* (Paris: Marc Ducloux et comp., 1849); Encrevé, *Protestants français*, 141-143. Interestingly, the Réveil was less a factor in Alès than at Nîmes or Montpellier. With a population of 25,000 in 1851, Alès was the second largest city in the Gard. It stood between the silk producing regions of the Cévennes and the coal mines of La Grand' Combe. It was the most heavily industrialized city in the region, with an unusual number of large firms, including a smelter and foundry. Its population was 30 percent Protestant and served by three pastors. Surprisingly, for a Reformed population of this size and diversity, Methodists and other independent evangelists were not much of a factor. The Reformed Church of Alès rarely appears in civil records and with little evidence of the battles that characterized relations between liberals and evangelicals elsewhere. Vidalenc, *Le peuple des campagnes*, 236-237; Savey, "Essai de reconstitution," 41-54. ADG 6M 111, Recensement de 1851. ADG 6M 770, Sociétés religieuses. It was not until 1856, that an independent evangelist stayed in the city. Samuel Mours, *Une siècle d'évangélisation en France, 1815-1914*, 2 vols. (Namur, Belgium: Editions de la Librairie des Eclaireurs unionists, 1963), vol 1.

63. ADG 4U5 350, Rapport du Commissaire de Police au Commissaire central de Police à Nîmes, Nîmes, 27 octobre 1866. ADG 3M 45, Listes électoraux; Petit, *Une Métropole protestante*, 65.

64. ADG 1M 607, petition, St-Mamert, 24 août 1854; Commis. de Police to Prefect, Sommières, 23 septembre 1854; petition, Valleraugue, 15 août 1853;

petition, Anduze, 7 novembre 1853; petition, St-André-de-Valborgne, 23 janvier 1854.

65. Margueritte-Corlay Hinsch-Armengaud, *Recueil des Lettres pastorales de Mme Armengaud, née Hinsch, précédé d'une notice biographique* (Nîmes: n.p., 1878) 2nd. ed., 12.

66. ADG 1M 609, Préfet au Commissaire centrale de Police, Nîmes, 29 décembre 1857; AN BB^{30}436, Procureur-Généraux au Garde des Sceaux, Nîmes. See also Jean-Claude Gaussent, *Les Protestants et L'Eglise réformée de Sète* (Nîmes: Lacour, 1993), 163-179.

67. Mme Planchon (née Lasalle), A Messieurs les Membres du Comité de la Société des Missions évangéliques à Paris, St-Hippolyte, printed in Jean Bianquis, *Les Origines de la Société des Missions Evangéliques de Paris 1822-1830, Volume III* (Paris: Société des Missions Evangéliques, 1935), 142. On the Comités des dames of the Société des Missions see Ibid., 54-154; Jean-François Zorn, *Le Grand siècle d'une Mission Protestante: La Mission de Paris de 1822 à 1914* (Paris: Karthala-Les Bergers et Les Mages, 1993), 642-660.

68. Emilien Frossard, *La Vie Réelle, ou Application du principe chrétien à quelques-unes des positions ou l'homme peut se trouver selon son age et sa profession* (Paris: Chez Delay, Libraire, 1843), "le Maître," 33, 41; ibid., "La Jeune fille chrétienne," 19, 27; ibid., "Le Jeune homme chrétien," 66, 72-73. "Une page de morale sociale," *Archives Evangéliques*, 1842 (11-12), 8.

69. Fontanès, *De la Lutte engagé*, 15.

70. Ibid., 16, 51-52, 55-60.

Chapter 6

1. Quoted in Stroehlin, *Coquerel fils*, 116. See also Vincent, *Protestantisme en France*, 14-33, 256-283, 306-356.

2. Karel Dobbelaere, "Community Formation and the Church: A Sociological Study of an Ideology and the Empirical Reality," in M. Caudron, ed. *Faith and Society*, 112, n. 2. Also, idem, "From Pillar to Postmodernity: The Changing Situation of Religion in Belgium," *Sociological Analysis* 51(1990): 1-13; idem, "Secularization, Pillarization, Religious Involvement, and Religious Change in the Low Countries," in Thomas M. Gannon, ed., *World Catholicism in Transition* (New York: Macmillan, 1988), 80-115.

3. ADG 42 J 48, Consist. de Nîmes, 25 août 1843, 18 septembre 1843, 1er avril 1844, 10 mai 1844, 24 mai 1844, 2 août 1844, 13 mai 1846. The consistory opened a free school of its own in the same neighborhood, but in 1846 it was noted that sixty children still attended Catholic schools "due to indifference or neglect." Ibid., 31 août 1846.

4. ADG 4U5-350, Procureur-Général to Garde des Sceaux, 4 avril 1863. Other examples are in AN BB^{18}1254 6767, Exhumation à Pont-l'Abée (Charente-Inferieure) d'une protestante enterée dans la cimetière catholique, juin-août 1838; BB^{18}1585-472, Incident à Cholet à l'occasion de l'inhumation d'un protestant,

septembre 1858; BB[18]1688-335,Violation de la sépulture d'un enfant protestant par le curé de l'Hommaize (Vienne), février-mai 1864. See also Thomas A. Kselman, *Death and the Afterlife in Modern France* (Princeton: Princeton University Press, 1993), 189-199.

5. ADG 42 J 25, B 74[4], Consist. de Sommières to the Consist. de Nîmes, Sommières, [?] Oct. 1845; ibid., Adolphe d'Espinassouze to Tachard., Salinelles, 3 octobre 1845.

6. ADG 42 J 60, Tachard to the Pasteur-Président of the Consist. de Sommières, Nîmes, 5 novembre 1845.

7. ADG 42 J 48, Consist. de Nîmes, 10 juin 1842.

8. ADG 42 J 94, G 24, Formation d'une Société de Prévoyance et de Secours mutuels, Nîmes, 10 juin 1842.

9. ADG 42 J 48, Consist. de Nîmes, 10 juin 1842. When Protestant workers tried to establish a retirement home and pension fund on their own the project failed for lack of support. ADG 42 J 51, Consist. de Nîmes, 19 février - 31 mai 1867.

10. Louis Chevalier, *Laboring Classes and Dangerous Classes in Paris During the First Half of the Nineteenth Century*, Frank Jellinek, trans. (Princeton: Princeton University Press, 1973). See also Katherine Lynch, *Family, Class and Ideology*.

11. William H. Sewell, Jr., *Work and Revolution in France*.

12. 42 J 94 , G 24, Formation d'une Société de Prévoyance.

13. Ibid.

14. On changing forms of sociability see Maurice Agulhon, *La Vie sociale en Provence intérieure au lendemain de la Révolution* (Paris: Société des études robespierristes et la Librairie Clavreuil, 1971); idem, *Pénitents et francmaçons de l'ancienne Provence (essai sur la sociabilité méridionale)* (Paris: Fayard, 1968); idem, *The Republic in the village*; Sewell, *Work and Revolution in France*; William M. Reddy, *The Rise of Market Culture: The Textile Trade and French Society, 1750-1900* (Cambridge: Cambridge University Press, 1984).

15. In 1903, the Société de prévoyance applied for government authorization as part of the legislative program leading to separation of church and state in 1905. Figures do not exist for Protestants in the working classes of Nîmes. The 1851 census indicated a total population of 53,619 of which 14,357 (26.77%) were Protestants. This census also gave a figure of 9,460 working in the city as non-masters in the fabrication and marketing of cloth and clothing, an industry in which Protestants are known to have been well represented. Applying the percentage of Protestants in the total population to the number of workers engaged in this industry provides a likely minimum of 2,648 as the number of Protestants employed in cloth manufacture. The 514 workers enrolled in the Société de prévoyance, therefore, constituted less than 20 percent of a low estimate for the number of Protestants working in the textile industry alone. ADG 6M 111, Recensement de 1851.

16. ADG 42 J 48, Consist. de Nîmes, 10 juin 1842, 12 août 1842, 18 novembre 1842. *Archives du Christianisme*, 10 (13 août 1842): 142. The editors

noted that "a consistorial work has a better chance of succeeding at Nîmes than a private one." See also Frossard's comments on the association repeated in Ingrand, *Histoire de la Maison de Santé*, 14.

17. ADG 42 J 48, Consist. de Nîmes, 2 septembre 1842, 16 septembre 1842.

18. Ibid., 4 août 1843, 1 septembre 1843, 17 novembre 1843, 23 février 1844, 11 janvier 1845.

19. ADG 42 J 96, Bilans, 1828-1834; ibid., Budget du Consistoire de Nîmes, 1847-1859; ADG 42 J 149, Journaux des écritures, 1840-1847.

20. ADG 42 J 96, Bilans, 1828-1834; ibid., Budgets du Consistoire de Nîmes, 1847-1859; ADG 42 J 149, Journaux des écritures, 1840-1847.

21. ADG 42 J 48, Consist. de Nîmes, 23 février 1844.

22. Pierre-Germain Encontre, "Epitre à Monsieur A. Monod sur le méthodisme"in Raymond Huard and Claire Torreilles, eds., *Du protestantisme au socialisme: Un Quarante-huitard occitan. Ecrits et pamphlets de Pierre-Germain Encontre* (Paris: Editions Privat, 1982) 152-153; idem, "Les gens comme il faut à l'Esplanade de Nîmes," 170, 171.

23. ADG 4U5-300, Procureur du Republic au Procureur-Général, Nîmes, 17 janvier 1851; ibid, 4U5-305 n° 113, Procureur du Republic au Procureur-Général, Alais; Comité provisoire de la Montagne, "Avertissement aux électeurs républicains du Gard: Circulaire n° 1," in Huard and Torreilles, *Du Protestantisme au socialisme*, 175. Ted Margadant, *French Peasants in Revolt: The Insurrection of 1851* (Princeton: Princeton University Press, 1979) 143. See also Agulhon, *Republic in the Village*, 109-111.

24. ADG 42 J 96, Administration et comptabilité, 1828-1859. Ultimately, the Mazoyer Succession yielded about 3,200 francs a year. ADG 42 G 48, Consist. de Nîmes, 14 novembre 1842. "Libéralité d'un catholique romain envers les pauvres de l'Eglise réformée de Nismes," *Archives Evangéliques*, 1842 (47-48): 15. The city of Nîmes also named one of its main boulevards for the general.

25. ADG 42 J 61, Règlement sur la Dotation Feuchères. Though dominated by notables and merchant-manufacturers the Consistory of Nîmes evidenced some distrust of large-scale production and wage labor. Despite use of the language of liberalism it was uncomfortable with the dependency of the employer/employee relationship as morally destructive and encouraging social-leveling schemes like those of the democ-socs. In their belief that economic independence was vital for developing a virtuous working class they tended to rely on traditional types of production. ADG 42 G 48, Consist. de Nîmes, 16 août 1844, 21 février 1845, 5 septembre 1845, 27 février 1846, 30 août 1846.

26. Ibid., 5 avril 1853; ADG 2 Mi 24-R 14, Consist. de Nîmes - Dons, legs, etc, 18 mai 1852.

27. He repeated this gift at least twice in following years. ADG 42 J 49, Consist. de Nîmes, 6 octobre1851, 24 décembre 1852.

28. ADG 42 J 47, Consist. de Nîmes, 14 mai 1847; ADG 42 J 56, Consist.· de Nîmes, 10 septembre 1853; ADG 42 J 49, Consist. de Nîmes, 24 septembre 1852.

29. *Archives Evangéliques*, 1842 (21-22): 15-16. Bib. SHPF, T 937, *Compte*

rendu au 31 août 1857 de la Maison de santé protestante de Nîmes (Nîmes: Lafare et Attenoux, 1857).

30. ADG 42 J 50, Consist. de Nîmes, 26 mars 1858. Puaux, *Oeuvres du protestantisme*, 259, 271-272, 276-277.

31. ADG 6M 770, Sociétés religieuses et de bienfaisance. For example, the Société des dames de couture pour les pauvres at Clarensac which the mayor said had operated more than twenty years and was "a veritable workshop."

32. Puaux, *Oeuvres du protestantisme*, 232-233, 260-261, 272-274.

33. ADG 42 J 47, Consist de Nîmes, 27 novembre 1840.

34. The practice persists to an extent today. Jean-Pierre Chabrol wrote about continuing the tradition when he buried his father alongside his ancestors on family land in the Cévennes. Chabrol, *Bonheur du manchot*, 47-48.

35. Quoted in Robert, *Eglises réformées*, 184, 230.

36. Kselman, *Death in Modern France*; Richard Etlin, *The Architecture of Death: The Transformation of the Cemetery in Eighteenth-Century Paris* (Cambridge, Mass.: MIT Press, 1984); John McManners, *Death and the Enlightenment: Changing attitudes to death in eighteenth-century France* (New York: Oxford University Press, 1985); Michel Vovelle, *La mort et l'Occident de 1300 à nos jours* (Paris: Gallimard, 1983); idem, *Piété baroque et déchristianisation en Provence au XVIIIe siècle* (Paris: Plon, 1973). Though challenged on some points Philippe Ariès' pioneering study, *The Hour of Our Death* (New York: Knopf, 1981) is still well worth reading.

37. For example "Des Grandes pécheresses en face d'un homme mort," *Archives Evangéliques* 1842 (5-6): 5-10; "Des morts part accident," ibid., (35-36): 1-9. One Methodist preacher not only led funeral services he did so even against the wishes of the family. ADG 42 J 48, Consist. de Nîmes, 19 novembre 1841. For examples of a softer approach to death see the notice on the death of Louis-Antoine Majolier, a Quaker from Congénies, in *Archives Evangéliques*, 1842 (13-14): 16, and "La mort heureuse de Marie Pau," ibid., (51-52): 1-12.

38. ADG 42 J 47, Consist. de Nîmes, 2 novembre 1838.

39. Ibid., 27 novembre 1840."

40. ADG 42 J 48, Consist. de Nîmes,12 mars 1841, 19 novembre 1841. *Correspondance pastorale*, juin 1846.

41. The Consistory of Nîmes refused a venture sponsored by the Prefect for the Catholic and Reformed Churches to cooperate in a municipal funeral company. The Prefect hoped this would help bring the two confessions together, but the consistory decided it was counter to their theological and economic interests, and would not be supported by the population.

42. ADG 42 J 181, Consist. de Vauvert, Lettre aux fidèles sur le mariage.

43. Pastor Emilien Frossard argued that if the church felt it was important to offer free primary education to all, there were even better reasons to make catecheses free. ADG 42 J 48, Consist. de Nîmes, 6 octobre 1837, 10 novembre 1837; ADG 42 J 65, Règlement pour le Répétition du Cathécumens.

44. ADG 42 J 47, Consist. de Nîmes, 3 mai 1839, 10 mai 1839.

45. AN F[19] 10440, dossier, Clement Ribard, Extrait du régistre du Consistoire

de St-Hippolyte,10 février 1854.

46. ADG 42 J 47, Consist. de Nîmes, 3 mai 1839.

47. ADG 42 J 48, Consist. de Nîmes, 28 novembre 1846, 9 mars 1848.

48. ADG 42 J 47, Consist. de Nîmes, 29 mai 1840. In 1854, the rate for pew rentals was raised to 7 and 9 francs a year.

49. "Réflexions sur la culte au sein des églises réformées," *L'Evangéliste*, 1 (1er avril 1837): 53-54.

50. Ibid.

51. "Culte. Réflexions sur le culte au sein des églises réformées - 4e article," *L'Evangéliste*, 1 (1er septembre 1837): 134-135.

52. ADG Chart. Clausonne, 90, G^{ve} Clausonne à E. Frossard, 7 juin 1842.

53. Jacques Marty, *La 'Correspondance pastorale' de Nîmes (1839-1848), coup d'oeil sur les origines du mouvement libéral et son rôle dans la vie religieuse des Eglises réformées* (Paris, 1924); Leonard, *Histoire général*, 3:240-241.

54. *Correspondance pastorale*, juin 1844: 3-4.

55. ADG 42 J 170, Conf. pastorale, 28 juin 1837. ADG 42 J 47, Consist. de Nîmes, 15 juin 1838, 7 février 1840., 29 mai 1840.

56. "Réflexions sur le culte - #2," *L'Evangéliste*, 1 (1er septembre 1837)' 134-135. ADG 42 J 47, Consist. de Nîmes, 11 octobre 1839. ADG 42 J 170, Conf. pastorale, 13 mars 1833.

57. ADG 42 J 47, Consist. de Nîmes, 9 septembre 1836. ADG 42 J 48, Consist. de Nîmes, 22 juin 1841, 8 juin 1846.

58. "Réflexions sur le culte au sein des Eglises Réformées - 5e article," *L'Evangéliste*, 1 (le 15 septembre 1837)' 146-147.

59. "Réflexions sur le culte - 4e article"' 134-135.

60. David Martin approaches this issue from the context of liturgical reforms in the Church of England. David Martin, *The Breaking of the Image: A sociology of Christian Theory and Practice* (New York: St. Martin's Press, 1979), 81-102

61. ADG 42 J 56, Consist. de Nîmes, 26 février 1853; ADG 42 J 50, Consist. de Nîmes, 27 janvier 1857.

62. ADG 42 J 170, Conf. pastorales, 13 décembre 1854

63. ADG 1 M 607, Commissaire central de police au Préfet du Gard, Nîmes, 26 avril 1855. A year later a meeting at St-Génies had upwards of 3,000 participants and one at Alès had more than 6,000. Ibid., Sous-Préfet d'Alais au Préfet du Gard, Alais, 25 août 1856; ibid., Commissaire de police au Préfet, Nîmes, 10 septembre 1856. A similar observance occurs each year in the *Assemblée du désert*, an open-air service held on the grounds of the Musée du désert near St-Jean-du-Gard the first Sunday of September.

64. In 1843, Fontanès complained about the shortage of qualified pastors, and urged his colleagues to give extra attention to directing promising youths towards the ministry. *Correspondance pastorale*, mars 1843: 4. Fontanès had the additional concern that with the general shortage of new ministers some consistories were forced to appoint orthodox pastors due to a lack of "tolerant candidates." Also Encrevé, *Protestants Français*, 993-994. Robert, *Eglises réformées*, 463-464.

65. ADG 42 J 48, Consist. de Nîmes, 6 juillet 1846.

66. Ibid., 5 août 1846.

67. Ibid. The consistory was assured that only a few scholarships would be given out and they would go to"carefully chosen subjects, and the manner in which they will be administered and supervised will necessarily attract the elevated class."

68. ADG 42 J 60, circular, Nîmes, 14 août 1846. ADG 42 J 48, Consist. de Nîmes, 12 septembre 1846, 7 décembre 1846, 19 mars 1847; ADG 42 J 60, circular, Nîmes, 2 avril 1847.

69. ADG Chart. Clausonne, 89, Gustave de Clausonne, "Discors à la Société Biblique de Nîmes, 1 juillet 1847."

70. ADG 42 J 47, Consist. de Nîmes, 4 décembre 1835. On this occasion the consistory felt the timing was not right due to the lack of "generally fixed ideas as to the form to give this power, the means to adopt in order to constitute it, and even upon the nature and measure of authority that would be conferred upon it."

71. ADG 42 J 65, C 32, Project d'Ordinance portant règlement d'adminis-tration pour les Eglises Réformées.

72. The project was developed and presented rather clandestinely, perhaps as an attempt to catch evangelicals by surprise. Its primary sponsors were Gustave de Clausonne and David Tachard. The *Archives du Christianisme*, however, attributed the writing of the project to Ferdinand Fontanès. This claim was not denied, though Fontanès did not actively participate in the campaign to have the project accepted. Encrevé, *Protestants français*, 181-185.

73. ADG Chart. Clausonne, 90, Commission de la Conférence Consistoriale du Gard à MM les Présidents, Pasteurs, Anciens et Diacres des Consistoires des Eglises protestantes de France; ibid., Pasteur D. Tachard et G. de Clausonne au nom de la Commission de la Conférence Consistoriale du Gard à *L'Espérance*, Nîmes, 10 avril 1848; ADG 42 J 48, Consist. de Nîmes, 23 juin 1848.

74. ADG 42 J 181, Consist. de Vauvert, 8 mai 1848; Serre, "Consistoriale de Lasalle," 86.

75. The Coquerels, outspoken liberals, ridiculed the consistories of the Gard for accommodating evangelicals. *Lien*, 2 septembre 1848: 355. Athanase Coquerel [pere] was also the most emphatic opponent to the inclusion of the extra delegate from the Gard. ADG 42 J 10, Assemblée générale des députés, 11 sept. 1848.

76. ADG 42 J 10, Rapport de la commission chargée d'examiner les cahiers des assemblées consistoriales.

77. Abraham Borrel lost a bid for President of the General Assembly by a vote of forty-three to thirty-seven to the liberal pastor from Lyon, Eugène Buisson. Gustave de Clausonne was elected as one of the two vice-presidents, receiving seventy-four votes. Ibid., "2ᵉᵐᵉ séance, 12 septembre 1848." Clausonne and Fontanès were both elected as liberal members of the commission. Ibid., "9ᵉᵐ séance, 20 septembre 1848."

78. Quoted in Encrevé, *Protestants français*, 208.

79. Arnal resigned in 1849. He spelled out his objections to the French

Reformed Church in a pamphlet entitled, *Ma démission* (Le Vigan, 1849). Frustrated by the Church's failure to enact far-reaching reforms he ended his explanation declaring, "I have acquired the conviction that a worldly church will support the most energetic of discourses so long as it does not take on practical significance in Christian ecclesiastical conduct. Today the world, a great imitator of Christian forms though internally opposed to the truth, gladly allows the servant of Christ the freedom to preach evangelical doctrines without shame so long as once he descends from the pulpit he does not bruise its prejudices or habits."

Epilogue

1. ADG 1 M 609, Préfet au Ministre d'Interieur, Nîmes, 27 mai 1859; ibid., Commissaire Central de Police au Préfet, Nîmes, 26 mai 1859; AN BB[18] 1598 n° 1694, Procureur-Général au Gardes des Sceaux, Nîmes, 28 mai 1859.

2. Mgr. Plantier, Evèque de Nîmes, "Le Synode de 1559", in *Oeuvres complètes de Mgr. Plantier, Evèque de Nîmes, tome 11. Mandements et Lettres pastorales: Controverses théologiques. Protestantisme* (Nîmes; Paris: Gervais-Bédot; Oudin frères, 1883), 1-52. Some of the responses to Plantier's pamphlet were, Les Pasteurs de Nîmes, *Les pasteurs de Nîmes aux fidèles de leur Eglise* (Nîmes, 1859), 4; Charles Dardier, *Réponse à la lettre aux Protestants du Gard, de Mgr. l'Evèque de Nîmes* (Nîmes, 1859), 7, 10; *L'Eglise réformée*, supplement to 10 juin 1859; Frédéric Desmons, *Réponse à la lettre de l'Evèque de Nîmes aux protestants du Gard* (St-Génies (Gard), 1859); Arbousse-Bastide, *Réponse à la lettre de Monseigneur l'Evèque de Nîmes aux protestants du Gard* (Puylaurens (Tarn), 1859). Plantier answered these pamphlets with two more of his own, only one of which he published. Mgr. Plantier, "Encore le Synode de 1559," in *Oeuvres de Mgr. Plantier*, 11: 56-137. The unpublished pamphlet is, "Les martyrs du protestantisme," in *Oeuvres de Mgr. Plantier*, 11: 295-336. AN BB[18] 1598 n° 1694, Procureur-Général au Garde des Sceaux, Nîmes, 26 juin 1859.

3. Ibid., 32, 38.

4. Ibid., 48. To prove his point he quoted the elder Athanase Coquerel's declaration, "from the ecclesiastical and disciplinary point of view, the ancient confession in this era has been foreign to the current body of Protestant clergy. It is a historical document. It concerns no one other than the Société de l'histoire du protestantisme français." Athanase Coquerel père, *L'Orthodoxie moderne*, (Paris, 1842), 62-63. Closer to home, Plantier referred to a similar sentiment expressed in the local Protestant periodical, *L'Eglise réformée*. AN BB[18] 1598 n° 1694, Procureur-Général au Gardes des Sceaux, Nîmes, 26 juin 1859. See also Plantier, "Encore le Synode de 1559," 56-69.

5. A proposal out of Paris had suggested moving the September communion to October as part of a yearly celebration of the Reformation. French Reformed Churches followed the Genevan practice of having communion four times a year. In most churches three of these occasions coincided with Christmas, Easter and Pentecost. The fourth communion sat by itself, usually in September, without any

special occasion associated with it. ADG 42 J 170, Conf. pastorale, 25 juin 1834. The Consistory of Nîmes had also decided not to have the Conference for Men in 1854 study the Reformation because it might become "an occasion for polemic." ADG 42 J 56, Consist de Nîmes, 13 janvier 1854.

6. G. de Félice, *Histoire des Protestants de France*, 7th ed. (Toulouse: Société des Livres religieuex, 1880), 688-697. Plantier, "Encore le Synode de 1559," 54-63. AN BB[18] 1598 n° 1694, Ministre des Cultes au Gardes des Sceaux, Paris, 21 juillet 1859.

7. *Lettre*, 1, 4; Dardier, *Réponse*, The Procureur-Général said these responses sold so quickly he was unable to secure copies for himself. AN BB[18] 1598 n° 1694, Procureur-Général au Garde des Sceaux, Nîmes, 26 juin 1859.

8. *Lettre*, 2.

9. Dardier, *Réponse*, 6-11, 22, 34.

SELECT BIBLIOGRAPHY

Primary Sources

Archives nationales

BB[18] 984 4302	Processions de la Fête-Dieu.
BB[18] 1001 5852	Enlèvement de mineure protestante.
BB[18] 1129 6221	Processions de la Fête-Dieu.
BB[18] 1168 1617	Enlèvement de jeune protestante.
BB[18] 1254 6767	Exhumation du corps d'une protestante.
BB[18] 1315 3998	Troubles politiques dans le Gard.
BB[18] 1414 7056	Prédications méthodistes, août - novembre 1843.
BB[18] 1425 9173	Incidents soulevés par l'exercise du culte protestante.
BB[18] 1585 472	Incident à l'occasion de l'inhumation d'une protestante.
BB[18] 1598 1694	Polemique entre Mgr. Plantier, évèque de Nîmes, et des pasteurs protestants.
BB[18] 1688 335	Violation de la sépulture d'une enfant protestante.
BB[30] 436	Cultes protestants.
F[19] 1779	Personnel des Pasteurs Réformées, an X-1858.
F[19] 10031	Statistiques, an XII-1905.
F[19] 10060	Etat civil des pasteurs, an X-1902.
F[19] 10094	Liberté des cultes, 1814-1874.
F[19] 10096	Proséslytisme, an XII-1856.
F[19] 10114	Ouverture des lieux de culte, Gard,1807-1884.
F[19] 10121	Réactions des consistoires aux événements politiques, an XII-1830.
F[19] 10122	Réactions des consistoires aux événements politiques, 1830-1848.
F[19] 10126	Conférences pastorales, 1836-1867.
F[19] 10170	Sociétés religieuses.
F[19] 10189	Discipline de l'Eglise Réformée, affaires de discipline, 1808-1898.
F[19] 10199	Faculté de théologie de Montauban, nominations des pasteurs, plaintes, etc., 1810-1878.

F^{19} 10389-10427	Dossiers personnelles des pasteurs, an X - 1909.
F^{19} 10433	Dossiers des pasteurs réservés en raison de doctrine, 1830-1906.
F^{19} 10436-10441	Plaintes contre pasteurs.
F^{19} 10200	Faculté de théologie de Montauban, votes des consistoires, 1800-1864.
F^{19} 10236	Renouvellement triennal des consistoires, 1837-1852, Gard.
F^{19} 10265-270	Renouvellement biennal des conseils presbytéraux, 1852-1882.
F^{19} 10343	Statistiques des votants en renouvellement, notes sur la population protestante de France, 1802-1895.
F^{19} 10347-428	Dossiers personnelles des pasteurs.
F^{19} 10432	Dossiers personnelles par raison de doctrine.
F^{19} 10434	Dossiers des pasteurs révoqué ou démissioné.
F^{19} 10440-441	Plaintes contre pasteurs, 1809-1882, Gard.
F^{19} 10926-927	Dissidence et sects diverse, 1809-1881.
F^{19} 10931	Réunions dissident, Gard, 1812-1900.

Archives du département du Gard

3M 35-45	Listes nominatives des électeurs et des jurés, 1830-1848.
5M 118-121	Epidémie de cholera, 1835.
5M 122	Epidémie de cholera, 1837.
6M 105	Recensement de la population, 1831.
6M 107	Recensement de la population, 1841.
6M 108	Recensement de la population, 1846.
6M 111	Recensement de la population, 1851.
6M 343	Surveillance des réunions et sociétés relgieuses, 1852-1870.
6M 692	Notes et observations sur les églises.
6M 770	Sociétés religieuses et de bienfaisance.
4U5 350	Cérémonies religieuses, sermons, plaintes, condemnations, 1846-1879.
V 345	Synodes: Délibérations pour l'établissement de l'organ synodale, 1837-1899.
V 347	Circulaires et correspondance. Tableaux des circonscriptions dressés en 1839.
V 348-349	Circulaires, instructions, correspondance et renseignements sur les pasteurs, X-1878.
V 353-362	Correspondance relative à la nomination, la confirmation et la présentation du serment, XI-1905.
V 491	Circulaires, correspondance relative au renouvellement biennal et triennal, 1812-1904.
V 492	Elections pour le renouvellement triennal des consistoires, 1812-1853.
V 500-503	Dons et legs multiple aux consistoires, aux établissements

charitables et hôpitaliers.

Chartrier de Clausonne

85-87   Travaux littéraires.
89   Société biblique.
90-92   Affaires protestantes.

Fonds du Consistoire de Nîmes.

42 J 1	Catalouge des archives.
42 J 10	Synodes et colloques.
42 J 25	Rapports avec l'autorité civile.
42 J 46-50	Registre des délibérations du consistoire, 1817-1859.
42 J 57-60	Correspondance du consistoire de Nîmes, copie des lettres, 1817-1856.
42 J 61	Copie des règlements délibérés en consistoire, 1805-1847.
42 J 65	Organization de l'église, 1819-1881.
42 J 70-71	Lieux du culte et temples, 1814-1879.
42 J 93	Charité, hôpital, assistance, Société biblique, 1806-1868.
42 J 94	Assistance et missions.
42 J 96	Administration et comptabilite, 1828-1859.
42 J 145-165	Comptabilité, 1819-1864.
42 J 170-171	Conférences pastorales, 1829-1878.
42 J 181-182	Consistoire de Vauvert, registre des délibérations, 1803-1860.
42 J 192-201	Additions et compléments, divers.

Archives of the Methodist Missionary Society

European Correspondence 4, cards 110-111.
European Correspondence 4, card 149.
European Correspondence 5, card 169.
European Correspondence 5, card 171.

Printed Sources

Arbousse-Bastide. *Réponse à la lettre de Monseigneur l'Evèvque de Nîmes aux protestants du Gard.* Puylaurens (Tarn): n.p., 1859.
Arnal, Emile. *Examen sommaire du project d'organisation des églises réformées, présenté au Consitoire général, dans sa séance du 8 juillet 1848.* Le Vigan (Gard): Argelliès, 1848.
_____. *Ma démission.* Le Vigan (Gard): Argelliès, 1849.

Aulard, F. A., ed. *Recueil des Actes du Comité de Salut Public avec la corréspondance officielle des Répresentants en mission et la régistre du Conseil exécutif provisoire.* Paris: Impimaire nationale, 1889-1933.

Berrian, William. *Travels in France and Italy in 1817 and 1818.* New York: T. and J. Swords, 1821.

Béziés, Timoléon. *Sermon sur ces paroles: Et Jésus leurs dit: Je suis le Pain de Vie.* Nîmes: Imprimaire de C. Triquet père et fils, n.d.

Borrel, Abraham. *Histoire de l'Eglise Chrétienne Réformée de Nismes.* Nismes: Bianqueis-Ginoux, 1837 & 1844.

Calvin, Jean. *Institutes of the Christian Religion.* Edited by John T. McNeil, and translated by Ford Lewis Battles. 2 vols. Philadelphia: Westminster Press, 1960.

Caron, Pierre, editor. *Rapports des Agents du Ministre de l'Interieur dans les Départements (1793-an II).* 3 vols. Paris: , 1933.

Cook, Charles. *L'Amour de Dieux pour tous les hommes, réponse à une brochure de M. le docteur Malan.* Valence, France: M. Aurelfrères, 1842.

————. *Cadeau à tous ceux qui craignet la mort.* Paris: Pihan-Delaforest, n.d.

————. *Les Devoirs du Ministère, sermon pronouncé à Nismes, le 23 aout 1735, à l'occasion de la consécration au saint ministère de MM. Le Bas, Hocart, et Rostan.* Paris: L.R. Delay, 1841.

Coquerel, Athanase père. *L'Orthodoxie moderne.* Paris: Cherbuliez, 1855.

Dardier, Charles. *Réponse à la lettre aux Protestants du Gard, de Mgr. L'Evèque de Nîmes.* Nîmes: n.p., 1859.

Desmons, Frédéric. *Réponse à la lettre de l'Eveque de Nîmes aux protestants du Gard.* St.-Génies (Gard): n.p., 1859.

Desmont, Jacques-Olivier. Letter to Reverend C. Smith, Nîmes, 10 janvier 1815. In "Lettres du Révérand Perrot et du Pasteur Olivier Desmont," edited by Frank Puaux. *BSHPF* 67 (1918): 221-222.

Encontre, Pierre-Germain. "Avertissement aux électeurs républicains du Gard: Circulaire n° 1." In *Du Protestantisme au socialisme: Un Quarante-huitard occitan. Ecrits et pamphlets de Pierre-Germain Encontre.* Edited by Raymond Huard and Claire Torreilles. Paris: Editions Privat, 1982.

————. "Epitre à Monsieur A. Monod sur le méthodisme." In *Du Protestantisme au socialisme: Un Quarante-huitard occitan. Ecrits et pamphlets de Pierre-Germain Encontre.* Edited by Raymond Huard and Claire Torreilles. Paris: Editions Privat, 1982.

————. "Les gens comme il faut à l'Esplanade de Nîmes." In *Du Protestantisme au socialisme: Un Quarante-huitard occitan. Ecrits et pamphlets de Pierre-Germain Encontre.* Edited by Raymond Huard and Claire Torreilles. Paris: Editions Privat, 1982.

Fanguin, Pierre. *Textes et documents sur l'histoire du protestantisme dans le Gard.* Nîmes: Archives départementales du Gard, 1983.

Fontanès, Ferdinand-Louis. *Discours pour le consécration de MM. Lavondès, Jalabert, et Amphoux à Nîmes, le 14 août 1828.* Nimes: Bianquis-Gignoux, n.d.

————. *De la lutte engagée dans les églises protestantes de France.* Valence,

France: Marc Aurel frères, 1842.

Frossard, Emilien-Benoît-Daniel. *Evénements de Nîmes depuis le 27 juillet jusqu'au 2 septembre 1830*. Nîmes: n.p., 1830.

_____. *Le Pastuer évangélique en présence du rationalisme moderne*. Nîmes: Durand-Belle, 1840.

_____. *Tableau pittoresque, scientific et moral de Nîmes et de ses environs à vingt lieus à la ronde*. 2 vols. Nîmes: Bianquis-Gignoux, 1834-1835.

_____. *La Vie réelle, ou Application du principe chrétien à quelques-unes des positions ou l'homme peut se touver selon son age et sa profession*. Paris: Delay Libraire, 1843.

Guizot, François. *L'Eglise et la société chrétienne en 1861*. Paris: Michel Lévy frères, 1861.

Hinsch-Armengaud, Margueritte-Corlay. *Recueil des Lettres pastorales de Mme. Armengaud, née Hinsch, précédé d'une notice biographique*. 2nd. Edition. Nîmes: n.p., 1878.

Hugues, Jean-Paul. *Rapport lu à la Conférence pastorale du Gard, le 8 juin 1854, sur cette question: A l'aide des articles du Concordat concernant tous les cultes, de la loi de germinal, des décrets de mars 1852, des usages généralement accepté dans nos Eglises, déterminer la discipline aujourd'hui en vigeur, et la comparer dans ses principales dispositions avec notre discipline historique*. Alais: Mme. Veirun, 1854.

Lamennais, Félicité de. *Essay on Indifference in Matters of Religion*. Translated by Lord Stanley of Aderly. London: John MacQueen, 1895.

_____. *Défense de l'Essai sur l'indifference en matiére de religion*. 2nd. Edition. Paris: Méquignon fils ainé, 1821.

Lamennais, Jean-Marie-Robert de. *De l'Enseignement mutuel*. St.-Brieuc (Côtes-du-Nord): n.p., 1819.

La Farelle, François-Felix de. *Eglise réformée de Nîmes. Démission de huit membres du Consistoire*. Nimes: Baldy, n.d.

_____. *Du Progrès social au profit des classes populaires non indigentes, . . . ou Etudes philosophiques et économiques sur l'amélioration matériel et morale du plus grand nombre*. Paris: Maison, 1839.

Laune, Paul. *Ma tentative de réforme et ma défense anticipée devant le Consistoire de Saint-Jean-du-Gard*. Alais, France: Vve Veirun, 1851.

Maison de santé protestante de Nîmes. compte rendu, 1857 (avec resumé depuis 1842). Nîmes: n.p., 1857.

J. Mavidal, E. Laurent and E. Clarel, eds. *Archives parlementaires de 1787 à 1860. Recueil complet des débats législatifs et politiques des chambres françaises*, first series. Paris: Librairie administrative de Paul Duport, 1867-1913.

Les pasteurs de Nîmes aux fidèles de leur Eglise. Nîmes: n.p., 1859.

Pédézert, Jean. *Cinquante ans de souvenirrs religieux et ecclésiastiques, 1830-1880*. Paris: Librairie Fischbacher, 1896.

Mgr. Plantier, Evèque de Nîmes. *Oeuvres complètes de Mgr. Plantier, Evèque de Nîmes. Tome 2. Mandements et Lettres pastorales: Controverses théologiques*.

Protestantisme. Nîmes and Paris: Gervais-Bédot, Oudin frères, 1883.

Rabaut, Paul. *Lettres à divers*. Paris: Charles Dardier, 1892.

Rivoire, Hector. *Statistique du département du Gard*. 2 Vols. Nîmes: Ballivet et Fabre, 1842.

Société d'évangélization parmi les protestantes disséminés - Nimes. Rappart 1839 à 1849. Nîmes: n.p., 1849.

Société protestante de prévoyance et de secours mutuels de Nîmes Règlement, 1842. Nîmes: n.p., 1842.

Société protestante de prévoyance et de secours mutuels de Nîmes. Séance anniversaire, 1860. Nîmes: n.p., 1860.

Thiébaud, Georges. *Le Parti protestant: Le progrès du protestantisme en France depuis vingt-cinq ans*. Paris: A. Savine, 1889.

Vincent, Samuel. *Catéchisme à l'usage de l'Eglise réformée de Nismes, suivi d'un abrégé de l'Histoire sainte, d'un petit recueil de passages et de quelques prières*. 2d ed. Nîmes: Gaude fils, 1817.

_____. *Observations sur l'unité religieuse*. Nîmes, 1820.

_____. *Observations sur la voie d'authorité appliqué à la Religion*. n.p., n.d.

_____. *Vues sur le protestanisme en France*. 2 vols. Nîmes, 1829.

_____. *Du Protestantisme en France*. 2nd edition. Paris: Michel Lévy frères, 1860.

Vincent, Samuel and Fontanès, Ferdinand, *Méditations religieuses*. Valence: Aurel frères, 1839.

Periodicals

Annuaire du Gard. Nîmes. 1830-1849.

Archives du Christianisme au Dix-neuvième Siècle, Jouranl Réligieux. Paris. 1833-1848.

Archives Evangéliques. Nîmes. 1841-1848.

Correspondance pastorale. Nîmes. Mars 1843, juin 1844, septembre 1845, juin 1846, décembre 1846, mars 1847, juin 1847, juillet 1847, août 1847, octobre 1847.

Religion et christianisme, recueil périodique publié sous la direction de MM. Fontanès et Vincent. Janvier-Juin 1830.

L'Evangéliste. Valence. 1837-1840.

Le Lien. Paris. 1841-1848.

Secondary Sources

Adams, Paul V., "The Determinants of Local Variations in Fertility in Bas-Languedoc and Roussillon during the Mid-Nineteenth Century," *Annales de démographie historique* 1990: 155-172.

Aguet, Jean-Pierre. *Les Grèves sous la monarchie de juillet (1830-1847):*

Contribution à l'étude du mouvent ouvrier français. Geneva: , 1954.

Agulhon, Maurice. *Pénitents et francmaçons de l'ancienne Provence (essai sur la sociabilité méridionale).* Paris: Fayard, 1968.

_____. *The Republic in the Village: The people of the Var from the French Revolution to the Second Republic.* Translated by Janet Lloyd. Cambridge: Cambridge University Press, 1982.

_____. *La Vie sociale en Provence intérieure au lendemain de la Révolution.* Paris: Société des études robespierristes et la Librairie Clavreuil, 1971.

Anderson, Lavinia. "Piety and Politics: Recent Work on German Catholicism." *Journal of Modern History* 63 (1991): 681-716.

Ariès, Philippe. *The Hour of Our Death.* New York: Knopf, 1981.

Baubérot, Jean. "L'évangélisation protestante non concordataire en France et les problèmes de la liberté religieuse au XIXᵉ siècle: la Société évangélique de 1833 à 1883." Thèse du 3ᵉ cycle, Ecole Polytechnique des Hautes Etudes, 1966.

_____. *Le Retour des Huguenots: La vitalité protestante, XIXᵉ-XXᵉ siècles* Paris: Les Editions Cerf; Geneva: Les Editions Labor et Fides, 1985.

Bebbington, David. *Evangelicalsim in Modern Britain: A History from the 1730s to the 1980s.* Grand, Rapids, MI: BakerBook House, 1992.

Bebbington, David, and Noll, Mark, eds. *Evangelcialsim in Britain, America and Beyond.* New York: Oxford University Press, 1992.

Benoit, D. "Le Synode de 1694: Etude historique et critique." *BSHPF* 1901: 337-368.

Berensen, Edward. *Populist Religion and Left-Wing Politics in France, 1830-1852.* Princeton: Princeton University Press, 1984.

Berger, Peter. *The Sacred Canopy - Elements of a Sociological Theory of Religion.* New York: Doubleday Anchor, 1967.

Bianquis, Jean. *Les Origines de la Société des missions évangéliques de Paris, 1822-1829.* 3 vols. Paris: Société des missions évangéliques, 1930.

Blackbourn, David. *Class, Religion and Local Politics in Wilhelmine Germany: The Centre party in Wurttemburg before 1914.* New Haven: Yale University Press, 1980.

_____. "The Catholic Church in Europe Since the French Revolution: A Review Article." *Comparative Studies in Society and History* 33 (1991): 77-790.

_____. *Marpingen: Apparitions of the Virgin Mary in Nineteenth-Century Germany.* New York: Alfred A. Knopf, 1994.

Bost, Charles. *Les Prédicants protestants des Cévennes et du Bas-Languedoc, 1684-1700.* Vol. 1. Paris: Honoré Champion, 1912.

Brown, Marvin L. *Louis Veuillot: French Ultramontane Catholic, Journalist and Layman, 1813-1883.* Durham, NC: Moore Publishing, 1977.

Bruce, Steven. *A House Divided: Protestantism, Schism and Secularization* New York: Routledge, 1990.

Butler, John. *The Huguenots in America: A Refugee People in New World Society.* Cambridge: Harvard University Press, 1983.

Carwardine, Richard. *Trans-Atlantic Revivalism: Popular Evangelicalism in*

Britain and America, 1790-1865. Westport, Conn.: Greenwood Press, 1978.

Chabrol, Jean-Pierre. *Les Fous de Dieu.* Paris: Gallimard, 1967.

————. *Le Bonheur du manchot.* Paris: Editions Robert Laffont, 1993.

Chamson, André. *Le Chiffre de nos jours.* Paris: Gallimard, 1954.

————. *La Superbe.* Paris: Plon, 1967.

Chartier, Roger. "The Two Frances: The History of an Idea," in *Cultural History: Between Practices and Representations.* Edited by Roger Chartier. Translated by Lydia G. Cochrane. Ithaca, NY: Cornell University Press, 1988.

Chevalier, Louis. *Laboring Classes and Dangerous Classes in Paris during the First-Half of the Nineteenth Century,* 172-200. Translated by Frank Jellinek. Princeton: Princeton University Press, 1973.

Cholvy, Gérard. *Géographie religieuse de l'Hérault contemporaine.* Paris: Presses Universitaires de France, 1968.

Cholvy, Gérard and Yves-Marie Hilaire. *Histoire religieuse de la France contemporaine, 1800/1880.* Paris: Privat, 1985.

Clout, Hugh D. *Agriculture in France on the Eve of the Railway Age.* London: Crom Helm, 1980.

Cook, Jean-Paul. *La Vie de Charles Cook, pasteur méthodiste et docteur en théologie, par son fils.* Paris: Libraire évangélique, 1862.

Coquérel, Charles. *Histoire des églises du désert depuis la fin de règne de Louis XIV jusqu' à nos jours.* Paris: A. Cherbuliez, 1841.

Cosson, Armand. "La Révolution de 1830 à Nîmes." *Annales historiques de la Révolution française,* 258 (1984): 528-540.

————. "L'Industrie textile à Nîmes: la fin d'une hégémonie (1790-1850)." *Le Mouvement social,* 133 (1985): 5-24.

Dansette, Adrian. *Religious History of France in the Nineteenth Century.* New York: Herder and Herder, 1961.

Deming, James. "Church and Charity in Industrial Society: The French Reformed Church and Public Assistance in Nîmes, 1830-1852." *Proceedings of the Western Society for French History,* 20 (1993): 239-248.

Deming, James C., and Hamilton, Michael S. "Methodist Revivalism in France, Canada and the United States." in Rawlyk, George A., and Noll, Mark A., eds. *Amazing Grace: Evangelicalism in Australia, Britain, Canada and the United States.* Grand Rapids, MI: Baker Book House, 1993.

Desan, Suzanne. *Reclaiming the Sacred: Lay Religion and Popular Politics in Revolutionary France.* Ithaca, NY: Cornell University Press, 1990.

Devlin, Judith. *The Superstitious Mind: French Peasants and the Supernatural in the Nineteenth Century.* New Haven: Yale University Press, 1987.

Dictionnaire de biographie française. Paris: Librairie Letouzey et Ane, 1979.

Dieny, Georges. "Essai sur la prédication de Rabaut de Saint-Etienne." Thèse de théologie: Faculté de théologie de l'Eglise Réformée à Paris, 1907.

Dobbelaere, Karel. "Secularization Theory and Sociological Paradigms: A Reformation of the Private-Public Dichotomy and the Problem of Societal Integration." *Sociological Analysis* 46 (1985): 378-387.

————. "From Pillar to Postmodernity: The Changing Situation of Religion in Belgium." *Socilogical Analysis*, 51 (1990): 1-13.

_____. "Secularization, Pillarization, Religious Involvement, and Religious Change in the Low Countries." In Gannon, Thoams, ed. *World Catholicism in Transition*, New York: Macmillan; London: Collier Macmillan, 1988.

Dobbelaere, Karel, and Billiet, J. "Community Formation and the Church: A Sociological Study of an Ideology and the Empirical Reality." In Caudron, Marc, ed. *Faith and Society - foi et société - geloof en maatschappij: Acta Congressus Lovaniensis, 1976*, 211-259. Gembloux: Duculot, 1978.

Dolan, Jay P. *Catholic Revivalism: The American Experience, 1830-1900.* Notre Dame, Ind.: University of Notre Dame Press, 1978.

Dubief, Henri. "Réflexions sur quelques aspects du premier Réveil et sur le milieu ou il se forma." *BSHPF,* CXIV (1968): 373-402.

Dubled, Henri. *Les Eglises protestantes de Gardonneque de 1802 à 1906.* Nîmes: C. Lacour, 1990.

Dugrand, Raymond. *Villes et campagnes en Bas-Languedoc.* Paris: Presses Universitaires Françaises, 1963.

Duport, "La Société populaire de Nîmes, 1791-1795." *Annales Historiques de la Révolution Française* 258 (1984): 514-527.

Edgar, William. *La Carte protestante. Le protestantisme francophone et la modernité (1815-1848).* Geneva: Labor et Fides, 1997.

Encrevé, André, ed. *Dictionnaire du monde religieux dans la France contemporaine.* Volume 5. *Les Protestants.* Geneva: Labor et Fides, 1986.

_____. *Les protestants en France de 1800 à nos jours: histoire d'une réintégration.* Paris: Stock, 1985.

_____. "Protestantisme et politique. Les protestants du Midi en décembre 1851." In *Droite et Gauche en Languedoc-Roussillon: Actes du collogue de Montpellier, 9-10 juin 1973*, 161-187. Montpellier: Centre d'Histoire contemporaine du Languedoc méditerranéen et du Roussillon, Université de Paul Valéry, 1975.

_____. *Protestants français au milieu du XIXᵉ siècle: Les réformés de 1848 à 1870.* Geneva: Editions Labor et Fides, 1986.

Etlin, Richard. *The Architecture of Death: The Transformation of the Cemetery in Eighteenth-Century Paris.* Cambridge, Mass.: MIT Press, 1984.

Fitzpatrick, Brian. *Catholic royalism in the department of the Gard, 1814-1852.* Cambridge: Cambridge University Press, 1983.

Ford, Caroline. *Creating the Nation in Provincial France: Religion and Political Identity in Brittany.* Princeton: Princeton University Press, 1993.

_____. "Religion and Popular Culture in Modern Europe." *Journal of Modern History* 65 (1993): 152-175.

Forissier, Marc. *Emilien Frossard, l'apôtre des Pyrénées.* Tarbes, France: Editions d'Albret, 1946.

Furet François and Jean Ozouf. *Reading and Writing: literacy in France from Calvin to Jules Ferry.* Cambridge: Cambridge University Press, 1982.

Garisson, Janine. *L'Homme Protestant.* Paris: Hachette, 1980.

Garrett, Clarke. *Spirit Possession and Popular Religion: From the Camisards to the Shakers*. Baltimore: Johns Hopkins University Press, 1987.

Gaussent. Jean-Claude. *Les Protestants et l'Eglise réformée de Sète*. Nîmes: Lacour, 1993.

Gildea, Richard. *Education in the Provinces: A Study of Three Departments*. Cambridge: Cambridge University Press, 1986.

_____. *The Past in French History*. New Haven: Yale University Press, 1994.

Godechot, Jacques. *La Contre-Révolution (1789-1804)*. Paris: Presses Universitaires de France, 1961.

Graetz, Michael. *The Jews in Nineteenth-Century France: From the French Revolution to the Alliance Israélite Universelle*. Translated by Marie Todd. Stanford: Stanford University Press, 1996.

Haag, M. M. *La France Protestante, ou vies des Protestants Français qui se sont fait un nom dans l'hisoire depuis les prémiers temps de la Réformation jusqu' à la reconnaisance du principe de la liberté des cultes par L'Assemblée Nationale*. Genève: Slatkine Reprints, 1966.

Hatch, Nathan O. *The Democratization of American Christianity*. New Haven: Yale University Press, 1989.

Hempton, David. *Methodism and Politics in British Society, 1750-1850*. Stanford: Stanford University Press, 1984.

Hobsbawm, E. J. *Primitive Rebels: Studies in Archaic Forms of Social Movement in the 19th and 20th Centuries*. New York: N. W. Norton & Co., 1965.

Hood, James N. "Patterns of Popular Protest in the French Revolution: The Conceptual Contribution of the Gard." *Journal of Modern History*, 48 (1976): 260-298.

_____. "Protestant-Catholic Relations and the Roots of the First Popular Counterrevolutionary Movement in France." *Journal of Modern History*, 43 (1971): 240-283.

_____. "The Riots in Nîmes in 1790 and the Origin of a Popular Conterrevolutionary Movement." Ph.D. diss., Princeton University, 1970.

Huard, Raymond. "Montagne rouge et Montagne blanche en Languedoc-Rossillon sous la Seconde République." In *Droite et Gauche en Languedoc-Rossillon: Actes du collogue de Montpellier, 9-10 juin 1973*, 139-160. Montpellier: n.p., 1975.

_____. *La préhistoire des parties: Le Mouvement républicain en Bas-Languedoc, 1848-1881*. Paris: Presses de la Fondation nationale des sciences politiques, 1982.

_____. "Souvenir et tradition révolutionnaires: le Gard: 1848-1851." *Annales historiques de la Révoltion française*. 258 (1984): 207-245.

Ingrand, Pasteur Samuel. *Histoire de la Maison de santé protestante évangélique de Nîmes*. Nîmes: Groupe Différence, 1986.

Jones, Colin. *Charity and bienfaisance: The treatment of the poor in the Montpellier region in 1740-1815*. Cambridge: Cambridge University Press, 1982.

Jones, Colin and Michael Sonenscher. "The Social Functions of the Hospital in

Eighteenth-Century France: The case of the Hôtel-Dieu of Nîmes." *French Historical Studies* 13 (1983): 172-214.

Joutard, Philippe. *Les Camisards*. Paris: Editions Gallimard/Julliard, 1976.

_____. *La Légende des Camisards: une sensibilité au passé*. Paris: Editions Gallimard, 1977.

Kselman, Thomas. *Death and the Afterlife in Modern France*. Princeton: Princeton University Press, 1993.

_____. "Funeral Conflicts in Nineteenth-Century France." *Comparative Studies in Society and History* 30 (1988): 312-332.

_____. *Miracles and Prophecies in Nineteenth Century France*. New Brunswick, N. J.: Rutgers University Press, 1984.

Labrousse, Ernest. *La Révocation de L'Edit de Nantes*. Geneva: Payot & Labor et Fides, 1985.

Lautier, G. "La sériculture et les industries de la soie dans le pays cévenol." *Bulletin de la Société Languedocienne de Géographie*. Série 2. 4 (1930): 79-86.

Lecky, W. E. H. *A History of England in the Eighteenth Century*. Vol. 2. London: Longmans Press, 1878-1890.

Lehning, James R. *Peasant and French: Cultural Contact in Rural France during the Nineteenth Century*. Cambridge: Cambridge University Press, 1995.

Léonard, Emile-Guillaume. *Histoire ecclésiastique des Réformés français au XVIIIᵉ siècle*. Paris Fischbacher, 1940.

_____. *Histoire générale du protestantisme*. 3 vols. Paris: Presses Universitaires de France, 1964.

_____. *Le protestant français*. Paris: Presses Universitaires de France, 1953.

Lewis, Gwynne. "A Cevenol Community in Crisis: The Mystery of *L'Homme à Moustache*." *Past & Present* 109 (November 1985): 144-175.

_____. *The Second Vendée: The Continuity of Counter-revolution in the Department of the Gard, 1789-1815*. Oxford: Clarendon Press, 1978.

_____. "The White Terror of 1815 in the Department of the Gard: Counter-Revolution, Continuity and the Individual." *Past & Present* 58 (1973): 108-135.

Ligou, Denis. "L'Eglise Réformée du Désert, fait économique et social." *Révue d'histoire économique et sociologique* 32 (1954): 162-163.

_____. *Frédéric Desmons et la Franc-Maçonnerie sous la 3ᵉ République*. Paris: Librairie Gedalge, 1966.

Liu, Tessie P. *The Weaver's Knot: The Contradictions of Class Struggle and Family Solidaity in Western France, 1750-1914*. Ithaca, NY: Cornell University Press, 1994.

Loubère, Leo A. *Radicalism in Mediterranean France: Its Rise and Decline 1848-1914*. Albany, NY: State University of New York Press, 1974.

Luckmann, Thomas. *The Invisible Religion: The Problem of Religion in Modern Society*. New York: Macmillan, 1967.

Lynch, Katherine. *Family. Class and Ideoι___ ..ι Early Industrial France: Social Policy and the Working-Class Family, 1825-1848*. Madison, WI: University of Wisconsin Press, 1988.

Marcilhacy, Christiane. *Le diocèse d'Orléans au milieu du XIXe siècle, les hommes et leurs mentalitès.* Paris: Sirey, 1964.

Margadant, Ted W. *French Peasants in Revolt: The Insurrection of 1851.* Princeton: Princeton University Press, 1979.

Marshall, Gordon. *Presbyteries and Profits: Calvinism and the Development of Capitalism in Scotland, 1560-1707.* Oxford: Oxford University Press, 1980.

Martin, David. *The Breaking of the Image: A Sociology of Christian Theory and Practice.* New York: St. Martin's Press, 1979.

_____. *Towards a General Theory of Secularization.* New York: Harper and Row, 1978.

Marty, Jacques. *La 'Correspondance pastorale' de Nîmes (1839-1848), coup d'oeil sur les origines du mouvement libéral et son rôle dans la vie religieuse des Eglises réformées.* Paris: n.p., 1924.

Maury, Léon. *La réveil religiuex dans l'Eglise Réformée à Genève et en France (1810-1850): Etude historique et dogmatique.* 2 vols. Paris: Librairie Fishbacher, 1892.

McLeod, Hugh. *Religion in the Age of Great Cities, 1830-1930.* New York: Oxford University Press, 1981.

McLoughlin, William G. *Modern Revivalism.* New York: Ronald Press, 1959.

_____. *The American Evangelicals, 1800-1900: An Anthology.* New York: Harper Torchbooks, 1968.

McManners, John. *Death and the Enlightenment: Changing Attitudes to death in eighteenth-century France.* New York: Oxford University Press, 1985.

Moch, Leslie Page. *Paths to the City: Regional Migration in Nineteenth-Century France.* Beverly Hills, CA: Sage Publications, 1983.

Mours, Samuel. "Essai d'évaluation de la population protestante réformée au xviie et xviiie siècle." *BSHPF* 103 (1958): 17.

_____. *Une siècle d'évangélisation en France, 1815-1914.* 2 vols. Namur, Belgium: Editions de la Librairie des Eclaireurs Unionists, Flavion, 1963.

Negre, Corinne. *Le protestantisme nîmois à l'oeuvre: Le diaconat 1561-1945.* Nîmes: Lacour, 1992.

Nord, Philip. *The Republican Moment: Struggles for Democracy in Nineteenth-Century France.* Cambridge: Harvard University Press, 1995.

Olivier-Lacamp, Max. *Les feux de la colère.* Paris: Gallimard, 1967.

Orentin, Douen. *Histoire de la Société biblique protestante de Paris, 1818-1868.* Paris: n.p., 1868.

Osen, James Lynn. "French Calvinists and the Statee, 1830-1852." *French Historical Studies* V (Fall 1967): 220-232.

_____. *Prophet and Peacemaker: The Life of Adolphe Monod.* Lanham, MD: University Press of America, 1984.

_____. "The Revival of the French Reformed Church, 1830-1852." Ph. D. diss., University of Wisconsin, 1966.

Peloux, Alfred. *La prédication du Réveil en France.* Montauban: n.p., 1908.

Petit, Pierre. *Une Métropole protestante en Languedoc: Nîmes 1802-1848, Chronique et Textes.* Nîmes: Lacour/Eruditae Indagationes, 1989.

Pitié, Jean. *L'Homme et son espace: L'Exode rural en France du XVIe siècle à nos jours*. Paris: Editions du centre national de la receherche scientifique, 1987.

Poland, Burdette. *French Protestantism and the French Revolution: a Study in Church and State, Thought and Religion (1685-1815)*. Princeton: Princeton University Press, 1957.

Poujol, Pierre. *La Cévenne protestante et sa plaine méridionale, tome I, De Louis XIV à Jules Ferry*. Paris: Librairie Protestante, 1963.

_____. "Socialistes et chrétiens (1848-1948)." *Questions de notre temps* January 1956: 1-60; December 1956: 1-79.

Pouthas, Charles H. *Une famille de bourgeoisie française de Louis XIV à Napoléon*. Paris: F. Alcan, 1934.

Price, Roger. *An Economic History of Modern France, 1730-1914*. Revised ed. London: MacMillan Press., 1981.

Reddy, William M. *The rise of market culture: The textile trade and French society, 1750-1900*. Cambridge: Cambridge University Press, 1984.

Robert, Daniel. *Les Eglises réformées en France, 1800-1830*. Paris: Presses Universitaires de France, 1961.

_____. "Documents concernant les origines de la faculté réformée de Montauban: Lettres de Benjamin Sigismond Frossard (1800-1810)." *BSHPF* 108 (1962): 139-165.

_____. *Textes et documents relatifs à l'histoire des Eglises réformées de France (1800-1830)*. Geneva: Labor et Fides, 1962.

Roque, Jean-Daniel. "L'Eglise nationale protestante de Nîmes de 1870 de 1870 à la vielle de la séparation des Eglises et de l'Etat." Mémoire de Maîtrise de la faculté des lettre de Montpellier, 1969.

_____. "Positions et tendances politiques des protestantes nîmois au XIXe siècle." In *Droite et Gauche en Languedoc-Roussillon: Actes du colloque de Montpellier, 9-10 juin 1973*, 200-202. Montpellier: n.p., 1975.

Roux, Théodore. *Le Méthodisme en France: Pour servir à l'histoire religieuse d'hier et d'avant-hier*. Paris: Librairie protestante, 1940.

Sabatier, Alain. *Religion et Politique au XIXe siècle. Le canton de Vernouz-en-Vivarais*. Vernoux: n.p., 1975.

Sahlins, Peter. *Forest Rites: The War of the Demoiselles in Nineteenth-Century France*. Cambridge: Harvard University Press, 1994.

Savey, Suzanne. "Essai de reconstitution de la structure agraire des villages de Sardan et d'Aspères (Gard) sous l'ancien régime à l'aide des compoix." *Annales du Midi* 81 (1969): 41-54.

Schram, Stuart R. *Protestantism and Politics in France*. Alençon: Corbière et Jugain, 1954.

Sentou, J. "Révolution et contre-révolution." In *Histoire du Languedoc*, ed. Philippe Wolff. Toulouse: Privat, 1967.

Serre, Bernard. "Le protestantisme dans l'Eglise consistoriale de Lasalle (Gard), 1802-1848." Mémoire de Maîtrise, Université Paul Valéry, 1979.

Sevrin, Ernest. *Les missions religieuses en France sous la Restauration 1815-1830*. 2 vols. St-Nandé: Procure des prêtres de la miséricorde, 1948-1959.

Sewell, William H., Jr. *Work and Revolution in France: The Language of Labor from the Old Regime to 1848*. Cambridge: Cambridge University Press, 1980.

Siegfried, André. *Géographie électorale de l'Ardèche sous la Troisième république*. Paris: Colin, 1949.

_____. *Tableau politiques de la France sous la Troisième république*. Paris: Grassert, 1930.

Siméoni, Joséphine. "Club et Société populaire à Nîmes." Mémoire de Maîtrise, Université de Montpellier, 1972.

Spitz, Lewis W. "History: Sacred and Secular." *Church History* 47 (1978): 18-19.

Sperber, Jonathon. *Popular Catholicism in Nineteenth-Century Germany*. Princeton: Princeton University Press, 1984.

Tackett, Timothy. "Women and Men in counterrevolution: The Sommières Riot of 1791." *Journal of Modern History* 59 (1987): 680-704.

Tilly, Charles. "How Protest Modernized in France, 1845-1855." In *The Dimensions of Quantitative Research in History*, ed. W. Aydellotte. Princeton: Princeton University Press, 1972.

Van Kley, Dale K. *The Damiens Affair and the Unraveling of the Ancient Régime, 1750-1770*. Princeton: Princeton University Press 1984.

Vidalenc, Jean. *Le peuple des campagnes: la société française de 1815 à 1848*. Paris: Editions Marcel Rivière, 1970.

Vigier, Philippe. *La Seconde République dans la région alpine, étude politique et sociale*. 2 vols. Paris: Presses Universitaires de France, 1963.

Vincent, Alfred. *Histoire de la prédication protestants de la langue française au XIXe siècle, 1800-1866*. Geneva: A. Cherbuliez, 1870.

Vovelle, Michel. "Essai de Cartographie de la déchristianization sous la Révolution française." *Annales du Midi* 76 (1964): 531.

_____. *La mort et l'Occident de 1300 à nos jours*. Paris: Gallimard, 1983.

_____. *Piété baroque et déchristianisation en Provence au XVIIIe siècle*. Paris: Plon, 1973.

_____. *Religion et Révolution: La déchristianization de l' an II*. Paris: Hachette, 1976.

Ward, W. R. *The Protestant Evangelical Awakening*. Cambridge: Cambridge University Press, 1992.

Weber, Eugen. *Peasants into Frenchmen: The Modernization of Rural France, 1870-1914*. Palo Alto: Stanford University Press, 1976.

Wemyss, Alice. *Histoire du Réveil, 1790-1849*. Paris: Les Bergers et les Mages, 1977.

_____. "Les Protestants du Midi pendant la Révolution." *Journal du Midi* 61 (1957): 310.

Willaime, Jean-Paul. *La précarité protestante: Sociologie du protestantisme contemporaine*. Geneva: Labor et Fides, 1995.

Woodbridge, John D. "L'Influence des philosophes français sur les pasteurs réformés du Languedoc pendant la deuxième moitié du XVIIIe siècle." Thèse de la 3e cycle. 'Université de Toulouse, 1969.

_____. "The Reformed Pastors of Languedoc Face the Movement of

Dechristianization (1793-1794)." *Problèmes d'Histoire du Christiamsme* 13 (1984): 77-89.

_____. *Revolt in Prerevolutionary France: The Prince de Conti's Conspiracy against Louis XV, 1755-1757*. Baltimore: Johns Hopkins University Press, 1995.

Zaretsky, Robert. *Nîmes at War: Religion, Politics, and Public Opinion in the Gard, 1938-1944*. State College, PA: Penn State University Press, 1995.

Zorn, Jean-François. *Le Grand siécle d'une mission protestante: La Mission de Paris de 1822 à 1914*. Paris: Karthala- Les Bergers et les Mages, 1993.

INDEX

Wilson, Brian, xix
wine. *See* viticulture
women's roles, 47, 49, 50, 57, 65,
    77, 105, 120, 122-124, 134, 144,
    145. *See also* gender
worship, xx, 22, 24, 27, 30, 33, 36,
    37, 39-42, 44, 48, 50, 54, 55, 57,
    60, 63, 65-67, 70, 73, 74, 79-81,
    84, 89, 91, 99, 101, 109-116,
    126, 128-130, 137, 146, 148,
    151-157, 165, 172, 174, 176,
    177

DATE DUE

DE 10 '04			

Demco, Inc. 38-293